Up from the Straits:
A Memoir

Up from the Straits: A Memoir

Myron Fenster

To order additional copies of this book, contact:
Xlibris Corporation
1-888-795-4274
www.Xlibris.com
Orders@Xlibris.com
83905

Contents

PART: 2

Part: 1

UP FROM THE STRAITS

A FTER A YEAR in Israel, we were homeward bound, first to Venice on a Greek ferry. The plan was to drive across Italy in our Peugeot and meet our ship for the U.S. in Naples.

In Haifa, about a dozen cars drove right up onto the Greek ship for the journey. The sleeping accommodations were adequate, if not luxurious, and for three days we ate fish, Greek salad and eggs. Twenty or so young students slept on the upper deck in the open air. We were jealous of them because the staterooms were quite warm and this was the middle of the summer. They seemed to be having a marvelous time, probably stayed awake half the night and seemed to be continuously partying. Our kids were still young so we did all our partying in the staterooms. The sea water filled our nostrils and our outlook: exhilarating.

Actually, our daughter Elissa, who was graduating elementary school, had flown home by herself so she could be there for graduation with her classmates. This, for her, was a great adventure and we managed to survive it also. Not quite fourteen and a twelve-hour flight! We did meet the stewardess and asked her to keep an eye out. It worked.

The most memorable part of that ferry journey to Italy was that as we neared the coast, we had to pass through the Corinth Canal. It's a very narrow strip four miles long and seventy feet wide. It's actually in the lower part of Greece, heading toward the mainland and Italy, which is a short distance away.

As you enter the canal, the boat docks for a moment and a special canal captain comes aboard. It's so narrow that it takes special skill to maneuver the ship through. He takes over from the Captain and for the next moments he becomes the 'Captain of the Narrow Straits'. No problem. When he finishes the job, he and the Captain have a short snort together and we are on our way.

What immediately came to mind was that verse in Psalms, "Out of the straits I called upon You. You answered me and set me free." It seemed to me thus, and the image has persisted. A graphic picture of our lives, maneuvering through the narrow straits.

It was a piece of cake for the captain and while it has taken awhile for us to learn how to navigate like him – we have enjoyed our cake with a drop of schnapps as well.

Navigating the narrow straits takes time and skill. If you are lucky, you are given the time, and with diligence you acquire the skill: I take it as a metaphor for this journey.

THE SOLACE OF SILENCE

S ITTING IN THE warm Florida sun in the middle of winter trying to regain perspective on 'after retirement.' The world seems in repose. And there is time to reflect.

So I read in the Palm Beach Post an article entitled, "Death Will Not Be Denied – But Love is Just as Powerful as Death." It tells of a 19th century tombstone upon which has been inscribed the words "FORTIS UT MORS DILECTIO – LOVE STRONG AS DEATH."

I am taken by it because the same idea is found in the Song of Songs in the Bible. Love is as strong as death, but death will not be denied. Since both have played such an important role, it is time to get my life into perspective. In effect, that's my story as well.

When I look back I am overcome with amazement. I have spent fifty-five years as teacher and a rabbi. Public utterance has been a way of life. I have given short speeches, long speeches, extra-long speeches – I have done it all. After awhile it becomes easy. But that is not how it all began.

Growing up in a family with a hard-working father and a loving mother was easy. But after awhile I came to realize there was something strange about our family relationship. We never really spoke about the high dramatic moments of our lives. Probably because they had been overlaid with sadness. Neither my sister nor I ever heard the details of that sadness.

To tell it I would have to go back to the beginning in Poland between the World Wars. The year of decision was 1920, shortly after World War I had drawn to a close. It was a time of great turmoil. Russians were returning from the battle, the Austro-Hungarian empire was breaking up and Polish anti-Semitism was surfacing again.

My father, Ira, lived in a small town, a village, they called it a shtetl in Poland, Strelisk. Life generally was peaceful but every once in awhile fierce men on horseback, cossacks, would ride recklessly, shooting their guns and enjoying the fear in the faces of the peasants, the shopkeepers and the small-time business people. Out of perversity they would sometimes shoot people before pillaging and raping. For the sport of it. That is who they were.

One of the young people who they shot at random on the street died immediately. It was my father's brother and he was dead before his twenty-second birthday.

They ran to tell my grandfather. By the time he got there the debauched murderers had left, leaving only the dead and bereaved behind. They took up the limp body of my uncle and buried it with appropriate prayers and weeping over their enormous misfortune.

By tradition they sat and mourned for one week, saying the kaddish, or memorial prayer, three times a day. Each time the wound in the heart was reopened for my grandfather and his children. The pain in the house was intense.

By the third or fourth day my father could not take it any longer and he told my grandfather that he was leaving the old world behind and going to the Golden Land of America.

This was no easy decision, nor was it easily received. His father understood that it had to be, but he was heartbroken. In one week he would lose one son to the cossacks and one to the New World. He told my father that he just knew he would never see him again. And he was correct. At the end of the seventh day mourning period my father was itching to get going. He was only nineteen but he was burning with ambition and energy and a fierce distaste for his home surroundings. My grandfather walked him to the railroad station a short distance from his home. They both were crying. It was a sad departure. Forty years later, my father recounted the event. He still could not help welling up in the telling of the walk to the train. Nor could I, in the hearing.

The train would take him to Lvov, a major city where my father's sister and her husband lived. He would stay with them a few nights and then move on. The New World was waiting. Like so many others, my father never wanted to speak about the events that brought him to New York. I do not think he ever told me about it. My mother did and as a kid in Brooklyn I heard the story like it had happened in the Wild West. It was remote. But the pain was real. And unspoken.

Two decades later the whole family he had left behind, siblings, nephews, nieces, cousins and his father all perished in the Holocaust. I remember reading vividly about these events when I was eleven years old and recognizing that my family was involved. We were living at the time on Ocean Avenue in Brooklyn and I had so many questions I wanted to ask. But it was never a subject that was spoken about.

My father had urged his family to join him in America. By then he was able to afford to bring them but their refusal was absolute. No strange new world for them.

And so I grew up in a home, a comfortable home at that, where the most defining event was never referred to. And then I went on to spending my life teaching and speaking and sermonizing and I never referred to it.

It took me a long time to summon my tongue to articulate some of the questions. Truth is I still have trouble in understanding how my father walked around and went about his business day-by-day without ever speaking to anyone about it. The insecurity and loneliness of coming to America, establishing himself and beginning the raising of a family, all was done in silence. I know that such is possible because I saw him do it.

It would have made me feel much more adult if he had shared his pain with me. I'm not naive enough to think I could have helped, but I think it would have made a difference if we were struggling together. Shared pain recedes faster.

Once when I was forty years old I was visiting a distant cousin in Tel Aviv, a man who had grown up with my father in Europe. Suddenly out of the blue he asked me where my folks had gotten my name and who I was named after. I drew a blank. "Of course, you are called after your father's brother who was murdered. Naturally."

I was dumbfounded. How come I never asked? How come he never told me? Silence ruled.

The strange irony of it was that he loved to talk and he did so excitedly and well, about his work, his customers, his success and failures. But never anything personal about the family back home.

The conventional wisdom has it that conflicts need to be aired, shutting them up is bad. Nowadays many have begun to question the importance of immediately venting a traumatic experience or situation. Supportive family and friends are crucial. Sometimes I wonder: is not there some aspect of biting the bullet and not immediately sharing it with others that partakes of heroism? Sadness did not permeate our home. So I don't fault my father for his reaction.

Still I wonder how all of that could have happened without conversation. How come it didn't just bubble over the top, the shooting on the street, the brutal deaths of the Holocaust, the ability to go on day by day without reference or mention, just seeing the task in front of you and doing it. For me if it has been an exciting day I cannot wait to share it. Given my background, how come?

So I speculate. When my father was young, living as he did in a small village of pious farmers, the only subject he ever really studied in school was the Bible. That was the only formal education he ever received until he came to America and learned to read and write in night school. One of the stories he was taught as a child was of Joseph the biblical dreamer, the slave sold down the river, who becomes second only to Pharaoh himself. Joseph the Provider in Egypt. He feeds his starving family and in the end is reunited with his father.

At a certain crucial point in the story as it is told in the Book of Genesis, Joseph's brothers bow before him petitioning for food. They don't recognize the now bearded dreamer, prematurely gray and handsomely robed in the velvets and silk of his office and with a small crown on his head. Joseph has watched them for awhile and now filled with emotion suddenly breaks down and reveals himself: "I am Joseph, your brother." Pandemonium breaks loose. His brothers and his entourage smell disaster and revenge, the scent of death. But it doesn't happen – Joseph composes himself, assures them that they need not worry. And then he speaks what is surely one of the most religiously profound sentences of the Bible: "And now my brothers be not sad nor fearful for your having sold me here – for God has sent me here for life-giving purpose. God has sent me before you to insure your survival on this earth and to save your lives. It was not you who sent me here, but God."

From this we learn that Joseph was a work in progress, starting as a precocious self-centered narcissist he had become now a responsible adult. Did he really accept that his brothers' rejection of him was a sign of God's providential love, that it was for his and their benefit? Or was it just to relieve their high anxiety of the moment?

And so to push it further and to try to find explanation, I ask myself whether my father saw himself as a kind of Joseph. He came to America on the back of a tragedy and went on to succeed in business and in life. Did he see all of this happening as some design of God, that after the tragedy, there would be new opportunities and unbelievable renewal possible. Europe was dead. Where else but in America? How else could he have proceeded without murmur or protest or breakdown? Did he see himself as a biblical shadow of Joseph?

And so out of all of this I come to the question of whether it is possible to experience a tragic event, suffer deeply from it and yet years later see it as a necessity to your own growth and maturity.

The questions that have stuck with me all of these years: Was there purpose or design behind all of this? And more to the point, could I be Ira, my father? Could we be Joseph? Let us see.

Is there such a reality as solace in silence? Isn't protest better? Ever since Abraham's plea on behalf of Sodom we have always thought so. Maybe it's time to reconsider. There may be moments in life you are better off just absorbing and going forward.

COMPLICATIONS

LOOKING AT A joyous picture on my wall adds to the perplexity. I see my father and mother looking young, confident, prosperous. My father is wearing a boutonniere in his lapel and my mother a small corsage. Placed on the table before them are silver teapots and servers. The place is the Waldorf Astoria, then and for some still today, the crown of all New York hotels. The occasion was the sixteenth birthday party of my sister Eleanor, a festive and happy time. The perplexity of it is that this was just a few short years after the revelation of the Holocaust had come out and a cataclysmic event had occurred to all of us in our family.

By this time we knew that as far as my father was concerned all was not going smoothly. On the surface he kept whatever inner tensions he had under wraps, except when he could not. That would be at night when, sleeping after a long and busy day, suppressed feelings would surface. There would often be nightmares and screams. By day he never spoke of them or described their content. From that the rest of us in the family learned that the unspoken could be far more scary than the shared. How long the night screams persisted I cannot say. But they haunted my mother who heard them and did not know what to do to get them to stop.

Looking at that picture on the wall, you never would suspect any of this. My father is wearing a toothy smile and my mother a wistful, dreamy, happy look. Suspicion is that it was not an act at all. They simply rejoiced in how far they had come after the turmoil.

The tragic event that occurred was without warning or preparation. Our closely-knit family was torn apart by the death of my brother Elliot at the end of March 1943. He was eight years old and died suddenly. We had no time to steel ourselves or to prepare for the shock. It all happened in one day and came as a traumatic event to my parents, to my sister and to myself. I think I can say without exaggeration, for Eleanor and myself we are still in recovery.

As for me at age sixteen, at first I did not know how to continue. I thought I too was going to die. I lay on my bed as if frozen. There was talk that he had died of a virus and that perhaps it was contagious. The official name was encephalomyelitis, which is commonly referred to as "sleeping sickness." He was at the end cycle of measles. He was getting better and twenty-four hours later he was dead.

Elliot had been sick five, six days. He was almost well. The fever had broken. Suddenly my mother comes down from his room, deeply troubled. She cannot rouse him. I go up to see for myself. One swift awful look. It is true.

The doctor is summoned. Shortly after the ambulance arrives. Night has fallen. The sight of the ambulance in the driveway sends a chilling fright through me.

He is whisked away. A restless night of waiting. He never awoke. By morning, he is gone. There were no medications, no time for anything. The cossacks have returned to our family.

The problem was that no one explained anything to me or the family, no physician, no social worker, no one. There was no antibiotic or inoculation. We were left to our own resources and we didn't really know what had happened. The only thing I had to fall back on, and it was a thin reed at the moment, was my earlier background and religious training.

It had not been meager, my religious training. It comprised of eight years of the best private Jewish parochial school available in Brooklyn. Our school was modern, progressive and even served a hot lunch daily. But to say that a clear and easily adoptable portable faith to live by was given to us would be an exaggeration. I felt nothing like a supportive hand touching my shoulder. I was trying to figure out what had happened and the whole episode made no sense to me whatever.

What I do remember is that Elliot was such an innocent sweet child. I used to love to try to teach him how to throw and catch a football in our finished basement. He was not very adept at it yet but I had great hopes for him. My mother used to say that he was the most helpful of children – always ready to jump in, go to the store, clean up. All I saw was futility and meaninglessness.

Remarkably my father held together. He arranged the funeral, went through the mourning without shrieks or sobbing. For me the hardest part was hearing him tearfully explain on the phone, which seemed to be ringing non-stop, saying the words, "we lost him. He is gone."

I overheard him and my mother discussing the funeral arrangements. They were speaking of the casket that had to be purchased which, according to the tradition, was to be a plain pine coffin. I remember my father saying, "We have to get the best we are allowed to. There goes his Bar Mitzvah and his wedding."

It has taken me a long time to see this clearly and in perspective. I can understand now my confusion, my sister's pain. But I still do not get my parents' reaction. Rarely did my mother refer to it. My father never. They virtually never went to the cemetery. I would say it was an unwritten taboo, that it was a subject not to be broached.

After that, I no longer needed to speculate on what my father felt when seeing his brother die suddenly. Different cause, but the same misfortune. Was there a family reservoir of strength from which I could now draw upon? Could I summon new energy as my father had? From where?

My brother had died shortly before the holiday of Passover, the time we celebrate the freedom of our people and the liberation from slavery. The seder at my grandmother's home in my youth was always an exuberant, noisy, gala affair. Not this one. I can still feel the sense of dread that was at the table that night. There were the four of us. That night was really different. Everything we ate tasted like the bitter herbs. We went through the ritualistic portions rapidly and finished early. That Passover was not the time of our joy.

Ironically, I was to read many years later that Alexander Fleming, the founder of penicillin, actually had made the discovery in the 1920's. Fleming was discouraged as to its efficacy as a cure and only many years later other researchers took up his original finding of the mold in the shoe and on the coat and brought it along to the point where penicillin was developed into a major health finding of the Twentieth Century.

Subsequently, Fleming and the others received the Nobel Prize. The year it came on the market and was available was shortly before my brother's death in 1943. Who knows what would have happened if the medication had been ready when we needed it. We were not to be that lucky.

But going back to the immediate period right after his death, I remember one bit of consolation. It did not dissipate the pain, but it made it more bearable. In keeping with the tradition, a group of people came to our house to pray with us morning and evening. We said the kaddish prayer in memory of my brother. A group would gather every day in our home. There was something comforting in the sense of community loss. At the end of the service people would come and squeeze our hand and mumble some words I did not quite get. But the intention was clear. They were telling us that they wanted to share the pain. And it helped.

Then I was trying to figure out what had happened. Was I also doomed? To me, it felt like the answer was YES. I had no energy to move – and saw no purpose in it. My life had fallen to pieces.

So now, many years later my wife and I, having the joy of a large and loving family and my having enjoyed a long, and some would even say, an illustrious career, I look back on all that has happened and I come back to the biblical Joseph. Can I say as he did that all of this happened for the best, that God arranged it all so that all of us who remain would be more appreciative of our lives and better people? Can I say that whatever God does is for the best and that we live in the best of all possible worlds? And that if my brother had not died I never would have felt the pain of so many other people and the powerlessness of the Holocaust and gone on to do whatever it is that I have done. Can I say all of that in honesty?

I cannot. To think that my brother died to shake me from my dreamlike complacency as a high school student and to provide me with greater focus and concentration on what I wanted to do and where I wanted to go – is appealing, but I totally reject it. I cannot possibly accept the thinking that would make it possible. He died so that I should live? It certainly is not fair to him, and to me it would be an awesome burden. Is my blood redder than his?

What about the biblical Joseph and his view, that God sent him to Egypt to be there at the right moment? I have not found the answer to these big questions that I am looking for. I still do not know the secret of the universe or the why of it all. The questions have long been with me and I have searched through the Bible and other sources for an answer. But knowing the questions has helped and knowing that after reading the Book of Job the questions are legitimate and the expression of them is also fair and even necessary. Job is a person of true Biblical proportion. I never saw myself as him, but his questions were mine.

Very often lately I come back to the memory of my father with renewed respect and love. I see it now that he was really the role model that I needed and the example to clear away some of the confusion. What was the response to the tragedies he had experienced? I saw the outward and reflexive part of his answer. He got up every morning full of energy and enterprise, ready to fill the day with effort, with hope and with success. His family had to be nourished and sustained and he was Joseph the Provider and he filled that role to perfection. It is still hard to believe that we each suffered the same fate, a dead brother, long before his time.

I still ask myself how do I repay my brother? It would be nice to see a neatly tied package, that he fed meaning into my life and into the life of my family. But the arithmetic just doesn't work. Was I really worthy of that sacrifice? Truth is I don't like to think about it. I try to submerge the thought of it. Like my father, I have also adopted the solace of silence. He never referred to it and neither do I.

And still every day internally I hear the command: Go forward! Do I owe that to thoughts of Elliot Fenster of blessed memory? How much of my life of today do I owe to him? A lot.

Somewhere along the line, the words of the old Psalm became my mantra: "A moment of trial in God's sight; weeping rules the night, but joy arrives in the morning,"

Looking back I ask myself how did I get off the bed and back into life. First I have to be grateful that I didn't fall into the many psychological traps that were out there. I never asked myself, "Is this a punishment for something that I did?" I never asked myself "Why me," though I often wondered "Why anybody?" Why is the world so constructed and God so silent that innocent eight-year olds can die within a few hours and their families remain completely bereft?

Nowadays they have a technical term for what apparently was happening to me at that time. They call it PTSD, Post Traumatic Stress Disorder. After the disaster of 9/11 many of the survivors of the Twin Towers and the families of those who did not survive learned about it. Now we know that such a traumatic event can bring on anxiety or panic and a lot worse. And that it can last a long time, accompanied by physical symptoms or lethargy, anomie or hostility. I was fortunate not to develop any obsessions, compulsions, psychosis or depression.

But anxieties I did not escape. They were with me for a long time, old antagonists, persistent combatants. It left me feeling that security is an illusion. The Evil One pounces without notice. Beware. Be ready.

The search took a long period of time. I wanted to reach the point where I didn't have to use my nose drops every four hours for my sinuses, or aspirin for my throat, or periodic naps during the course of the day. At one point I was able to say to myself: I don't need this any more – get beyond it.

CHILDHOOD FLASHES

O THER FLASHES OF the past influence me. A number of early memories still rattle around in my head. One of them has to do with my grandmother on Kol Nidre night. Kol Nidre night inaugurates the most awesome day of the Jewish calendar which is Yom Kippur. It is a day of fasting, penitence and the making of resolutions for the year ahead.

This took place on East 12th Street in Brooklyn not very far from the school I attended as a youngster. My grandparents had bought a house there which remained in our family for eighty years. As she was getting older, our family came to live with her for awhile, as did my other aunts and uncles. My grandfather had already died and while her mind was always active, her strength was fading.

On this eve of Yom Kippur on Kol Nidre night, she had gone to the small synagogue around the corner from the house on Coney Island Avenue. Our family had gone to a large modern Orthodox synagogue a few blocks away. By the time we got home it probably was 10:30 at night. She was not there. My mother sent me around the corner to see what had happened and to bring her home. I will not forget walking into that small synagogue that night. There were two or three people still praying, still engaged. One was my grandmother. "Grandma, it's late, come home with me now." Today we would say that my grandmother was "cool." She called me by my Hebrew name, Mordecai. "Sit down" she said, "on Kol Nidre night you don't run out of the synagogue. Stay and say a few prayers, it'll do you good."

At that hour at my age, I was not in much of a reverent mode, so shortly thereafter I urged her homeward. But the message came through to me. Later, I must have told it to my congregation many times. My grandmother was not one to rush out of the synagogue. Did that affect me? I don't know, but I do still tell the story. I have never forgotten the awesome silence in the synagogue on that Kol Nidre night. I search for it every year.

Around the same time another incident occurred which has burned itself into my memory. It occurred at the school I attended, the Yeshiva of Flatbush, which I would describe as a progressive educational institution. Its students were from solidly middle class homes. But some things always remain the same. On this particular day our teacher called in sick. Naturally, the ten-year olds in my class and myself were overjoyed. A substitute showed, brought in by our principal. The principal, Joel Braverman, warned us about behaving with the substitute. We all listened carefully and, of course, the moment he shut the door pandemonium broke out. The teacher finally quieted us down for awhile, did some teaching, but it didn't last long. The noise factor was high, so high in fact that it brought the principal back into the room.

Now the principal was livid and asked the substitute to point out the kids that were causing the disturbance. It wasn't me because I was daydreaming about something or other. But it was the son of what was reputed to be the wealthiest family in the school. The teacher pointed out the culprit. Braverman began what probably would have been a few choice rebukes. But before he could get very far into it, this kid blurted out, "Braverman, f – you." A sickening silence permeated the room. Personally, I thought the ceiling would fall in the next moment. But before we could recover, Braverman moved. He ran over to this child of affluence and bango, smacked him across the face with an open-palmed hand and a resounding clout, which I sometimes still hear in the middle of the night. Truthfully, I don't even remember what happened after that. It seemed to me like all hell broke loose. But it's quite possible that the kid never reported it at home because it didn't exactly resound to his favor. It bespeaks of an altogether different time. It did shake me at least into the reality that the world was not always this dreamy pleasant, fantasy-like place I had constructed for myself.

The beginning reality came when I graduated elementary school and began attending James Madison High School, at that time one of the premier schools of Brooklyn.

PAIN AND JOY

B EFORE THAT, AS a youngster I had a serious illness but it turned out okay. I had hoped that it would be repeated with Elliot. But it wasn't.

My childhood was essentially unselfconscious and without pain. I was a chubby, dreamy, generally happy youngster until a knawing earache felled me at age eight. No antibiotics available. The ear drained for a few days and then closed up. The infection was still within.

I had a hint something was radically wrong when my distant cousin, the doctor, showed up to examine me. In those days you undertook nothing serious medically until a family member was consulted. Of course, that he was a urologist, was no deterrent. But he confirmed serious trouble.

My parents were both ill with fever and flu. They told me I was going to the hospital only to take x-ray pictures. They couldn't go but my Uncle Mike would have his chauffeur drive me and he would come along as well. I took to the idea of the limousine, and I was fine with my Uncle Mike. All of that was to change.

It was all very confusing and was to get worse. Once on the gurney and in the operating room, a nurse began shaving my head. "I'm here for x-rays." No one spoke.

A moment later a chloroform mask was clapped over my mouth. Anesthesia. "You're making a big mistake. Take that off me. I'm going home." I kept protesting until I dozed off and they did their work. Successfully, thank goodness. But I have never forgotten the awful feeling that a terrible wrong was proceeding. How did I get into this? How do I get out of it?

Some hours later I awoke. My head ached. I touched it. Bandaged. I looked out. There were bars on the window. Another giant mistake must have taken place. Why was I in jail? What had I done?

The nurse appeared and began to explain. I was going to be fine in ten days. And your parents are going to be here tomorrow. And before you know it, you'll be playing football again. Now just close your eyes and rest. And despite its traumatic beginning, it all turned out exactly that way.

But when I come across one of those books that tell youngsters about going to the hospital, I smile inwardly. Ironically, I was born too soon.

A few weeks after my operation when things began to return to normal, we were getting ready for our annual summer retreat. I was then quite young and my head was bandaged from the mastoid operation. But the previous summers we had gone to a bungalow in Far Rockaway for the summer. These were the days before air conditioning so the ocean breeze provided a little relief from the heat. My aunt and uncle and their family had a place close-by, as did many friends that formed a warm community. I remember those summer journeys as a happy and nourishing time.

However, this one year my mother warned me not to go into the ocean because of the draining which still continued from my ear. But my older cousin Alvin Samter and I would walk the beach and before I knew it, the ocean was too intriguing to abstain. The Atlantic Ocean has always had a special drawing power over me, especially that part at the end of Brooklyn where we lived and in those summer places where we stayed. We always lived within a fifteen or twenty minute drive from the Atlantic.

When I was young, on Sunday morning frequently my father would say, "Let's go to the boardwalk." I think he liked to look into the ocean that had brought him to America. He was entranced, I think, by how far he had come. Now he was taking his oldest son for rides in automated cars in a recreation park, and other delights which I lapped up with great relish. I remember looking at him when the ride was finished and the motor would be shut off. He knew I was looking for a nod that I could go around again. No problem.

Actually, there was a time as I grew older when I would take the trolley in front of my house down to Sheepshead Bay, walk across the wooden bridge into Oriental Beach where I had a season pass. The whole experience was marvelous. I was eleven. At the beach you had a locker and you could go swimming in their pools or the ocean, there was entertainment. I still remember seeing Betty Hutton, Vincent Lopez, and Spike Jones before they had achieved their fame which came their way later.

But the summer right after the operation presented a great challenge. I finally succumbed and jumped into the water, careful not to get my head wet. Such, at least, was my intention. But after the first few moments, feeling more comfortable, I began jumping the waves. Growing even bolder I moved further into the water until one wave sailed over my head. My bandage was soaked and I ran out. I knew I couldn't go home, so my cousin and I walked around for hours, lying on the beach, buying popcorn and coke, and waiting for it to dry. It finally did and, as I recall, my mother never really discovered it. But I was scared as could be when we had to go back a few weeks later to have the head band changed by the surgeon and happy to hear that it all looked quite good. From this I learned that jumping high is often very good, but also could be dangerous.

Those summers in Far Rockaway made a strong impression on me. I remember the vendors coming around in the morning, shouting their wares: "I cash clothes." I had no idea what that meant, but it sure sounded exotic. In fact, I never saw anybody doing business with him, but I can still see his face and hear his voice. Not all the memories were good ones. Every once in awhile there would be a small gas explosion from the stoves that were used in these bungalows, which apparently were not that safe. But all in all I have fond memories of it.

My sister Eleanor, who later turned out to be quite a public relations specialist and co-partner in one of the more prestigious Manhattan firms, found the beginning of her entrepreneurial career on the beaches of the Rockaways. She would spend hours searching in the sand for Coca Cola bottles, washing them out and gaining 2 cents a bottle. I never had to ask her for money, which she always had, but I surely admired the way she knew how to put it all together. And I still do, especially when we spend time on Fire Island at her house, her family and mine, once again so near the heart of the Atlantic Ocean.

So now I see more clearly that my early life was much taken up with pain, sickness and early death. They scared the hell out of me. But there was the other side as well. It showed me a glimpse of heaven.

Having subsequently been involved in hundreds of rites of passage, I know how central Bar/Bat Mitzvah times are in the life of the family. I remember my own vividly. It took place at the Young Israel of Flatbush. But I hadn't really met the rabbi, Solomon Scharfman, till shortly before my big day.

For me, our first meeting was memorable. He was young and after a few minutes of conversation, noting that I was tall (and presumably strong) challenged me to a hand wrestle which he promptly won. OK, how about a repeat? He let up a little and the second round was mine, but he emerged victorius from the rubber match.

He was the first rabbi I really got close to in any way; it was a wonderful introduction. And truth is I have used the same ice-breaking device with young people on many occasions. Except with young ladies. There I try charm. I hope it works. Rabbi Scharfman's moment certainly worked with me.

In readying me for my Bar Mitzvah, my teacher informed me boldly that I was a hopeless monotone. Minimum singing for you. But he added, for compensation, I like your speaking voice. As a result, I wound up with two speeches on the day of my Bar Mitzvah: one in Hebrew, the other in English.

Looking around the crowded synagogue that morning I wondered who would understand my Hebrew speech. Certainly not my cousins or my family. But I plowed ahead nonetheless. Sort of what I faced many times in the future. My knees were quaking, but my voice was steady. My teacher, my parents were happy.

The luncheon at the synagogue afterward was marvelous. I remember everyone treating me as if I were a young prince. I liked it. One of the waiters asked me if I would like "an orange blossom." I had no idea then, or now, what the ingredients were but I enjoyed my new status. A rite of passage.

I also remember the joyous singing at the luncheon and a speech made by the President of the Young Israel, Mr. Simeon Gross. To this day, every time I see his children, Elliot and Eleanor, as I often do, the picture of this warm and dignified man comes to mind. My Bar Mitzvah remains a standout in memory.

Nowadays, Bar Mitzvah celebrations at times get out of hand; they are over the top. Mine wasn't, a tribute to our community.

While still quite young, another perplexing event happened.

We were living on Ocean Avenue where I would take the trolley car to Avenue J, less than a ten minute ride, and walk to school. It was my habit to put on my skullcap and study the day's lesson in the Bible or the Prophets on the trolley.

On this particular day, I was deeply absorbed sitting in my seat. I didn't particularly notice the man standing above me. Apparently he had been observing my study for a few moments. "Listen sonny, this is America, take off the yarmulke" he ordered.

I was stunned, but obedient. I was eleven. Complying, I took off my skullcap and put it in my pocket.

I have often thought of other possible responses, like, "Look here you weak-kneed Jew, flake off" or "My dear sir, because this is America I wish to exercise my right to be what I am and not take crap from guys like you" or "Buddy, I have two words for you and they are not "Happy Birthday."

I said none of the above or anything else. By then I had been taught to respect elders in age, if not in wisdom. I have always been embarrassed by my compliance and still am. All I can say is – I was eleven.

Every once in a while someone will ask me, "Why don't you wear a yarmulke all the time? My answer should really be: "find that fellow that told me to remove it. It's his fault."

Fortunately, my childhood was not without its humorous side as well. This could best be illustrated by an event which happened when I was eleven. Lying on the floor of the bedroom, I heard my mother call asking me to wash up for dinner. I don't move. Second call, same reaction. My mother appears, "Why don't you get up and wash your hands?" No answer. I must admit there must have been some mystical alignment of the planets that led to my obstinacy. I cannot account for it otherwise.

My mother came into my room and began to lift me bodily from the floor. I wasn't tiny, but neither was she. Feeling the pressure, I gave out with an "Aw sh___." She did not hesitate; she strode into the bathroom, brought out a cake of soap, and before I knew what hit me, shoved it into my mouth and pushed it around. My protest was done. I got up silently and removed myself to the kitchen.

Six decades later I can still taste the soap. Since then I have tried to adopt cleaner speech. I still have no idea where that expletive came from.

In many ways, my mother had a profound influence on my life. She spoke clearly and articulated thoughtfully. And I have never heard a curse or expletive leave her lips. She taught us well. Thanks, Mom!

JAMES MADISON HIGH

MY PARENTS HAD always taken an active interest in my schooling and especially my mother would monitor me carefully. But she was always very supportive. While I was playing football at Madison High School, I can never forget her appearing at one of our games with a small Madison flag in her hand which she waved excitedly when I went by with the team. I was reminded of it many years later in viewing Arthur Miller's "Death of a Salesman," where they also had these small Madison High flags. If I remember correctly, that game in the play was taking place at Ebbets Field. In high school we too played at Ebbets Field.

The focus of this incident was that you were not supposed to leave the school during the course of the morning. But we lived right around the corner and so my mother would prepare a hot lunch for me every day and I don't know if I was aware of the rules or conveniently forgot them, but I would go home for lunch and then come back to school. I was able to do that because when you are on the football team they didn't make you take the gym class, so I had that free time.

One day inevitably they caught me. I was brought up to the office of the principal who knew me and my family and said he was surprised that I had violated the rule and he would have to call my mother to come up. My mother Beattie arrived and I will never forget the scene in the principal's office. He explained that I had violated the rule. My mother listened patiently until she finally exploded. "Mr. Blumstein, do you mean to tell me that my son has to eat what you are serving in the cafeteria instead of the nourishing and well-prepared lunch that I have for him at home? You ought to be ashamed of yourself for calling me up here for such nonsense." With that she walked out in a huff. Of course when I came home that night she did say perhaps I better stop doing it because they seem pretty upset. But she didn't back down. The support was right there.

My football career was short-lived. I was scheduled to be on the first team in my senior year, but I left to attend Yeshiva College. My coach, Mike Torgan, shook his head in disbelief. No one had ever left his team to become a rabbi.

However, the athletic field at Madison High gave me a boost that I still feel. It was before the season started, we were scrimmaging with Erasmus High. They seemed bigger and stronger than us, but it wasn't a regular game – so it hardly mattered. The coaches were sorting out their players.

At one point the coach sent me in. "Watch out for that big guy, he runs hard." As luck would have it, minutes later the big guy is heading toward me, the ball cradled to his chest, his legs pumping.

It seemed awful quiet to me, like the world stopped to watch. I didn't see anyone else on the field, but him and me. This was the moment of decision. I hesitated for a split second, but dove at him fiercely. Unbelievable. I brought him down, as clean a tackle as I ever made. Never mind my Bar Mitzvah. Today I became a man.

The next moment the assistant coach is running onto the field all excited, pounding my back, telling me I made the team. That very day they were handing out jerseys to the squad. The future rabbi received one and even slept in it that night. Forget the playing fields of Eton – my choice is Madison.

One of the other normal things I did as a teenager was to join some of my friends who were heading for downtown Brooklyn for jobs as ushers in a giant movie theater called the RKO Albee. Since I had never worked in my life it seemed like it would be fun. Especially when they gave me the uniform that I would wear, and more particularly, the coat and hat I would wear for Saturday night. The head covering was something akin to what a drum major would wear and the coat also had epaulettes with gold strings hanging from it.

As I remember it, there were large groups on Saturday night trying to get into the movie. My job was to stand in the lobby with another usher and alternately we would loudly proclaim: "For a shorter wait for seats, kindly use the stairway to your left – the stairway to your left for a shorter wait for seats." The stairway brought people up to another major gathering center on the balcony floor and our spiel was meant to indicate that there you would have to wait a shorter time until seats were available.

This legendary proclamation was accompanied with a gesture, pointing to the stairway and a wiggling of the fingers. Of course, I was wearing white gloves. It was also a very special privilege to be given that job which everybody was vying for because of its relative ease and not having to push the crowds back. Only guys who looked like football players were chosen. My grandchildren still love when I do my usher routine – "for a short wait for seats . . . . kindly use the stairway to your left." It still moves me as well.

It didn't last very long. I was making thirty seven & a half cents an hour, which was a fair wage for those days. I often bought lunch for a quarter. It consisted of a tuna fish sandwich with lettuce on rye bread, a side portion of potato salad and a coke. All for twenty-five cents!

The reason the job didn't last long was that my father didn't like it. I would come home late at night and then have to go back again on Sunday. After a few weeks of driving me downtown to the job, he asked me how much I was making there. When I told him, he said, "Good, I'll pay you more to stay home." That was the end of my ushering career. But it did give me the opportunity to find my voice, so to speak, and while that oft-repeated statement of the shorter wait never helped me in my rabbinic life, it did give me some indication of how you control crowds. And I still love to imitate my sixteen year old self.

SUMMERTIME IN PENNSYLVANIA

AFTER MY BROTHER'S death, the light came in the summer of 1943 and of all places, it began at a summer camp in Pennsylvania. That summer enabled me to go from confusion over Elliot's death to a clarity in my own life. I needed to connect to others in order to heal myself. I wanted to get back into life. It was as if someone threw an anchor to me which I grabbed onto before drowning. Could it be that from my pain I would discover my redemption? Did my Redeemer live?

But given my background I see now that there was something more. I felt keenly even though I was still a teenager, the pain and powerlessness of my family and of my people. I also began to have nightmares about the Shoah – the Holocaust as it is called. I couldn't quite understand then, nor do I understand even today, how the world and even the Jewish people sat there and allowed their young and old to be burned up alive while Roosevelt was smiling with his pince-nez and cigarette holder and Churchill was chomping on his cigar, taking baths and drinking whiskey. Both were excellent statesmen and eloquent orators. Why not put those talents in the service of my people?

Why didn't one million Jews from New York and all over go to Washington, sit down in front of the White House, and refuse to move until something was done? I have no question in my mind that would have done it. The planes were flying daily over Auschwitz but never bombed them. People by the thousands were pouring in and going out in a chimney of smoke. And few were disturbed by it. Every landmark of civilized behavior and moral restraint was trampled in service of the idol Moloch. The Bible strongly protested this barbarous practice of passing the child through the fire. (Lev. 18:21). The Nazis didn't accept the prohibitions. No culture, no religion, no decency could ever condone it. And yet: Deafening Silence.

In fact, there was one attempt at public demonstration with the goal of influencing President Roosevelt.

Later I learned that on October 6, 1943, four hundred mostly Orthodox rabbis gathered, under the leadership of Rabbi Eliezer Silver, and tried to meet Roosevelt at the White House. They failed. It was the only attempted rally at the height of the Holocaust to save European Jews.

If there was any guilt I was to sense it later, realizing that in 1943 I was at camp studying those texts that I intuitively believed would carry me through.

Almost a half-million people were arriving at Birkenau-Auschwitz from Hungary and most of them were killed upon arrival. That is where the infamous Dr. Josef Mengele stood at the entrance and pointed people to life or death. And during that time I was enjoying the sun and the lake, eating substantial meals and having a good social time. The crematoria were going twenty-four hours. I have often wondered about those who pushed the button, or pulled the lever, bringing death into the crowded rooms of the gas chambers. It did not take long for the screams and the death cries to die out. What did these inhuman humans do during those moments? What had ever happened to the Germany of Beethoven, Heine, Brahms? Did they look away unable to watch the sight? Did they sing a Wagnerian solo? Did they just watch in fascination, in sadism and obscenity? Did those people then finish their work for the day and go home to the comfort of family and dinner? Apparently, they did. Incomprehensible.

Among those they put to death in a camp in Lvov was my aged grandfather, whom I had never met. To this day I think of him often, of his fear and confusion and, I hope, of his strength. I am still filled with pain and anger in recalling his memory. No text or explanation has ever helped me to understand the enormous perversity of his murder. God didn't do it. The Nazis did. How could God remain silent? How did we?

Out of those disturbing thoughts and moments this awesome charge came to me. Young people like you, have to see that such powerlessness never again happens. We need many to work to reach that goal. Be one of them. I have tried.

FIRST STEPS

WHAT HAPPENED AT camp that summer of 1943 was that I was invited to explore the Bible with a fellow counselor who was a few years older. We began to study together. How it came about was completely by accident, if one could speak of complete accidents. This was a fellow by the name of Jacob, a religious guy from a yeshiva in Baltimore. Looking back, I owe him a great deal. Somehow or another on one of the very first days of camp, we were thrown together and after learning that I had eight years of elementary education in a religious atmosphere but was now attending a secular high school, he said: "How about if you and I study Bible together a little bit during the rest hour every day?" I don't know where he came up with that idea, but he turned out to be a first-rate outreach teacher before that term had ever come into existence.

Rest hour in camp comes after lunch. It is a daily respite from a heavy schedule of morning activities, of baseball, basketball, tennis, soccer, whatever. And so we met. The problem was there were occasions that by the time he arrived, I had fallen asleep. I was carrying on this vigorous schedule and of course counselors wait until the little ones go to sleep so they can have some social activity at night. This meant that oft-times during the day we were a little sleepy and sometimes even groggy.

But Jacob persisted. After awhile I realized how much I was enjoying our study together. It was invigorating. Was this the anchor that I was looking for? He never suggested the next step but I came to it on my own. I saw it as an extension of what I had earlier experienced at youth services at school on Shabbat morning, that sense of envelopment and embrace.

We were reviewing the Book of Leviticus, the third book of Moses, Chapter 19, often referred to as the "Holiness Code." I was taken by the smooth joining together of the ritual and ethical tradition. As Jacob was teaching it to me, the aspiration of holiness impacted: not to withhold the wages of the day laborer – not to curse the deaf, to rise before the aged – to love the stranger as yourself, and to remember that you were strangers in the land of Egypt – to love your neighbor for (he/she) is like you. I was feeling personally addressed. The commandments were simple and for me. But now I heard the thunder of Sinai in them. I wanted to go further.

I enjoyed learning, not only for the intellectual component. It was speaking to my soul; it was nourishing a part of me that felt very much in need.

It was that summer after my brother had died – and it could be the events were related – that it dawned on me that I had found a plan for my life's work, to become a rabbi. Truthfully, I didn't know I was looking for some deeper design. But it came nonetheless.

As I look back, I ask myself what exactly was it nourishing? I have no doubt I was discovering my spiritual dimension, the stuff that feeds the *neshama*, the soul. All my life my physical needs had been more than adequately cared for. Now I was learning that we do not live by bread alone and that here I would be out on my own. It took my brother's death to bring that dramatically home to me. I did not realize it but I was searching for a stronger connection to God and to the tradition. And I found it. With Jacob's help.

It was obvious to me right from the start as soon as I made up my mind I wanted to be a rabbi, that there was a big gap between my intention and the reality. First of all I would have to tell my parents and that might not be too easy. My mother had me take Latin in high school so that I could become a doctor. My father had built up a business so that I could take it over. I didn't envision smooth sailing ahead.

I was also sixteen years old and somewhat impatient to get going. I decided to write home, at least I knew that would give me a few weeks to mull it all over and to prepare my arguments. Three days later, summoned by a loudspeaker, the inevitable return call confirmed my worst fears. I raced up to the office, my heart pumping rapidly. My mother conveyed immediately her displeasure by asking me if I had come down with a fever.

She informed me that my father was outraged. I made a simple point on the phone. I would be home in a few weeks; let's wait until I get there and we could discuss it. "Nothing is going to happen right now, so you and Dad please relax."

Arriving home a few weeks later, the situation had not improved. My family was respectfully traditional, but a Rabbi? Where is that coming from?

There had been no rabbi in my family heretofore. At that point I had no model or mentor. I was no one's disciple. A life of pious poverty had no appeal to my family, nor in truth, to me. There were, of course, still nostalgic memories of Europe for my father, but as time went on they were fewer and less well remembered. In fact, most of them were dour.

In America my father had become a businessperson, one man with the energy of two. He plied his trade relentlessly. In his mind, I was to be the inheritor of the business. Now I was throwing it all over for some foolhardy and elusive goal. He couldn't quite understand why I would choose to be a *schlepper* when I could be a success?

Once, in a fit of exasperation, he told me that in Europe the Rabbi lived in isolation and poverty. "Do you think I came to America to see my son become a Rabbi?" What hurt was not really that I had no answer; it is that I had no role model for the kind of rabbi I was interested in becoming.

I fumbled feebly to explain that I had no head for business. Frankly, I also had little interest. I didn't consider it beneath me (for it had made a comfortable life possible), but in fact, if anything, it was beyond me. I could see myself swimming relentlessly upstream in one place. I told my father that if I went into the business that he had patiently built up over many years, I would probably bury it within two.

None of these comments on my part had any resonance within the family, but my mind had been made up. I persisted. I proceeded to inquire how one gets admitted to the Talmudical Academy, the High School division of Yeshiva University. (Actually at that time it was still Yeshiva College). There was no problem as far as the High School was concerned and I transferred there for my senior year.

The Rabbinic department of Yeshiva University, however, was quite different There, a body of knowledge and Talmudic learning were prerequisites. Though I was a graduate of the Yeshiva of Flatbush, in those days there was no Talmudic learning in elementary school and for three years I had been at Madison High School in Brooklyn, where of course my Jewish studies had languished. At Madison High I was engaged in playing football, but now all of that was to change. Yeshiva College had no football team.

Seeing that I would not be deterred, my father came with me to YU, and we spoke to Dean Samuel Sar. He said that it would be possible for me to gain entrance into the Rabbinical Department if I studied twenty-five folios of Talmud and knew them well within the next three months.

At that point a tutor was assigned to me to prepare for the entrance exam. I remember him as a short fellow named Sol with a lot of energy and complete dedication to the task. He offered me no pep talks, no compliments or sermons, just straight teaching. I have also never seen him in the last fifty years though I often wonder where he is today. Meanwhile I was taking to his teaching more than I ever expected. Our subject was Talmud Baba Metzia which is filled with torts and damages, legal concepts, acquisitions and commercial dealings. It was unlike anything I had ever studied before. Later on I came to the conclusion that there were other parts of the Talmud that I enjoyed much more. But at that moment I had no choice. The material of Baba Metzia filled my days and occupied my nights. At the end of three months I discovered that I passed with flying colors and was placed in the Rabbinical School of Yeshiva University. It was for me then, and even now in retrospect, a day of great triumph. I was on my way.

A routine was quickly established. All week long I would live up near Amsterdam Avenue and 187th Street, around the corner from the school. On Friday I would come home and be there for Shabbat. That in itself proved to be quite an interesting experience.

On Shabbat in our home, my father left early, my sister and my mother were out doing one thing or another, and I was left home by myself. That proved to be a bonanza to me. I loved it. I would go to our nearby synagogue in the morning, come home, have lunch, sit and study, take a walk, take a nap, and be with my internal thoughts all day long. Those Sabbaths were really an island of spiritual repose and quiet. They confirmed my intuition that I wanted to continue on that path.

I really gained a great deal of strength from those Sabbaths. But my parents didn't quite get it. They used to chide me, asking how I could be home by myself all day. That is the part of this story, which, thanks to my mother, turned out to have a happy ending.

One Saturday afternoon in late spring, my mother came home around six o'clock and I was there by myself. No one was home. She saw my head in a book and said, "What is that you're always studying?" I said, "Mom, this time of year, we study *Pirke Avot* a text of the Mishnah, with very relevant and concise advice about life, Torah, manners, and about aspirations." She said to me, "Okay. Teach me some of that *Pirke Avot*."

I didn't have time to be nervous or to prepare. But it was probably the most important test I have taken in my life. My mother was intuitive and wise beyond her education. She was an American-born woman who had been out in the world, in business, before her marriage. She came from a large family, parts of which had gone on to academic distinction. It was always held up to me that my uncles had gone to Harvard, and my cousins had gone to Cornell. I was going to Yeshiva College. I had a lot to prove.

So we opened the book and we began to study. Truth be told, I don't even recall the passages I presented to her. I probably was so uptight that I did it by rote, or by good luck, or however. We went on for about twenty minutes. At the end of that period she closed the book and said, "You're okay! That's good stuff. You know what? You're going to be a good Rabbi." That was the beginning of my Rabbinic career. Convincing my mother that *Pirke Avot* was worth studying and teaching.

Whatever degree or distinction I have received since, none will ever compare to that moment. I also learned an important lesson that day. A supporting word or gesture at the right moment can sustain a life.

Still I ask myself where did it come from, beyond intuition, beyond Jacob and Sol and the supportive environment; there needed to be something more.

There had been brief flashes of spirituality that I had seen and that had spoken to me. A cantor, when I was very young, after singing a Kol Nidre service whose face shone with holiness; the way my grandmother double-kissed her prayer book in simple piety after the silent prayer was done; the earnest way my father recited the kiddush on Friday night, long after we had eaten. But he had just come home after a long day, signifying the onset of the Sabbath day for him. Those occasions had stirred me to a world beyond the mere physical. They were the stirrings of the soul – the early nourishment of the *neshama*.

Possibly most important for my future involvement was my participation in a young people's service on Saturday morning at the Yeshiva. I had been chosen to be the *gabbai*, a kind of young sexton. I would give out honors, roll the Torah, call the people up to the bimah.

I can recall running to the school to be there on time on Saturday morning. I also recall my father dropping me off and driving to work. (As a rabbi we always told parents that was a no-no.) Yet, it was the high point of the week, giving me the early basis of what it was like to be involved in leading religious services. I loved it. Still do!

WHO CALLED YOU?
I CALLED MYSELF

INTUITIVELY, I KNEW as soon as Elliot died and I felt my center dissolving, that both people, texts, and traditions could help. Where this came from I cannot say. But it was present and powerful.

Very often in those days and subsequently, I would be asked, "when did you get the calling to be a Rabbi?" It sounds like a fairly appropriate question. But I never liked it. Many clergymen and others speak of receiving or sensing that God is calling them, urging them to speak, or preach in the hope of leading their people to a higher ground.

I was and am always embarrassed by that question. How can you answer that without sounding ridiculous? The truth is I called myself. Beyond tragedy, I wanted to feel that my life was headed in some positive direction, that I was searching for some spiritual experience. I believed it was there, but at that point I hadn't found it. Still, I was exhilarated by the prospect that the Divine Presence, or the Shechinah, would favor me with a visit if I searched long enough. I was exalted by the prospect then, and still am to this day. It is fun to increase your speed when you know where you are going.

It is true that I had neither the background, nor the tradition, to become a Rabbi. My Mother told me after many decades of service that my Grandmother could not believe that the likes of me would become a Rabbi.

She had an old-world model in mind which I certainly did not fit. Strangely, she felt that playing touch-football on the street hours without end with my friends was no preparation for a rabbinic career.

While nobody expressly challenged my aspiration, I was aware of the skepticism. I had it myself. I guess it helped fuel my desire, and made me realize I would have to study harder, concentrate more, and just plain prove myself.

I certainly did not come to my decision of being a Rabbi trailing clouds of glory. I recognized that I was dreamy and unconcentrated. But knowing it did not help me to overcome. Fantasy is no substitute for the facts. My teachers wanted the facts. I was unable to supply them. Again and again, they told my parents that they sensed my potential but I was not living up to it. I would have loved to, but I had no clue as to how to do that.

I could and did sit in front of an open book for hours. I would see the print, and read it without absorbing the words. I suspect there are a lot of people like me at some time in their lives. My advice to them would be the same as I adopted – keep reading, keep talking to people, be curious, don't give up, and the rest will follow. If it is meant to be it will come. In a way, it was a good thing that I was dreamy, and that fantasy was my constant companion. If I had been realistic, today I would be selling bakery supplies. There is no crime in that, but it is a lot less of an interesting life.

During the Shoah, in 1937, I was 11 years old, and we were living in Brooklyn. Even I knew what was happening. Like Rip Van Winkle we slept through the Holocaust. The perversity of it still haunts me. The enormous monstrosity of what people are capable of still makes me shudder. Apparently it is possible for some to shut off all compassion and all emotion when it comes to other human beings. They are completely unaffected. I still don't get it. No reading of the Book of Job has ever helped me to understand the horrific things that happened to good people. It is so unfair, and represents a fatal flaw in our world.

If that is so, how can you speak of faith, and how does one maintain it in the face of evil incarnate? The words of the Forty-Second Psalm were powerfully descriptive. They applied to me: "As a heart pants after the waterbrooks, so does my heart pant after you, Oh God. My soul thirsts for God, the living God; when will I see your face?" I could never claim that I put the pieces of the world together so that I understood where everything fits. But I can say, that I felt God's Presence and impetus in my life. And that made all the difference. Not all the answers can be found like in a Regents preparatory booklet. But if you discover the questions, you can keep working at them for life. You learn to live with fragmentary insight. And keep going.

THERE IS A DIFFERENCE

A YEAR OR so after beginning my rabbinical studies, while I was still going home for the weekend, suddenly my attention was diverted to a young lady who was living next door. My mother had pointed out to me that she was tall and attractive and that I should really take her out. I resisted mightily. With good reason I claimed that if it didn't work out it could be embarrassing. "Do you want to move out of the neighborhood? Right now you have good relations with your neighbors. Don't you want that to continue?" My mother was undeterred by any of these arguments. She was nothing if not persistent and in the end she prevailed. We went out and I did pursue it further, and now that Ricky and I have been married more than fifty-nine years, I could also view that as a very blessed turn of event in my life after some of the tense and difficult times that preceded it. Without her, I know I couldn't have accomplished anything. As Neil Diamond sings, "You are the best part of me – the best I am or ever will be." That fits.

Our first date – tennis on a public court. Big time spender. But Ricky was always a good sport.

Truth is I had discovered the world of femininity at an earlier age. We were living in a small apartment on Ocean Avenue when my mother brought in a young woman to help in the house with the kids. I guess today we would call her an au pair. She was blonde, eighteen and from a small coal town in Pennsylvania. I was eleven and knew very little about male and female differentiation. In the school I attended there were few girls. In our class of twenty-five we had four. They played virtually no role in my life.

All of that was to change, but not dramatically. Years later I asked my mother, "How did you come to put Helen in my room?" My mother was astounded. "You were still wet behind the ears" was her response. That was true. But suddenly hormones began to flow that I didn't even know existed.

We were getting ready to move to a lovely private house in the same neighborhood on 28th Street. It was impressive with a high lawn and many rooms. But before the move, we were living in a smallish apartment. All the kids were sleeping in the same room, including Helen.

That first morning she was with us, she rose early and began to dress. I awoke, to see her take off her pajamas and began to get dressed. She didn't realize I was watching. It was a revelation, but I squinted so as not to be seen, as if I had done something wrong. I hadn't and I liked what I saw.

Our au pair Helen stayed with us for a long time. She was at one and the same time an older sister and a substitute female companion, keeping us company when our parents were not at home. She was with us on-and-off for the next seven or eight years, and she came back to us for a stint after Elliot died.

There never was any intimacy between us, but I always knew that she was there. I also knew that I was a kid and she was an adult. She would tell us about many boyfriends, and often would come home very late at night on her day off.

So by the time my mother began to point out the girl next door, I had begun to think of the future and even of a family. Four children, sixteen grandchildren, and sixteen great-grandchildren later, I must admit that my mother knew better what was good for me than I did. But of course I had to come to my own conclusions in my own time. It was like deciding to become a rabbi. I needed to feel that it was my own decision. Happily Ricky agreed.

Of course being a rabbi's wife was not an easy path for her. We both came from a similar style background. Her father had been born in Europe as had mine. Her mother had been born in America as had mine. Our homes were traditionally oriented but not in the European sense. There was already much accommodation to what you might call the American way. Sabbaths were observed on Friday night with candles and a festive meal, but there was no such atmosphere on Saturday itself. Dietary laws were observed at home, but not outside. Religious education was of value but not at the expense of general education or music or sports. If I was taking a giant step forward by going for the rabbinate, Ricky needed a jump and a leap.

But with one exception she never buckled. And I must say that in my opinion and in the eyes of others she has been an example to many. But while we were still in our early years and I was a student at the Jewish Theological Seminary, the wives of some of our teachers decided to help out these young women. They planned an evening for them when they would come together for do's and don'ts and for general hints about success in what is often a fish bowl existence.

As it turned out at the end of that evening, I almost lost a fiancee.

The problem was they made the rabbinate sound somber, strictly academic and soulless. I saw it as a joyful opportunity for being with people and teaching them in close companionship with fervent prayer and enthusiastic song. They also held up the ideal of the rabbi's wife – they called her the *rebbitzen* – as being a mine of information, also on duty 24/7, being a Hebrew-speaking surrogate rabbi. It did not wash, they had not done me a favor. I still recall the aftermath, there was pain and there were pleadings. They had missed the main point which is that if you do something not out of duty but out of desire and anticipated pleasure, all of the difficulties recede.

For both of us our lives have been a challenge. But also fun. And I think there is an element of surprise – look how far we have come!

This leads me to reflect on leadership, its sources and its goals. The more I experience the world and speak to young people, there is a truth that I see more clearly than before. This is the advice that I give them. If at all possible, go for your dream, no matter how difficult or far-fetched it might seem. But if it turns out that your dream was not quite correct for you, switch gears and go for another. There is nothing comparable to believing in what you do and enjoying it. Once you have found that, stick to it.

I have known many people for whom their day-to-day activity is drudgery and boring. Continuing along that path will burn you out. Of course in every job there are high moments and lower ones. You have got to take into account the whole picture. If there are difficult and irritating small details, don't sweat it. Try to see the big picture every day. Keep alive your sense of wonder and of grandeur. Keep the goal in sight.

Given my background I have never forgotten what a stretch it was for me to become a rabbi. I don't even know where such an idea began. I didn't have the background and I didn't come from the right family. I didn't even have a mentor or an example of the kind of rabbi I would want to be. And yet sixty years later I am still excited by the prospect – still learning, still hoping to get better at it. I have retired five times and still am trying to answer the bell for the next round.

The best thing parents can do for their children is to help them find what they really like and encourage and nurture their dreams. Tell them to keep at it – and keep their nose clean. They should do this, unless the youngster's dream is to be a full-time gambler or a rapist. Anything humane, decent and desirable should be encouraged.

WITH THE BOYS

IT WAS THE time of Andy Hardy movies with Mickey Rooney, innocent mischief.

I was eighteen and attending Yeshiva College. My Madison High School friends and I would come together on the weekend when I returned home. By this time I was punctilious about my observance of the Sabbath. None of my close high school friends were. I learned to order a lettuce and tomato sandwich in a Chinese restaurant.

Often we would gather on Saturday night. One of the guys, Aaron Jortner, (the first of us to pass away a half-century later) had a car. We used to refer to it as our Roger Toughy roadster. Its shape was like a box and its body like a tank. The boys would wait for me in the alleyway of my house because I couldn't leave until it got dark. But by May that would be 9:00 at night and of course these young buckaroos were impatient. They would start honking the horn. Often I would hear, "Hebe, – come on down, it's dark already, you idiot." After a few honks I would open the window from my room on the second floor and call down, "I will be out in ten minutes and if you guys don't stop honking the horn, I'm going to call the police," which of course I couln't do until the Sabbath was out anyway.

Thus we would begin our trip – to nowhere. As we drove some would open the window and pound the paneling of the outside, calling out "Let's go Shtume – don't fail us now." Shtume is the Yiddish word for the silent one and this silent one never spoke back, just kept going forward.

We thought the whole experience was hilarious and outlandish. We saw ourselves as serious kids coming from solid family backgrounds who needed to let off a little steam. This we did quite often until the following experience happened which helped dissipate our enthusiasm, certainly mine.

One Saturday night we were cruising around the Hi Ho Casino on Ocean Parkway. The Hi Ho was considered to be risqué – it certainly was trendy. There were six of us in the car. Of those who were there, none was ever to go to jail, to be indicted, or to get into any trouble of any kind. Solid citizens all. Quite the opposite, one became an internist with a very large practice, and four other physicians with him. One became a pediatrician, another a State Supreme Court Justice, and another a land developer who in the end, as he would like to boast, "could buy and sell all of his big-shot friends." And then there was this future rabbi.

But this night and the strength of being together, we stopped to invite a young lady into our car. She accepted. I swallowed hard; I had no taste for this thing at all. As a rabbinic student I didn't know how this was going to turn out. I was concerned. Before you knew it, we pulled away. She didn't seem particularly frightened, a lot less than I was. We drove a bit and then finally one of us blurted out, "Look lady, you know what you are here for, put out or get out." I almost died on the spot. Fortunately, she became indignant, told us to stop the car immediately, which we did, and she got out in a huff. I don't know about the others, but I can honestly say I heaved a sigh of relief. I love my friends from high school and to this day we still meet in hilarious reminiscence. But that is one incident that nobody ever brings up. We were skirting on the edge of disaster. We averted it.

AND OTHERS

S O MUCH OF my early background was tied to my friends and to our mutual unfolding. Because of my background and the schools I attended, I always felt somewhat apart. But in retrospect, I see it differently. So much of my younger days were spent in activities and outlooks that were typically Brooklyn and growing up in the '40's. Only later did I opt out. At the beginning, I was happy to be part of it.

I was reminded of that whole period watching Paddy Chayefsky's "Marty." It was fun up to a certain point. Then, like Marty, I wanted to get beyond it.

One of the events that I recall, while I was already a rabbinical student, was sleeping over at Murray Strober's house. Murray was always someone with whom I enjoyed spending time because there was always some fun and frolicking attached to it. Actually, Murray was a serious student who was admitted to Harvard Medical School after only three years at Columbia College. Murray was 6'4", a basketball player, and when told to present himself at the medical school for an interview, he had to borrow a rain coat and a tie for his trip to Boston. But he must have made a good impression because he sailed through. Murray was a Brooklyn original. He still is.

Sleeping at his house that night, I was impressed not only with the good time that we had, but Murray always read a book for an hour or so, no matter how tired he was. It became my life-long habit as well.

When Ricky and I finally started talking, the first thing we did was play a game of tennis together with our other friend from 28th Street, Ronnie Levine. It's strange looking back how Ronnie and I would refer to Ricky as the 'handicap' and the one who had to take her on their side. I long ago stopped playing tennis, but Ricky has continued and has become a much better player than I ever was. Of course, I take credit for the teaching.

But it all began with a long period where I completely ignored her. When it was finally time, I asked her out for our first official date. Debbie Weinerman, who lived nearby, was having a party on a Saturday night and I inquired whether it would be okay if I brought Ricky with me. Debbie was a friend and an advisor and I wanted to get her opinion of this young lady who lived next door. And so we went.

Debbie Weinerman subsequently married my good friend Stanley Harwood. Today we refer to him as Judge Harwood, formerly of the State Supreme Court in New York. Unfortunately, Debbie died some years ago and since I had officiated at their wedding and like all our friends shed many tears at her death, Stanley asked me to eulogize her. There were a large number of family and friends, judges and lawyers and high county officials present that day. I swallowed hard, but decided that out of loving respect to her memory I would have to tell this story. It may not speak so well of my worldliness, but it does remind me of her warmth and love for all of us.

Shortly after that first date, I asked Debbie if I could come over to her house because I had a problem that she could help me with. Blatt had taught me how to dance, awkwardly to be sure, but I could get by. Now I had to learn how you kiss a girl, and I had no idea how to do that. Where else would I go but to Debbie to have her demonstrate. In retrospect, I cannot believe it myself, but she proceeded to show me how one does that, delicately and passionately. All the boys knew that Debbie had the warmest and most delicious kiss. Not that she ordinarily offered them around so liberally, reserving them for Stanley, but we knew her abilities. I have always been grateful to her; first of all for not laughing at me and second, for doing such a good job. She was a special person who is still missed. Out of respect, I hope I learned well. She was a great teacher.

There are many aspects of our lives together that I would recall about Stanley Harwood, who was my neighbor across the street. I have chosen this even though it is the most painful but also pleasurable in remembrance.

One other incident in Stanley's life is still a powerful memory. Stanley's parents, Ben and Hannah, who I knew well, were not part of any synagogue and never attended, even on the High Holidays. That was unusual in our neighborhood.

Stanley and his brother Ted were nominally Bar Mitzvah, but that was it. One day Stanley told me a most unusual story. He woke up at midnight, went into his parents' room and saw his father standing silently in prayer. He was astounded. There was never any hint before of such activity.

His Dad explained: I can't go to synagogue anymore, but I pray in my own way, every day. When I was ten, my rabbi in class in Europe, hit me on my head with his ruler, it knocked off and broke my glasses. My parents couldn't afford another pair. I vowed never to return to synagogue again!

The lesson was not lost. The messenger is responsible for the message. Both are judged. I have tried to remember it all my life!

Nowadays, Stanley is married to Cathy. She is a lovely woman and I wish them both good health and long life together.

One of the other people I admired most from my early days was my friend for the last sixty-five years, Stanley Blatt. We started out in Brooklyn together. He also lived on Ocean Avenue. My first memory of him was when we were playing basketball with the other kids at Cunningham Park on East 16th Street and Quentin. I went up for a rebound off the basket, grabbed the ball and came down. But as I did, I sprained my ankle. Within the next five minutes it blew up the size of a balloon and I could barely walk.

Blatt was undaunted. He took my arm and put it on his shoulder and started practically carrying me home. I was overwhelmed with gratitude. "Stanley, you're a leader, you should be a doctor, you're gonna be a doctor." He looked at me like I was crazy. But it was one of the few times in my life when I turned out to be a prophet, because I have know him as an excellent pediatrician, who many people consult even about adolescent and adult problems. I once met a lady who told me the story about her young son who was running a high fever and she called the doctor and he came running over to the house. By that time doctors no longer made house calls. Her son had to be rushed immediately to the hospital, but within a few days returned home. His life had been saved because of the quick and early diagnosis. I asked her who her doctor was. "Stanley Blatt."

The next time I saw Stanley I asked him how come he had made the house call. His answer was most logical, "I know this woman for a long time and have taken care of her other children. She's not the alarmist type. When she told me she was very worried and the kid had a high fever, I knew I had to move. And it's a good thing I did."

They used to say of Fiorella LaGuardia that he once remarked, "When I make a mistake, it's always a beaut." I am happy to say that when I make a prediction, at least in this case, it turned out to be a beaut! When our kids were sick with a strep throat or whatever, and they were uncomfortable, I would often turn to my friend Dr. Blatt. Once I remember distinctly when our son Jonathan was about fourteen and ill I went downstairs to see how he was doing. He had only one request. "Get Blatt," I always received special joy when Jonathan's son Michael tells me he has just seen Dr. Blatt and he took care of his problems. All of that from a beginning with a sprained ankle at Cunningham Park! A healer then and now.

To this day Ricky and I enjoy being with Stanley, his wife Myriam and son Steven. We like to hang out together. Their other son Joel is married and has a few kids living in Denver. Recently the whole family was reunited in Denver. Actually, Ricky and I went out there and I officiated at Joel and Robin's wedding. While we were there we visited Aspen and Boulder and environs and saw the stone climbers, the rappellers. They go straight up with ropes and pulleys. I admired what I saw but didn't attempt to emulate it. I must admit to being most comfortable with my feet on the ground.

But the business of impulsive prediction can be a problem. Fortunately it has worked for me at crucial moments. When we moved to 28th Street in Brooklyn from Ocean Avenue, a short distance, Blatt came to see me. Someone had forgotten to teach me the social graces. In my head I heard the music and the tempo, but it did not communicate the message to my feet. "Stanley" I beseeched, "teach me how to dance."

I can still recall the serious tone with which we both approached the mission. No one was home. We put the music on in the living room, Blatt showed me how to take the lead, and we started trying to do the fox trot. I was moving, but clumsily. Blatt was whistling. What can I say? I never advanced beyond the two-step. But some years later, Ricky added a few additional touches to my limited repertoire. I still enjoy dancing with her, but I'm afraid my feet never quite got it. But I still hear the music in my head.

As we were coming out of the house that day, a dark brunette was emerging from the house next door. I kind of gave her a half wave. Blatt said to me, "Who is that?" "Stanley, that's the young lady I am going to marry."

Now I know it sounds a little bizarre, indeed it was. The truth is that I had never spoken to her. My mother, of course, had keenly observed what I had chosen to overlook. Later on Ricky claimed to have been watching me for six years, faithfully waiting for the day. In her mind's eye, she intuitively knew tht one day I would ask for a date. And that's precisely what happened. Too shy to ask directly, I wrote from camp that summer and arranged to meet with her when I returned home. After a few fumbling starts and misses, we did get together. First for tennis, then for Debbie Weinerman's.

But one aspect of his story that really set my friend Stanley apart was the way he got into his life's work. In high school he wasn't an outstanding student. Nor in college. Except that he bonded with his Biology professor and started working in his laboratory. He found he was good at research and loved doing it.

Meanwhile, he had to support himself. He started by placing cigarette machines in apartment house buildings, such as ours, in the neighborhood. He had made the contact with then a small time builder, Sam Lefrak, who would become a major builder in Queens. When it came to cigarette machines in his buildings, Stanley was his man.

But Stanley was unfulfilled. His professor told him to go on to study medicine, and making a living out of cigarette machines bothered him anyway. It was the late '40s but awareness was increasing.

Stanley took a great leap and left for Lausanne in Switzerland. They had open admission for med schools, but once you were in you had to keep up. Many flunked out. Stanley first had to learn French, a daunting task, especially the medical terms and had to work hard at it. He did it all. The school turned out excellent physicians. Stanley is one of them to this day.

That intuitive prediction, however, has become festooned in our genes. Let's hope it will always work for us.

Years later our son Jeremy was visiting with his friend in Kansas City. They went to see the Gibian family whom the friend knew from high school days. Ellen had been a classmate. Apparently they didn't announce their coming so when they got there, Ellen was not at home. Instead, her parents showed Jeremy a picture. Now I realize it doesn't sound rational, but Jeremy said it clicked in his head immediately. "This is the girl I am going to marry." Of course, he never said anything to her parents or to us or to anybody. But within the year it was accomplished. Do I recommend this predictive process to others? No, I do not. It could be catastrophic. Fortunately, in our family it has been magnificent. Thanks, God.

The tales of my high school group would not be complete without a description of my friend, Howie Hoffman, who we always called Chaimburick, for reasons long ago forgotten.

Chaim was a tall, loose, handsome basketball player for Madison High School and later for George Washington. He went on to score a great success with his life as a land developer, property owner, business entrepreneur. Going back to the 80's he owned a large house with a pool in Scarsdale where once a year "all the boys" and their spouses would go to frolic, retell and embellish ancient tales. Those were special times.

Howie came from the poorest family of all. I still remember the crowded, dark apartment which he, his parents and sister shared on Ocean Avenue. Not exactly a McMansion.

Blatt still tells the incident of Howie's Bar Mitzvah on Saturday morning at a local synagogue many years ago. Blatt went, but Howie never showed. Years later he explained that he had no suit to wear. There wasn't enough money for the traditional serge for the Bar Mitzvah. The rabbi had offered to buy him the suit when told of the problem. Rabbi Alexander Alan Steinbach was then the President of the New York Board of Rabbis and a generous presence in the community. Howie's father, hearing about it, nixed it immediately. "No son of mine is going to accept charity." Instead – No Bar Mitzvah.

We still promise each other that some day he will come to Jerusalem with me and be a Bar Mitzvah at the Western Wall, and have a Kiddush at the King David Hotel. It hasn't happened yet, but there is still time.

I never preached to my high school buddies, but I always had high hopes for them. I still do. Someday I am going to see Howie Hoffman and Murray Strober attain Bar Mitzvah status, I do believe!

UNEXPEDTED VISITORS

THE VERY NEXT summer I took my first plunge into the rabbinical world by getting a job for the summer as a counselor and camp rabbi. A friend who had held the job the summer before and who was not going back recommended me and the camp director signed on to it. I was then seventeen years old. An auspicious beginning. At least for me.

Of course a rabbi at a summer camp is not exactly the most prestigious person on the campus. In addition to my regular counseling duties it really meant that I was to conduct services on Friday night for no more than forty-five minutes and again on Saturday morning for no longer. While the campers all arrived solemn and dressed in white, the service itself was diluted and it was hoped would not be too burdensome. I signed on to that as well.

Neither the campers nor the staff were interested in lengthy disputations on religion or theology. Most had their minds focused on a nice swim before lunch.

Nonetheless, for me it was an awesome opportunity. And I can see that expression on my face in the picture I have of the first service I conducted. I see myself dressed in a linen robe and prayer shawl, wearing a skullcap, with a long-sleeved shirt, a tie. My face is set in a quite serious mode and I am squinting into the sun. But the outstanding feature that I see is my hair, rising in the style of the pompadour favored by the young in the 40's. As far as I can remember, I am not imitating anyone – since neither Elvis Presley nor the Beatles had not yet been heard from. The thick hair and the full lips are prominent.

But the most memorable part of the day was yet to come. The campers were filing into the bare benches that had been provided for the service. They were already wearing the languid look that accompanied the service. I had rehearsed the five minute sermonette over and over again in my mind and thought I had it down pat. Suddenly, a group of oversized guys appeared and started occupying the front seats. I couldn't believe my eyes. My friends, "the boys of summer" were there, six feet and taller, on the small benches. There was Strober, Harwood, Blatt and Hoffman. They had made their way up to the Catskills. They had come to see my debut as rabbi.

But before I could settle in to enjoy their coming, they began the razz, not screaming, but not exactly whispering either. "He's no rabbi, he's a fake – what school did he graduate? Don't believe him." I got the joke immediately, but I'm not sure anybody else did, or even heard what they were prattling. Since they quieted down, the service continued. Truth is that after those first shocking moments I was glad they had come. Ordinarily they were never quiet enough to listen to any homily that I was about to offer. But now I had a captive audience.

I remember distinctly what I said that day; it was a well-known story of the simple shepherd boy who whistled in the synagogue. It tells of a poor peasant lad who never had the opportunity to learn and did not know the letters of the alphabet. The prayer book was way beyond him. But his heart was overflowing with gratitude and awe for the opportunity to care for his sheep in the sun, to lead them to places where they could feed, to brooks of water. He gave vent to all of these feelings by issuing a long, loud, deep whistle in the synagogue. There are many versions to the story, but according to the original one, the Baal Shem Tov himself, recognizing the young man, stood up before the congregation and said, "Do not chase him out – this young man's whistle just broke the block that has prevented our prayers from reaching the heavens." The Baal Shem was reminding the congregation that a prayer of deep meaning in whatever way is always acceptable to God. Mechanical prayer is not the way to go.

Of course, the homily caught the attention of the listeners, and I am happy to say that nobody got up the following week to whistle in the synagogue. The point had been made at the very beginning. Prayer is the service of the heart – to be spoken in utter sincerity, with the hope of reaching its destination beyond. Concentrate and speak to God. You may not get an immediate answer. But you get a hearing.

At the end of the service my friends all gathered around me and I had a few brief moments with them before they left and I had to go back to caring for my youngsters. Looking back upon it, I am grateful to them for the time they took out to come, and even for the jocular approach which turned out to be less than disastrous. They are true friends.

Over the years I have given sermons to hundreds of assembled congregations. It is true the first was probably the most difficult – but it was also the most rewarding. I had passed the test of fire. First with Mom, then with the boys.

COMING TOGETHER

A S I LOOK back I am amazed how in that new environment, as a full-time Rabbinical School student, I was still able to carry on other interests as well. I became a reporter for our high school newspaper there and later in college, an editor of the Commentator, the undergraduate newspaper. Meantime I was reading Dos Passos' USA, Farrell's Studs Lonigan and John Steinbeck's Grapes of Wrath, all of which gave me a focus of the world in which we were living and peppered up my social activism. Especially Steinbeck. I remember being transfixed at the ending of his books, "Grapes" and "Of Mice and Men." We were living in affluent Flatbush, but this was taking place in real time.

Of course, truth be told, my excursions into Latin and Greek were a disaster. Sorry to say so was mathematics and especially trigonometry. My reaction to it was the same as my idea of going into the business world. No patience and no head for it whatsoever.

However, in college I loved every course I could take in philosophy and psychology. After I was admitted to the Graduate School of Columbia University, I thought awhile of getting my PhD in Philosophy and actually completed the course credits. But the idea of focusing on one subject and writing a thesis about it, which would take any number of years, had no resonance in me at all.

Actually, I was absorbed in philosophy but did not see where it was going in my own life. I voraciously read the Platonic Dialogues and loved

Socrates and his search for justice, wisdom, truth and the rest. But I was attached to the Bible infinitely more because they did not try to find out what was abstract justice or fairness or right: they teach us instead what to do to achieve it. But I never regretted studying and immersing myself in the works of Plato or Aristotle and later thinkers like Kant and Spinoza. They were the walls off which I bounced my own burgeoning philosophy, which I was learning in the Bible, Rabbinic literature and contemporary culture.

When it came to that search for understanding, I always came back to my own situation. In effect I was trying to translate some of the words of the psalm, "The heavens are the heavens of the Lord, but the earth He has turned over to the children of flesh." (Psalm 115) So the problems of this world and God's working within it became my focus. I always understood the psalm to mean that it is our job to bring as much of heaven down to earth as we can. No promise of ultimate solutions. Just an earthly agenda, and if you are fortunate, time to explore it.

In the meantime the discovery, crucial to my emergence, that the subjects I enjoyed could be pursued relentlessly. I had no trouble concentrating. They included philosophy, literature and psychology. I soaked them up. My cultural horizons were opening up and I found traveling through them a sheer delight.

Other courses that fascinated me were Political Science and surprise of all, Biology. I was told by my advisor that I must take a science and so I chose something with which I had at least passing acquaintance, namely the human body. To my great surprise I enjoyed it and did very well at it. Then there was also a course that we were required to take called Hygiene. It was taught by a very sweet man who was a physician and I believe a survivor. He attempted to give us many insights into the proper working of the human body, but he capped it off with a line that I shall never forget. Neither will any of the many students who heard it over a number of years. "Boys, remember that you are Yeshiva students. You are going to be rabbis." And at this point he voice would rise in tone and intensity. "And boys, be very careful what you are doing down there. It is crucial that you be careful what you are doing down there. That is all I am going to say." Most of us, including myself, had trouble hiding the laughter. In those days that was about as far as you went. It was enough to give a warning, "to what you are doing down there." But I suspect that of others as well as for myself it worked. We learned how to control 'down there.'

At this stage as a young rabbinical student I was given to introspection. But the more I pondered, the more inscrutable did God's ways seem to me. It was a constant effort. "Search God's face continually." Many religious people stress the incomprehensibility of God's ways. If you want to understand God, you need to have a mind like God's. I have heard all of the arguments. I know all of the medieval proofs for the existence of God. I understand them all and truth is I have used them all. But it still is not enough.

In more technical terms, the sense of the transcendent God sustained but also frustrated me. The immanent God within the world and ourselves was not enough to satisfy. My faith was strong but searching. Was it in God that I believed, or in purpose to life? Is there such a sharp distinction between the two? At one and the same time I felt God was with me, but I was still exposed or vulnerable. I had found my anchor, but it was moving in the water. And so then, as now, I was in search. Continually.

But when I look back at my beginnings, I realize how far I have come. In high school before the defining events in my life, I was taken up with football and horsing around with my friends. And then the black days when I felt I had sunk into a hole. But in the direst moments there was something urging me on. A feeling that if only I would persist I could do more; I could get better if I keep going.

This became my mantra: "His anger is for a moment, His love is for a lifetime. Tears may linger for a night, but joy will come with the dawn." (Psalm 30). I said it every day. It worked for me. I had known the tears. And the joy. After the fall, the spring had come. I had willed myself back to health.

WESTERN INTERLUDE

SHORTLY BEFORE I was to graduate college in 1948, I decided to leave Yeshiva University and spend a semester at the University of Arizona in Tucson. Recently on a weekend at Fire Island with my sister Eleanor and brother-in-law Alex Holtzman in that very mellow atmosphere, we did a bit of reminiscing. Since Alex and I had met in Tucson and had actually traveled to California together, I had to answer the question in 2006 of why I had decided to Go West in 1948. Ricky knew the story but no other members of the family had heard it. I guess I was embarrassed, though right now I would question the need for that.

The fact of the matter is that a good friend of mine from our earliest days together in Flatbush had moved with his family to Tucson. They had purchased a large home with a pool and a garden house nearby. The garden house had amenities and whatever one would need for a comfortable visit. My friend, Herbie Pion, invited me to come out and spend time with them. He knew that I had been ill that winter; there were huge snowstorms in New York. My parents knew about my sinus problems and about Herbie's offer. Ever since Elliot died, they were indulgent of my symptoms. They readily agreed that it would be a good idea and so I spent three nights and four days on a slow train to Tucson. It was a great adventure. It was also, besides summer camping, my first foray away from Brooklyn.

But there was a large looming fact which I had not disclosed. I was the Editor of the Commentator, the undergraduate newspaper of Yeshiva

College. The President of Yeshiva University was a thirty-two year old Greek and Talmudic scholar by the name of Dr. Samuel Belkin. It was said of him that he was the youngest college president in the United States. There were pressures there from the Orthodox community on the right that wanted the school to adhere more strictly to a traditional line. Given my background and predilection, I chafed under some of the new restrictions that he had put into play. I had not grown up in the Orthodox world and while I was attracted to significant segments of it, I still hadn't yielded my personal right to pick and choose.

I began to write a series of articles speaking of my dissatisfaction with student life at both the rabbinical department and the college. The first article I wrote had to do with curriculum. During the course of our morning study in the rabbinical department, once a week or so a mashgiach would come into our class and speak to us for about a half hour. I guess you would say he was a spiritual counselor to try to keep our minds focused on the straight and narrow. He was against TV, movies, dating or, in general, against the integration of Judaism with the American way of life. He was European but I must say also that he seemed very gentle and even sweet. Nonetheless, it was a total disconnect. I used to listen to this man in admiration but in disbelief. Did he really expect to get through, speaking in Yiddish of which I understood very little? To me it seemed like he was from another world.

So I wrote this article in which I said that the idea was a good one but its application was not. There was no mention of his name but everyone understood. He had visited all the classes in the rabbinical department. Many of my classmates agreed; most were silent. All I suggested was that the role of the mashgiach should be someone who could speak more directly to American kids. I guess that was the beginning of my road to Tucson.

The conflict became more intense when I wrote against Dr. Belkin's new restrictions. Here I was smart enough, by some intuition, to co-opt the student body president and vice-president who signed the editorial together with me. The three of us were called into Dr. Belkin's office. I must say that I did not see myself as a rebel; I was just writing what I though was needed and that the student body was calling for. Dr. Belkin did not quite see it that way and he told us that he was thinking of expelling us from the school. To me specifically he said that Dr. Churgin, the kindly head of the Teachers Institute, had suggested to him not to do that, saying that I was a good student, serious, and not about to take on the establishment. So that saved me. But Belkin kind of indicated that we better shape up rapidly and not try anything like that again.

It was just about that time that Pion was writing from Tucson. And I made the connection. To hell with all of this. I would head out there and enjoy myself in the sunshine of Arizona for a semester. Which is what I did.

I cannot describe adequately the contrast between Yeshiva College and the University of Arizona. It is not that I disliked the Yeshiva where I had learned a great deal and to which I feel a strong sense of debt to this day. It is just that Tucson was extremely laid back in those days. Most of the students wore cowboy hats and boots, especially those in the School of Agriculture, a major presence on campus. Those were the days when boots were in, long before sneakers. In the morning when we would begin classes very often someone had gone into the mountains early and put together a snowman and brought it down to the campus. By noon it was a puddle of water. The sun was strong and warming. And the campus was beautiful. And the people friendly.

The university had a great basketball team that I loved to watch. Its captain was Morris Udall, later a U. S. congressman and once briefly a candidate for the presidency of the United. States. His brother Stewart was a member of the Kennedy Cabinet. Morris had been a good friend of my brother-in-law Alex Holtzman whom I had met at the University. Not being endowed with prophetic insight, I didn't know then, that years later and independent of our friendship, my sister Eleanor and Alex would meet and marry. When Udall hoped to make it to the presidency, Alex tried to help by running a fundraiser for him at their apartment in Manhattan. Unfortunately, it didn't help. He would have been the first star varsity basketball player to be president. Bill Bradley also failed.

At Arizona I requested the opportunity to take a very full program, more than is usually permitted. I explained to my advisor that I was accustomed at Yeshiva University to start classes early in the morning and finish late at night. By contrast, I felt that the program I was taking on would be simple. He agreed only on the tentative proposal to evaluate after the first marking period. Since I had choices, I took courses I was interested in, that had not been offered at Yeshiva. I did well and was allowed to continue.

One of the offerings which was not given back home and which I found here was a course in Logic in the Philosophy Department. I was happy to be able to take it. It was not easy but I liked it, and since in our class there were no articulate, outstanding students, I would often be in discussion with the professor.

One day the professor announced an exam for the following week. To me it sounded just fine. I would be looking forward to it. One of my classmates approached me and asked if he could study with me for the exam. It turned out that he was living not far from my bungalow residence. We agreed to meet. I knew absolutely nothing about him except that his family name was Matthews. It didn't register with me.

We met in the main house and were reviewing our work for about half an hour when he spotted a Chanukah menorah on one of the tables. This eight-branched candelabrum is very often exhibited throughout the year, even though it is attached to the holiday of Chanukah. He inquired what that was. I explained that it was a Jewish ritual object used in December for the holiday observance. He listened quietly. Then, his face flushed. Five minutes later he told me he would have to leave immediately. I didn't protest nor did I resist. He left. For all I care, he flunked the test. But I didn't.

Later I discovered that he was the son of the publisher of the Arizona Daily Star, who had opposed the rise of the State of Israel in his newspaper and may not have been a great friend of the Jewish people. He left in a huff and I do not recall that we ever spoke again. In my mind, it was not philosophic behavior. For all I could see, he had failed logic.

While at the university, I had decided to take a course in Irish Drama. I'm not sure I knew why, except that the subject intrigued me and it was being given at a convenient time, 2:00 p.m., right after lunch. The time turned out to be crucial.

Our teacher was an old Irish actor who knew his Sean O'casey, Lady Gregory, Abbey Players and Theatre exceedingly well and was happy to transmit its spirit and content. One problem. It seemed that lunch before class was not so much to be eaten as imbibed. I don't know if he ever came into class completely sober. Some days he seemed dead drunk. He was able always to start the class by calling on someone to tell about this or that play that had been assigned reading. Within minutes he was completely asleep. As the student droned on, he continued sleeping. Miraculously he had trained himself to wake up when the voice stopped. It worked every time. We had trouble believing it, but it always worked.

When my turn came I felt no need to follow the accepted pattern. In fact, I felt foolish even attempting to do so. Instead, once I was sure he was out of it, I proceeded to simulate a Dodger-Yankee game ala Mel Allen in the early 40's, using Pee Wee Reese, Duke Snider, Dolph Camilli, Cookie Lavagetto and the rest from Brooklyn, and Joe DiMaggio, Tommy Henrich, Bill Dickey, Phil Rizzuto and the rest for the Yankees. I would continue my false commentary for fifteen, twenty minutes. Then suddenly I stop. The teacher awoke, tells me it was very good; class is over.

But one thing I did learn from the experience was to enjoy O'casey and Irish Drama. I try never to miss a play in New York, on Broadway or off, and as a result have enjoyed many a joyful evening in the theatre, all the while reminiscing over my 'spirited' professor. I may not have learned very much about play construction, but it did create an abiding interest in the Dublin Theatre scene.

But I also recall most favorably our trip to California – Alex, Herbie and I. The road in those days was long and deserted. So there was time for getting to know each other better and enjoying a bit of togetherness. At a diner at which we stopped, I tasted hominy grits for the first time. Immediate disconnect.

Imagine my surprise later at my newly-acquired brother-in-law, which we have been now for half a century, who introduced me to that delicacy.

While in Hollywood for those few days, we decided to imbibe a little bit of its spirit and culture. We didn't have gobs of money so we looked for those places where we could hang out that didn't require much. We were not big drinkers but there were those bistro-type bars where you could buy a beer and nurse it for an hour or two while taking in the sights. I don't know how we found the exact places to go, but in one or two of them there were actually movie stars. For a kid from Brooklyn to see real-life those you have seen on the screen is a miraculous transformation. Especially in the days before TV when movie stars dwelt in some mystical realm beyond the touch of humans.

Summer was already approaching and Tucson was getting beastly hot. The natives were leaving for the mountains. It was time to head back home and graduate from Yeshiva University. There was that tall brunette that was waiting and she and her parents came to my graduation. After that we all went to a famous kosher restaurant at that time and celebrated. Shortly after, we were to be married. Ricky was not yet twenty-one and I was not yet twenty-two. It's been a long and successful journey. The detour to Tucson was only temporary. I had not become mesmerized by a different way of life. Exciting events called to me from New York.

Ricky and I were married. The wedding at the East Midwood Jewish Center in Brooklyn was magnificent. There were a few hundred people present. It was a festive occasion. My parents beamed. My in-laws were happy.

The bride and groom were filled with excitement and joy. The "boys" were my ushers, all decked out in tails. What a sight! And our short honeymoon stay at the Waldorf was starry-eyed.

My in-laws had gone all out. Their other daughter, Beulah, was to be married a few weeks later. Her husband, the late Alvin Raphael, was Robert Redford when the latter was still a boy. Alvin was a terrific guy who unfortunately suffered much before he died. I still miss him. Too bad he never got to see his beautiful family unfold. But who knew what awaited us in the fall of '48. Life seemed to possess infinite possibilities for expansion.

MOVING ON

AFTER FIVE YEARS at Yeshiva University, I left voluntarily to attend the Jewish Theological Seminary. By then I had graduated the college and was studying solely for the rabbinate. In my daily practice I was really nominally Orthodox. But I had not been brought up that way and, truth be told, my heart was not in it.

I also felt that if the goal was to reach American Jews, Conservative Judaism had a better chance. Its emphasis on modernity, not just on tradition, appealed to me. I seized at the opportunity to lead a full-blown American life, without limitations, except those directly affecting my faith and practices, of which I gave up nothing.

The curriculum at JTS was much more to my liking. Emphasis was on Bible, Hebrew literature, Midrash, Codes and not just Talmud. My teachers included famous scholars of international reputation, like Drs. Finkelstein, Kaplan, Marx, Lieberman, Boaz Cohen, Hillel Bavli A. J. Heschel and Shalom Speigel. Classes were lively, filled with questions, often heated discussions and resolutions. Oftimes it was tense. But it was never boring. I had found a home.

I especially admired Mordecai Kaplan and Robert Gordis. Both were academics while serving as rabbis in congregations. They found time to do both. They served as an ideal example for us, to conserve your time carefully, husband it, so that it was possible to serve more than one master.

This I hoped to do as well. I had been offered an academic position, but had turned it down.

Later I was to discover that for me to serve two masters was virtually impossible. A certain type mind is drawn to academic study. Only on rare occasions, from my observation, does it combine readily with the gifts of popular homily and homoletical dexterity. Proper academic study requires a great deal of time and tenacity. Not everyone is capable of it. Add talent to the equation as well.

One of those gifted persons, whom unfortunately I never met, nor even heard, was the late Rabbi Milton Steinberg who died in 1950 while I was still a student at the Seminary. I have recommended his book "As A Driven Leaf" to at least a hundred friends, students and family over the years. It is still, a great achievement.

Steinberg's enduring legacy, to my mind, comes in his posthumous work "The Anatomy of Faith" lectures he was giving in Theology at his home synagogue, The Park Avenue Synagogue in New York City. We were already living in Mt. Kisco, so it was very difficult to attend the class at night. But I remember when he died, tragically and prematurely, walking the streets of Mt. Kisco reading lines to Ricky from his various writings. They were pure poetic outpouring of his faith which helped me to find mine. Many years later I realized that my own critique of Kaplan gained momentum from his. But, of course, I didn't have his words before me when I wrote in 1955.

Often I go back to Milton Steinberg's essay, "The Theological Issues of the Hour." While I was deeply concerned in those days with the issues he presents, the meaning of God, Revelation and Torah, and the role of the Jewish People, and all three of them became abiding concerns of my life, without resolving it, in time something intervened. It was the preoccupation with the practical and political issues of the Jewish people whom I was serving and how to put together a strategy for our future. I began to sense something which later became an obvious fact to me, that all the talk and debate about ritual, and Shabbat, and prayer is important and necessary. But none of it is a substitute for the living reality of engaging yourself and experiencing, rather than talking about such concerns. I learned a great deal when I read the story of Franz Rosenzweig, the brilliant German Jew who was engaged in deep dialectics about whether or not to remain a Jew, until he decided to go to a synagogue on Kol Nidre night in Berlin at a crucial moment of his life.

What he experienced there, the depth of piety, the fervor, bodies wrapped in a tallit, the singing of the prayers of repentance, hearing the plaintive tone of Kol Nidre asking for forgiveness and renewal – all of this made a permanent impact upon his life and transformed it. No longer did he need to argue and debate. From that point on he wanted only further depths of experience and to come to know the many levels of observance that he had never known or heard of before.

So it was around this time that I became disaffected with the theology of my teacher Mordecai Kaplan. Kaplan, coming as a young man from Europe, was deeply impressed with the pragmatic and naturalistic style. He was a great follower of William James that for an idea to be true it had to be observable in action or conduct. Kaplan sought to strip Judaism of supernaturalism and miracles and railed against any idea of God that would make him a "bearded grandfather in the sky, sitting on a throne listening to prayers."

All of this was very contemporary in the decade before the Second World War when the full dimension of depravity and evil in human nature came to the fore. Earlier Kaplan was responding to the mood of his time. Christian Science was attracting many Jews. The Society for the Advancement of Ethical Culture on Central Park West had been founded by the son of a rabbi and was not concerned with custom, ritual or observance, but went directly to the heart of the ethical enterprise, of humanism, which certainly has a worthwhile and attractive goal. Kaplan founded a congregation also on the West Side of Central Park and he called it as it still remains, the Society for the Advancement of Judaism, to direct attention that Judaism contained humanistic ideals, but it was also culture, land, language, religion and people. In fact, he coined a term "Jewish Peoplehood" by which he means a semi-mystical view that all Jews throughout time and history are connected, which harks back to the Midrash which speaks of the souls of all Jews throughout history being present at the Covenant of Sinai. (Incidentally, that would always move my friend, Shlomo Carlebach, to say when he met somebody for the first time, "We are not strangers, I think I remember you from Sinai.")

At that point, something was disturbing me within. Kaplan had asked me to join the editorial board of his magazine, The Reconstructionist, and I found it quite satisfying to help put together its editorial policy of day-to-day issues that confronted Jewish life. But increasingly I found his religious outlook and theological position cloying. As I look back, I am not quite sure where it all came from, but I wrote a very sharp critique to Kaplan of his concept of God. He published it in the Reconstructionist Magazine and later placed it in his book "Questions Jews Ask." Every now and again I meet someone who tells me that he found himself moved by the chutzpah of this young rabbi standing up to his teacher, who by then was a major figure in American Jewish life. As I read my comments now, which I still use in courses I give in modern Jewish thought, I do not feel like I want to take back a single line. Some of it was quite sharp, such as "your concept of God I see as causing a hardening of the arteries that lead to the Jewish heart. For this reason many, reversing the trend, can stand with you with their head in the synagogue, but their hearts outside of it." What I was pointing to was the lack of the personal aspect of Jewish theology, the reducing of God to definition, the taking away of the sense of prayer in the presence of God. It was not yet particularly popular in the 1940's, but became more so as the enormous depravity of man and the need for spiritual fulfillment became obvious in the years ahead.

Kaplan naturally answered the letter in the magazine and in the book and reiterated his long-held position that God is the stimulus to each of us to pursue the good, the holy and the beautiful. But as to "Someone" out there to whom we could relate, there he was more skeptical. And so at that time I began to find Franz Rosenzweig and Martin Buber far more evocative of my own religious striving. The years have not changed any of that.

A syllogistic God is for them, and for many of us, hardly a replacement for the God we experience and the God we pray to. For all of its pragmatic appeal and intellectual strength, it cannot replace the Living God of Abraham, Isaac and Jacob.

BROOKLYN INTO SUBURBIA

T HE FIRST POSITION I was offered as a rabbi was in Mt. Kisco, Westchester County, New York. It was then a bucolic, backwater suburb and I was still a student at The Jewish Theological Seminary. The year was 1949 when we took our young daughter Elissa and moved to about thirty miles from New York City. For Ricky and I who came from Flatbush this seemed like the real country. The town was small, picturesque, with the train station in the middle. I took the train daily to 125th Street in New York City to attend school.

The trip itself was highly instructive. I would get off in Harlem on the East Side. Often if there was time I would save the money of a token by walking clear across 125th Street to Broadway and 122nd Street where the Seminary is located. There was one luncheonette where I would often stop and have a cup of coffee, all in very neighborly surroundings. In the 70's and 80's people were astounded to hear that because by then Jews or white people didn't always feel welcome in Harlem.

And so today when I drive through Harlem, as I have over the last half-century, I am happy to see that a whole new face is being presented to the public. Gentrification. A new set of upscale stores are on both sides of 125th Street, and former President Bill Clinton has his office in one of its most prominent buildings. Quite a change from the early fifties when I first came to know the area.

Truth is I was woefully unprepared to assume the role of rabbi in 1949, or even that of a student rabbi. I had a great yearning to live as a Jew with my family and to teach others the same. But I had not yet been given the equipment to do the job.

My transfer from Yeshiva University to the Jewish Theological Seminary was a smooth one. Five years at the Yeshiva had prepared me quite adequately for a rabbinic career. I had imbibed more than the Talmud and other subject matter. I had admired the style, taken on the zest for learning and for translating the insights of the Jewish tradition into the contemporary world.

Oftimes I would hear those rabbinical students, more advanced than me, practice their sermons with their tutors, whetting my appetite to try my hand at it. I was not quite there yet. But it was soon to come.

The way I came to my first position was quite quixotic. Wolfe Kelman tapped me in the Seminary cafeteria. "I have the perfect job for you. You replace me in Mt. Kisco." He had been serving as Interim Rabbi.

I protested that I wasn't ready. This was only my second year in what I thought would be six at JTS. (Actually, I was ordained after four). "Don't worry. We'll drive up. I'll tell you everything you need to know on the way." And so it was. Of course, it took four additional years at Mt. Kisco to really "get" me what I needed to know.

One of the things that haunted me when I was in Mt. Kisco was the idea I would not be taken seriously because of my age (I was 22) or that I would be seen as a sports jock who came tangentially to theology and religion. It was a problem that I had hoisted onto myself because I had played football in high school and freshman basketball in college.

One of the problems was that Ricky had been given this magnificent sports car, a shining Buick convertible, by her parents. It was so resplendent that I was embarrassed to drive it. But for the first weeks in Mt. Kisco I did. Then I immediately traded it in for a lower-scale-working-man's Pontiac with two doors, which seemed more appropriate. It didn't raise eyebrows and it didn't enable the people to see us coming.

Much different than I expected, the hardest part of the job was relating to people with problems and knowing what advice to offer them. I focused intently on the question and tried to listen carefully. Over the years I have heard hundreds of different situations and trying to remain as honest as I could be, offer some helpful suggestions.

Almost the first problem I met with put me way out of my depth. A youngster was to be Bar Mitzvah within a month or so, but unfortunately his father left the house just at that time and became preoccupied with another woman. The question was how do we explain all of this to the youngster. Both the father and mother brought him to my office so that I could make the explanation. How do you explain something you don't understand yourself? But that particular situation was like a metaphor for what was to occur in the future. People want support rather than advice about what they are doing.

What they really were worried about with this young man was how he would do on the day of his Bar Mitzvah. The biggest hurdle of all is standing up there looking out and seeing your family and friends and wondering if you are really ready for all this or am I about to blow it? Assuring the youngster that he is well prepared and just do the best you can is the most honest and important thing you can do for him. The same is true of young ladies or for families in general.

I discovered already in Mt. Kisco at an early age that when you are a rabbi the community also needs engagement and involvement. I was both young and inexperienced but I was the only rabbi in town and therefore the representative not only of my congregation but of the community. If you are determined to do the job correctly, there is no abandoning that role. Early on I often found myself with Christian colleagues who had decades more experience than I. Those colleagues struck me as being first-rate. There was the Methodist minister, and the Presbyterian and Episcopalian and the Catholic as well. And of course our discussions ranged from the local to the universal. Truth is I listened carefully and watched them intently. There is a certain clergyman's universal discourse, the shared problems and tensions of anyone who deals with a congregation. In a large measure those do not vary from one faith to another.

Ever since that experience I have been able to identify strongly with clergy of all faiths. To this day and to give it a contemporary setting, I understand quite well what someone who lost a sibling, a cousin, a child, parent or spouse, is feeling after the tragedy of 9/11 and how rabbi, priest, minister need to help. It is not difficult for me to understand why years after 9/11 the families have not been able to absorb their loss. There is no easy closure for a tragedy of that dimension. When you grow up in a culture that speaks of every person being entitled to life, where you are taught that humans are sacred – the image of buildings collapsing, with people jumping out of windows, with charred bodies and an atmosphere laden with dust and ashes for many miles, it is not easy to erase those images. To me, the terrorist mind, like that of the Nazis, is completely off the charts. How to expunge them is a problem. How do the survivors survive? How do you get up from the dust and start over again?

When it happened to me, brooding was not the option. I did that for awhile, tested it and finally discarded it. I was so young I didn't know all of the resources that were open, things I could fall back upon. What I did know was this big black hole I had fallen into and had to crawl out of. I have always tried to lead others along the same path. To try and turn away from confusion toward the positive. And pray for an opening. When you are hit and knocked down, get up, dust yourself off and keep going. If you continue to lie there, chances are you'll be hit again. This became a defining compass for me, akin to Daylight Saving Time, "If you fall back, spring forward."

All of this colored my discussions of theology with my fellow clergymen. Actually they were much older than I, but it could be that I had given more thought and expended more energy on trying to understand what happens to us on the path of life. In a real way the sadness of my life helped.

Looking back, support systems are crucial: family, community, tradition. When I turn to Scriptures I read words often that were deeply meaningful to me and could well serve others. As for God, "You hid Your face and I was terrified – later You changed my sackcloth for a robe of joy – those who seek the Lord will rejoice." I found that all of this was true, but it took time and patience and help from Above. Thanks God, they were forthcoming.

JOB, MY FRIEND

IT WAS AROUND this time that I began to be caught up with the Book of Job in the Bible. Later at the Seminary under the mentoring of Robert Gordis, exploring this book became a passion. It is to this day.

It was quite natural that I would be drawn to Job. His questions were mine. Why suffering to good people? What happened to their reward? The slick operators of the world so often prosper. How come? Bad things happening to good people is an everyday occurrence. That the Bible dealt with this subject was itself a boon. Not off bounds. Not, "Don't ask questions!" Instead – Probe! I did. I still do.

What I admire most about the Book of Job is the ending, the so-called answer as presented in the last chapters. The beginning of the book is familiar. Job suffers a series of tragedies rapidly succeeding each other. At the beginning he clings to his integrity and to his faith but once what happened to him really sinks in, he begins to question. At first he curses the day he was born and as the fog of his mind begins to clear his most persistent demand is that he be presented with a bill of particulars as to what went wrong. His friends come to console, but they spout platitudes that do not help. Job insists, "Though God slay me – yet I will trust in Him! For I know my Redeemer lives – From my flesh, I will yet see God." (13:15, 19:25) This faith he never yields. He will see the goodness of God in the land of the living.

When his friends arrive to console him, things take a turn for the worse. They persist in the old-fashioned way to affirm, "No punishment without sin." You're suffering, no doubt it is a result of your missteps.

In fact, the friends go even further, suggesting Job thank God for his suffering, a sure sign of God's love. Job throws up his hands in exasperation. "With friends like these – " Actually, he is ready to throw up.

And then the last chapters where God does in fact appear to Job. God does not directly answer Job's questions. In fact for many readers the answer seems abstract and without direct meaning to Job's situation. Yet afterward Job is happy and content. How come?

As I understand it, the Book of Job has been placed in the Bible – in and of itself an act of great courage – to announce two important insights. The most valuable is to teach that pain or death is not necessarily the result of sin. This reverses a long-standing tradition and is indispensable in the evolution of religion.

Death as the wage of sin had been taught by many pious observers of life. Both Jews and Christians have heard many varieties of it. Job challenges the equation and thereby liberates many guilt-ridden and unnecessarily burdened people. We may not be able to explain evil, in which case we need not adopt convenient but incorrect answers.

Job clings to his innocence demanding a bill of charges. His friends insist that he has sinned. Job insists they are wrong.

The truth is that there is no satisfactory answer, even for the person of faith, to the persistence of evil in the world.

Job's vindication is that through it all he intuitively knew he was going to make it through. He may not understand what happened, he certainly doesn't accept it with equanimity. But he persists.

Martin Buber has struck precisely the right note; "The true answer that Job receives is God's appearance only, distance turns into nearness, that his eye sees Him. (42:5)' Nothing is explained, nothing adjusted: wrong has not become right, nor cruelty kindness. Nothing has happened but that man hears God's address." If you were to ask me what effected the transformation in my life, I would not have been able to say it then, but it was precisely this sense that I had not been deserted. Not by God, not by my family, not by my people. Dimly at first, louder later, I too began to feel addressed. By God, by my people and family and shortly thereafter, by the happiest turn in my life.

This sense of being sustained might be seen as wish fulfillment or self-delusion. Perhaps, but I did not feel that. I was sensing the strength of my tradition, my forbears, "the merit of Biblical fathers and mothers" and all the rest through the ages. I felt they were all rooting for me – pushing me to go on. I felt it then. I feel it now.

Whenever I record my debt and my identity with the Book of Job, especially as Martin Buber interprets him, I recall the English romantic poet William Wordsworth. Jacob, back in Camp Delawaxen days opened up my religious appetite: Wordsworth sharpened my spiritual sense.

It began while I was a student of English literature at Yeshiva College. My teacher was Mr. Fleischer, whose first name I don't believe I ever knew. But he made a deep impression because of his strong love of the Romantic Poets of England, and Wordsworth in particular. I can still see him in class, a good-looking man, dressed in a dark suit with a white shirt and tie. It was pointed out to me that he was not quite fashionable because he always wore brown shoes with a dark suit. Today I understand it is quite acceptable. But I can still see him, a half-lit cigarette in his mouth, his head tilted slightly to the side, his eyes dreamy, as he would read Tintern Abbey to us. Viewing this majestic Wye River after an absence, the poem declaims how,

> "Oft, in lovely rooms and 'mid the din
> Of towns and cities, I have owed to them
> In hours of weariness, sensations sweet,
> Felt in the blood, and felt along the heart;
> And passing even into my purer mind,
> With tranquil restoration: good feelings, all,
> Of, unnumbered pleasure: such, perhaps,
> As have no slight or trivial things
> On that best portion of a man's life,
> His little, nameless, unremembered acts
> Of kindness and of love. Nor less, I trust,
> To them I may have owed another gift,
> Of aspect more sublime: that blessed mood
> In which the burthen of the mystery,
> In which the heavy and the weary weight
> Of all this unintelligible world,
> Is lightened – that serene and blessed mood,
> In which affections gently lead us on,
> Until, the breath of this corporal frame
> And even the motion of our human blood
> Almost suspended, we are laid asleep

In body, and become a living soul;
While with an eye made quiet by the power
of harmony, and the deep power of joy,
We see into the life of things.

Seeing into "the life of things" became a calling, a lifelong passion. Job and Wordsworth became my co-conspirators. Our search continues.

MACLEISH'S J.B.
AND THE BIBLICAL JOB

ARCHIBALD MACLEISH'S PLAY, "J.B." did more than win a Pulitzer Prize for its author and draw large audiences to his long running show on Broadway. It helped to restore the Book of Job, from which MacLeish derived his material, to a rightful place of honor in the life and letters of our time.

This we will want to acknowledge and applaud. It is fit and proper that a generation like ours, that has seen and suffered so much and now seems to be striving for a viable faith, turn to this Biblical repository of ancient wisdom. For the Book of Job is concerned with the ultimate issues of our existence, the relationship between God and man, nature and evil in the world we inhabit.

Our acknowledgement, however, is tempered by a reservation. "J.B." is fine as far as it goes, but it does little to interpret the Book of Job properly or to correctly locate the perspective from which it was arrived at and ordered.

MacLeish's, "play in verse," concerns itself primarily with the incidents that make up the first two chapters of Job's Prose Prologue. Beyond that there is some reference to the concluding portions of the Book without an attempt to point to their poignancy or underscore their religious significance. The author's own conclusion seems to come in the last moments as J.B.'s wife Sarah speaks:

"Cry for justice and the stars
Will stare until your eyes sting. Weep.
Enormous winds will thrash the water.
Cry in sleep for your lost children
Snow will fall . . . .
       Snow will fall . . . .
You wanted justice and there was none
Only love."

I take it that by this MacLeish means to describe what is for him the basic neutrality and impassivity of the universe to man's dreams and desires, his failings and faults. "The candles in churches are out," he says. His conclusion seems to be that love between man and man is the only basis for personal consolation and hope. Beyond that – nothing.

In truth, this interpretation of the Book of Job is in keeping with some of the scholarly writing on the subject. MacLeish on this score is in good company. The late Prof. Robert Pfeiffer of Harvard University held the view that in the Book of Job, "God is too exalted to be affected by human deeds." Renan went further when he declared, "The essence of the Book of Job contains nothing particularly Hebraic." It is to a consideration of these claims that we now turn.

The Book of Job is the story of a man suffering the duress of personal affliction. His family and his fortune have both been destroyed and his body is plagued by a painful Oriental disease. Not having read the arrangement with Satan that has been made in the Prologue, Job has no idea why this unfathomable darkness has suddenly descended upon him.

And now the author's keen artistic and religious sensitivity take over. He does not attempt to inhibit Job. Instead his humanness commands that Job bemoan his fate, "curse his day" and freely bespeak his unhappiness toward his friends who instead of consoling only further provoke him. In the intensity of his pain, Job even dares to question God's ways in the world.

This is so because the Biblical Job is no patty-cake or pablum inquiry of the tender hearted. It is an intense probing of the deepest problems that beset the human mind. As the book unfolds, Job's vexation increases and with it his spirit of rebellion. And it is easy to mistake this for a denial of the Hebraic concept of God.

But it is worth noting this about Job's protest. It is an eminently healthy-minded attitude. Job does not fall prey to the hydra-heads of moral lassitude, obsessive guilt on the one hand or moral callousness on the other. Job does not blame himself nor does he say to hell with the world. Instead, he clings to his own integrity and is not ready to surrender his interest in the life around him.

Job's cry is bitter but it is exalted. He demands to know how he has sinned. There is a divine quality to his unrest, which MacLeish fails to convey in his modern counterpart of the Biblical hero. Job cannot understand why the good God's ways are translated to him in such uncompromisingly evil dress and so he persists in his probing.

Furthermore, we believe that the author of Job has subtly interwoven into his work the Hebraic faith that God, "is close to all who call upon Him in truth". This is Job's undaunted hope. Job believes ultimately God will hear him. The hypocrite, however, is doomed. "Will God hear his cry when trouble comes upon him?" Job asks rhetorically in a passionate Credo of Integrity in Chapter twenty-seven.

The friends try to dissuade Job from this belief. Eliphaz questions, "Is it any advantage to the Almighty that thou are righteous, is it a gain to Him that thou makest thy ways blameless?" (22:3), implying God's little concern with the fate of man. But Job will not buy it. Instead he holds fast to his faith.

> "I would speak to the Almighty-
> I desire to reason with God,
> This shall be my salvation,
> That a hypocrite cannot come before Him." (13:3,16)

Job is not easily shaken, he still believes that he can speak to and reason with God, that the Almighty is not conspicuous by his absence from the affairs of man, that God is not mortally smitten to contemplate only Himself. "Cry for Justice," MacLeish says, "And the stars will stare until your eyes sting." "I know my redeemer lives," Job would counter, "even if He arises last upon earth." Job never abandons his belief in the possibility of divine communion and dialogue.

And then when the fullness of his plaint has been spoken and the way paved for his acceptance of the Divine Will, the clouds darken over, the skies part and God does indeed answer Job, speaking to him out of the whirlwind. Job has maintained that God is concerned, that He can be reached and here He is, in the glory of His Presence to speak to him directly.

"Weep," MacLeish has written, "and enormous winds will thrash the water." But in Job the winds do more than thrash the water. They bring forth the presence of the Lord. Come what may Job now knows, with the certainty of a faith cast into the fire to emerge pure, that God has not deserted him. In the face of this divine concern, the pain recedes and is assuaged.

The Biblical Job holds forth to us this bright, indeed incandescent possibility, the promise of at least a meeting with God, a promise that does not bring automatic fulfillment but is nonetheless luminous in its prospect. For it holds forth the hope of opening heavenly channels of communication. Man is not smitten with devastating silence. He can speak. This is not only a basis for consolation, it is the groundwork of the Biblical faith. 'God's greatness' as the Psalmist has said, "may be unsearchable." But, "His tender mercies are over all His work."

MacLeish's J. B. begins in despair and ends in his grasping the hand of his fellow man. The Biblical Job goes beyond this, he reaches out into the night to discover the presence of the Living God. Feeling the strength of God is Job's consolation. It was mine as well.

THE VILNA INFLUENCE

A S I LOOK back, one incident in Mt. Kisco is prominent in memory. I do not know to what extent it shaped my entire outlook, but it certainly made a strong impact upon me at the time.

All week long I would go into New York City, attend classes at the Jewish Theological Seminary, tried to read and do my work on the trains both coming and going home. One of the most powerful influences upon my thinking at that time was Dr. Mordecai Kaplan. Dr. Kaplan was a follower of the naturalistic school of theology. He believed that God's signs were manifest in the world and in each of us. He was less certain about the power of prayer to affect the universe and to be heard in the fashion which most people understood it. He warned against picturing God as a "bearded grandfather in the sky," saying that all of that had to be reinterpreted in the light of technology and science in our time. Be he went one step further.

With passion he proclaimed his belief that the old-fashioned biblical view of God was unacceptable to the modern mind. And to try to force that onto our people was to do a disservice because then they would reject the whole package as outdated and antiquated. He believed strongly that ritual, which he called sancta, still had a very important role in religious life. Further, it was his contention that the Jewish people are at the center of our faith, and not God necessarily or even Torah. All concepts are to serve the Jewish people and whatever enhances that goal is valuable and worthwhile.

Having heard all of this during the week and still being in my early education as a rabbi, my tendency was to repeat it in one form or another in my sermons and discussions on the weekend with the congregation. The practice in Mt. Kisco was that on Friday night the service was brief, followed by an Oneg Shabbat, which meant that we all sat down around a table with some singing, tea, and discussion.

I can never forget the discussion one night and the remarks spoken by a woman whom I admired very much for her piety and candor. Her name was Bertha Smilkstein and I can still see the lovely smile on her face as she spoke. But her words were very disturbing to me: "Rabbi, I was brought up in a simple Jewish home in Vilna. My parents and my family were not philosophers. They were pious people who practiced the teachings of what they had learned. They taught me the same way. Now I hear you talk in a fashion that leads me to believe that our prayers are not heard in the way that I had thought. And that I have no reason to expect an answer to them. If I believed what you said here tonight, I probably would not be coming to the synagogue over these last years and would not continue now. It is easy to take away someone's faith, but what are you going to replace it with?"

The statement was spoken without anger or hate. But it was spoken with a sincerity that could not be denied. Did it cause me to change my outlook and my belief? Truthfully, I think it did. I took it very seriously and the words echoed in my head for many days thereafter. My break with Dr. Kaplan's thinking had many sources, but it is quite possible that the initial stimulation was given to me on that Friday night, by that simple woman of Vilna, who spoke her heart out on Shabbat.

Nonetheless, Kaplan's teachings had a permanent imprint on my outlook. He had studied with the famed educator John Dewey and hoped to bring a pragmatic approach to Judaism, rejecting asceticism, obscurantism and supernaturalism. "Define precisely what you mean by God, Torah and the Jewish People", he would probe and push his students, often verbally tying them up in perplexity.

THE NITRA RAV

W HILE STILL IN Mt. Kisco a very positive experience took place when I visited the Yeshiva Farm Settlement on the outskirts of the town. There I met Rabbi Michal Baer Weissmandel, a European sage who had been through the war and bore its marks on his body and mind. His story is at once chilling and compelling.

The Nitra Rav. He was one of those holy people you are privileged to meet. I first became acquainted with him in Mt. Kisco in 1950. I was serving the congregation in town and he was the head of a Yeshiva Farm Settlement on its outskirts. Depending on how you looked at it, his story was depressing or fascinating.

Rabbi Michal Baer Weissmandel was part of that group of pious Jews who managed to survive the war and came to America to try to begin their lives over again.

Many people do not believe that up until the Second World War one did not see chasidic figures in their special garb on the streets of New York. The elementary school that I attended, the Yeshiva of Flatbush was in an intensely Jewish area, but if a chasid was seen walking down the street in the special dress that sets them apart and that is now familiar to everyone, then he would have stopped traffic.

Weissmandel was given this farm settlement by a donor because they had been in villages in Slovakia and they were closer to the farming way of life than they were to urban dwelling. The way of life in Williamsburg or

Crown Heights was foreign to them. This very large Brewster estate which they had been given was filled with all the amenities, flower beds, barns, guardhouses and a huge main house. The new tenants were not capable of tending to the estate that they had been given. It began to look tacky. There were complaints. Before you knew it there were public protests and a move to dislodge the Yeshiva Farm Settlement. Let them relocate in Williamsburg – our property values are at stake.

Sentiment was building up against the Nitra Yeshiva. Rabbi Weissmandl decided to act decisively. He sought and obtained an audience with Billy Rose, the master showman, who then was living on a large estate in the Mt. Kisco area.

The rabbi once described the meeting with Rose for me. He knew that his only chance was to appeal to Billy Rose's inherent American sense of fairness. Briefly describing their miserable plight in Europe, he explained that they had come to Westchester County to live peacefully. They were not out to convert anyone to their ways or to impose themselves in any way. Twenty-five were left. He described how he had always heard that in America there is freedom to pursue your own course, as long as you don't interfere with anyone. That's all he wants to do, he emphasized.

Billy Rose took up their cause at the next public meeting. Never referring to his own Jewish roots, he made the case for the "American thing to do" and he carried the day for the Yeshiva. They are still there pursuing their way forty years later. Thanks to a fellow who believed in the American way.

Meanwhile a new type of American student then suddenly began to be attracted to the European way. A person of basically non-religious outlook who turns himself inward to a more spiritual and religious change is called a Baal Teshuva. It was there at the Yeshiva Farm Settlement that I met my first of that genre. These were young people, some from the south shore of Long Island and elsewhere, who were turned off to American materialism as they saw it and turned on to the Jewish spirituality as they understood it. As I reflected upon it in a certain way, that is exactly what I had done, but of course it was not a 180 degree turn that I had taken. Rejecting the home environment in which you are bred and searching for something more, is not always applauded by your parents or those who surround them. Very often there is a break at the beginning. And I met a number of those at that time as well. It takes sensitivity, on both sides, to prevent that break. Thankfully, it hadn't happened to me. My parents didn't want to break off from me. I certainly didn't relish the idea. We had managed a merger.

Rabbi Weissmandel never encouraged tension between children and parents. Just the opposite. He was a kind and gentle man who spoke softly and had been through all the gates of hell. A certain mystique always surrounded him. Stories circulated about how he had jumped from a train heading for Auschwitz in 1944. They say he hid a coil of emery in a loaf of bread, and used it to cut a hole in the train taking him to the concentration camp and then jumped off. But I never spoke to him about it nor questioned him. The story was told that when he jumped from the train, he had left his wife and children behind.

I was attracted to Weissmandel and to the sources of his spirituality and often spent time with him. He visited Ricky and me and our young daughter. I remember that we served him fruit which he ate slowly and deliberately, cutting it into small pieces. We felt completely at home with him.

We studied Talmud together and spoke in Hebrew. I believe he was fascinated by my knowledge and love of the Hebrew language. His was gutteral and literary, and he had a special Talmudic lilt and quality as he spoke. We would walk together under the lovely spruce trees of the settlement and then emerge from the cool shaded areas into the warm sunlight.

He often spoke of America and where it was heading. It always seemed to me as if this man, who knew very well that European Jewry was dead, wanted to convey to a young American rabbinical student that a transfer was taking place and that this process had to continue if there was to be a future.

Looking back, I see he was infinitely patient with me. Once he asked me to explain my religious outlook to him. He knew that I had graduated from Yeshiva University where I had studied Talmudic texts for five years. He couldn't quite comprehend how someone with that background would choose to strike out on, for what was for him, a new path. The only Judaism he knew was Orthodox.

Actually, I wanted to say straight out that the Austro-Hungarian empire into which he had been born was no more, and that his native Czechoslovakia was now dead and buried. How would it be possible, however, to refer to one's painful past which included an entire family which was lost?

The difficulty was that there was a dialectic side to our discussion. I did attempt in a way to convey to Weissmandel the emerging and changing nature of the Jewish tradition of which I was beginning to learn. In those days we used to use fancy terms like, "evolving religious tradition." It was my contention then, as it still is, that all religious traditions have to combine the contemporary and the modern into them or else they are lost. He was bidden to preserve the past. In America, our eyes were focused on the future. I had unbounded respect for Rabbi Weissmandel, but we inhabited different worlds.

Weissmandel listened intently to my presentation, with a faint smile on his face. I know he didn't agree with me and yet he never refuted a single word. What made his style attractive to me was that he had this encyclopedic mass of Jewish texts plus deeply held convictions, such as he was prepared to give his life for. I knew furthermore that he was not timid about expressing his point of view; in some of his letters and his books a hot fury bursts forth when he felt American Jews were not doing enough to help save the Jews of Europe. But he never allowed his demeanor to descend into meanness or deprecation. I believe that it was his desired intention to find the sparks of holiness within each person and to, "blow on the coal of their heart" to help bring out their inner spiritual being. As such, he was a good model because that is exactly what I had been trying to do. But in most parts of my life I had the fear that I was not getting through.

The Nitra Rav gave me the strength to believe that you can make an impact if you persist, even if you are not abrasive and don't push too hard. He will always remain in my mind as an outstanding example of a scholar saint. He made a lasting impact on me.

In the meantime, our first born, our daughter Elissa, was getting older. Soon she would need a kindergarten with Hebraic content. Also, our son Jonathan was born, a few blocks from our home, in the Northern Westchester Hospital. Our family was growing. We felt it was time to move on. Our student days were coming to an end.

FINAL EXAMS

FOR FOUR YEARS I was the student rabbi at Mt. Kisco, traveling back and forth to New York City daily. Graduation was drawing close. A huge obstacle remained.

Final examinations in half a dozen major subjects. Oral exams with the professor, one on one. Freak-out time.

Every student knew that if any one of our teachers wished to fail us, it would be easy. You find a weak area and keep boring in. The prospects were terrifying. The whole enterprise could go down the drain. Years later at the students' insistence, such tests were eliminated in favor of written exams. But I was not that lucky.

My first oral exam was to be with Dr. Alexander Marx, a German professor of the old school and co-author of a classic text in Jewish History.

This was not going to be easy; I had not been an attentive student in this class. Through the years I was to learn how fascinating the people and leaders who made up history could be. But then it was mostly the facts and figures, dates, expulsions, wars – stuff that did not command my attention.

But passing history was a must. Marx could tell in a moment if I was bluffing. What to do? To me, the resolution was simple. I would have to memorize, as best I could, his "History of the Jews." If you have ever held the book, you know how thick and forbidding it is. But there was no other way. I had not come this far to be tackled by the Procurators of Rome in Palestine.

For more than a month I studied, sometimes as much as ten hours a day. By the time of the exam, I was much more confident than I had been. You know what? I might yet get to be a rabbi!

I was invited to Dr. Marx's home. His study was filled with books, ceiling to floor. Awesome.

All proceeded well the first minutes. Whatever he asked, I knew. Piece of cake. All that studying was not for naught.

Then suddenly the cruncher. He posed a question, I readily presented the answer. "No, no, sorry Mr. Fenster, but there you are wrong." I was stunned. I was certain I was correct.

Suddenly, I hear myself react. "Forgive me professor, but in your book on the first page of Chapter 12 you say exactly what I have quoted."

Marx quickly turns to his History. He reads briefly. I am hardly breathing. He shuts the book with two hands. "Well, I have changed my mind since I wrote that."

Now he looks at me hard. Who is this nut who can recite the chapter and page by heart? I immediately squelched any look of triumph, considering it to be a disaster.

A moment later the exam concluded abruptly. "You pass." I thanked him profusely and shook his hand vigorously, grabbed my coat and ran out of the house.

I didn't anticipate the rest as being so difficult but that first oral is etched in my memory forever. Who knows, I could still be struggling to memorize the list of procurators.

Right after that, a strange series of events intervened. My father, then age 51, came down with colon cancer. In those days it was considered, in most cases, like a death warrant. Before the operation my father called me into his office to make sure it was understood that I would take care of my mother and sister. The insurance policies and other assets would provide the financial means. That aside, I was far from ready to see my father crumble before my eyes.

The operation was set for the eve of Passover at the Beth Israel Hospital in New York City. The surgeon was to be Dr. Leon Ginsburg, who my father found and who turned out to be one of the leading surgeons of his time. He taught at Mt. Sinai Medical and kept operating into his seventies.

But he was a maverick. I waited patiently until the operation concluded, after many hours. He exited to tell us that he removed all the cancer he saw. Nervously we asked, "Is he going to be all right?" Ginsburg turned to me and not unkindly answered, "You're a rabbi, aren't you. Well, pray."

My father recovered. Actually, he died thirty-four years later and not of cancer. Dr. Ginsburg became his guru. Once they told my Dad years later, that he needed a prostate operation; he said not before he spoke to Dr. Ginsburg, who told him "Ira, do it." And he did.

All of this was happening while I was taking my easier oral exams. I was putting off the big ones, in Talmud with Prof. Saul Lieberman, and in Bible with Prof. H. L. Ginsberg, for the end. But the operation interceded. I needed a minimum of a month to prepare for those exams and I just didn't have it. My father had asked me to help in business while he was recuperating. There were checks that had to be collected, or so he thought, in person. I would have to go, in his place, to do the collecting.

I didn't look forward to it. But while he was recovering in the hospital and at home, I would call him excitedly when a substantial amount came through. It made him very happy. His customers were very kind. The collections were good. Had I missed my calling?

Meanwhile I had put in for late examinations in Talmud and Bible, explaining why it was necessary. I could take the exams in the summer and still graduate before the new class was welcomed in September. Everyone cooperated.

It turned out, much to my surprise, that both Lieberman and H. L. had summer homes on Martha's Vineyard. So that July with much trepidation we ventured forth, staying at Hyannisport on the mainland and taking the ferry over to the island. If all went well we even envisioned a few days of recuperation afterward in Hyannisport.

Ricky decided to come along to the Vineyard. No sense waiting in anxiety: we could do it together. Getting off the ferry, who was there to greet me? I couldn't believe it. The Rector of the J. T. S. himself, one of the leading Talmudic scholars of his time. Not only that, but he drove from there to his home. No one at the Seminary even knew that he drove, that he kept a car on the island, or anything like that.

"How was your trip" he asked pleasantly. "Fine, fine, I stammered. We are staying on the mainland and took the ferry here." "What do you mean we? Where is your wife now?" "Well, she is looking at the stores on the Island and we made up to meet later." Lieberman put on a grave visage. "Fenster, you come here for a final test in Talmud. You don't know the first principle. 'Ishto K'gufo' – a man's wife is like his own body. You send her out on her own. That's enough to fail you!" Did I detect a smile on the wizened professor's face? I did not laugh.

Once settled in his house, Mrs. Lieberman was ready to serve lunch. Steak. I couldn't believe it. I couldn't get a grape down if my life depended on it, and there was a thick slab of meat in front of me. Somehow we got through it.

Now by ourselves in the living room. "Fenster, I know that you know all the material. I don't need to ask you any questions." Indeed I did know most of it by heart, by virtue of constant repetition.

I heard myself saying: "Oh no, professor, you're not going to get away with that. I've been preparing for weeks, please ask me something." He did. I answered. Graduation time seemed closer. I still can't believe that reaction that came out of me. Foolhardy.

H. L. had me trace the Biblical Exodus route. It was not easy, there were complications and some confusion. But that too I knew by rote.

I had made it. A rabbi at last. Ten years after that summer in camp, I was legitimate. A real rabbi. No joke! On the ferry back to the mainland, Ricky and I celebrated with a coke. My eyes glazed over. The road was open before us.

It led of all places to Newark, N. J. to one of the largest congregations in the state, Where I spent two years with one of my mentors, Dr. Joachim Prinz.

A RABBI WHO FOUGHT BACK

IT WAS A brief episode in my unfolding as a rabbi which did make a marked impression upon me despite its brevity. We lived in Newark, the heart of a metropolitan area, and I was the Assistant Rabbi at Temple Bnai Abraham. I was still in my twenties. The Senior Rabbi was Dr. Joachim Prinz who had come from Berlin and established himself in New Jersey. Prinz was a colorful personality who had to wend his way through the troubled waters of the early Nazi period. As I remember it, he told me that high Nazi officials would come to his synagogue, which was one of the largest in Berlin, often to monitor what he was saying to the congregation.

This was still in the early period, between 1933 and '38 and the S.S. were not always in uniform. One fateful night right before Hanukkah, he wanted to speak of the evil specter that he believed was rising up before them. But as he looked out into the audience he saw some of the hostile and unfriendly faces that he knew. Immediately he switched his remarks from the oppressive Nazi regime to the Greek-Syrians who dominated Palestine in the Second Century before the Common Era and under whose aegis the Hanukkah story took place. The prayer that we say at that time is one of gratitude for, "turning the wicked and the many over into the hands of the few." He escaped censure, but of course the congregation understood precisely what he was talking about.

Other times there were attempts to stop and disgrace him. The congregation prayed that decency would prevail over power. It didn't.

In 2007 excerpts from his Berlin diary began to appear. In them are many of the stories Prinz had told me in Newark in 1953. Some are harrowing. Some are almost hilarious. Those were historic times and Prinz was the man to respond heroically.

Prinz' life had been difficult but he had an indomitable, triumphant spirit. He was glad to be working creatively within the community. I learned much from him, certainly in the field of social activism, but we had many theological discussions besides.

In the last years Phillip Roth, who comes from Newark, has made Prinz's name popular, especially in his book "the Plot Against America." In that part of the novel, Roth was telling the truth.

I also have a very vivid memory of going with him to visit in a house of mourning. It was not a long trip but on the way I was reading J. D. Salinger's "Catcher in the Rye" which had really just come out a short time before. And then I came upon a special part of Holden Caulfield's early life at boarding school, at the church service, and when I read it I exploded in laughter. Just at that moment we reached the house but I was in no shape to go in, So I told Prinz that I would meet him inside just as soon as I had gotten myself together. It was no longer than ten minutes before that was to happen. The passage describes how his friend is in church when suddenly a loud fart is emitted and the service stops. I showed it to Prinz, but he didn't think it was quite as funny as I did.

That was not difficult to comprehend. Prinz had lived through harrowing times in the early Nazi period, trying as best he could to counsel his congregation to leave Germany while it was still possible. He decided to come to America. His last service in Berlin was announced.

Here I depend on testimony presented years later at the trial of Adolf Eichman in Jerusalem by Salo Baron, eminent, long-time professor at Columbia University in New York. On the day of the departing service for Prinz in Berlin the synagogue was full. In the lobby prior to the service some of the youngsters were running around. Inadvertently one of them stepped on the foot of an adult in the lobby. It happened to be Adolf Eichman, now in full uniform, polished boots and all.

Eichman flew into an instant rage. He grabbed the youngster by the throat and began choking him. Witnesses attest that had he not been pulled away, the child would have died.

The story is shocking but not surprising. Berlin in 1938 was a dangerous place. Prinz and his family managed to leave. Many years later we met up in Newark.

Prinz and I were dissimilar in many ways. He was short and I was six foot tall. He didn't like taking pictures that made us appear like Mutt and Jeff, so I would stand on the step below. He was a European intellectual with a PhD. in art history. I was a young rabbi from Flatbush with a B.A. from Yeshiva College. Yet, I learned a great deal from him. He had also learned to start life over again after pain.

One of the times that I was invited to the Prinz home for lunch, Ricky was unable to join me. They served a souffle. The firmness of the arch in front of me was most inviting. Trouble was, I had no idea how you eat it. It was not a dish which I had seen in Flatbush. I watched Joachim and Hilde carefully and followed suit. It was delicious, a real treat. Though I have since been searching, never found another one quite as good.

Prinz was a dramatic speaker who knew how to rapidly present the essence of his thought. He always had a good peroration. I hope I learned well. I certainly listened intently.

When I listened to him speak, I tried to pick up pointers. Our religious outlook differed. But I learned a great deal nonetheless.

When I left after two years, it was on the best of terms. Prinz installed me in Jackson Heights and, in fact, at Shelter Rock, eleven years later. He was a loyal friend and mentor.

The move to the suburbs focused my mind better on what was to become my agenda over the next years. It would accurately be: 'Theology and Social Concern'. I reflected through the prism of my personal life, the spiritual and religious tradition that I had come to revere. Social action was in a sense the marching orders for those who were ritually pious. Every morning in prayer the emphasis was on those "who bring peace and order between a person and his friend." Saying that, I sense that now I had to go out and do it.

MCGINLEY

CERTAIN EVENTS WHILE I was at Temple Bnai Abraham in Newark made a lasting impression upon me.

One of them had to do with the very first Saturday after our moving. Dr. Prinz, then the President of the American Jewish Congress, called on Wednesday to tell me that he has been called to Berlin for an important meeting with Adenauer. The whole subject of the future relationship of the Jewish community to Germany was on the agenda.

That all sounded easy and logical. The problem was that there were going to be four Bar Mitzvah boys on Shabbat morning in the synagogue. I would have to officiate. It was to be my first plunge into the water over my head, since my mastoid operation.

At Mt. Kisco which was up to then the totality of my rabbinic experience, I had perhaps four Bar Mitzvah boys a year. The task was daunting, there was more than just a little apprehension as we approached it.

So, I am standing on the bimah that day, associating the names with the faces of the boys. This tall one is Steven, the blonde is Michael, the kid with freckles is Jonathan, and the short one is Howard. As I looked at it, if I made a mistake and mixed them up the synagogue ceiling would collapse.

Actually, the synagogue itself was quite imposing. Legend had it that it was built by wealthy fur merchants and bootleggers and the affluence of Essex County. The synagogue was made of imported Italian marble with a huge Ark for the Torah which was operated by pushbuttons. Its main feature, however, were two thousand permanent seats, five hundred in the balcony and fifteen hundred on the main floor. On many occasions such as the one I anticipated at my inaugural, most of the seats on the main floor would be occupied.

I might add, parenthetically, that this early experience of having to address large numbers of people gathered in the synagogue was to prove valuable to me later on. At Shelter Rock on the holidays there were also two thousand people in the expanded sanctuary-auditorium when the folding doors between the two were removed. This I did for many years, which was also a good rehearsal for my sixteen month stint at Temple Israel in Great Neck. There, on any given Sabbath morning, anywhere from five to eight hundred people could be in the synagogue.

If those numbers did nothing more for me, they certainly guaranteed my concentration. Knowing that I was going to take the time of so many people, I worked long and hard to make sure I had something worthwhile to say. My credo was and is: never take any statement casually, you never know who is listening, you never know how deeply they may possibly be affected. A further kicker: do nothing to remove a person's faith unless you replace it with something stronger. Telling people that God does not hear their prayers or that the Exodus never took place, or that the Israelites were not gathered at Mt. Sinai to hear the Ten Commandments – I would have no part of that. Often biblical passages have to be reinterpreted and you must point that out when you are doing so, but there must also be a strong message that comes through the biblical history, the teachings and the values. And they should not be neglected.

I am not sure I had that all fully developed in my mind on that first Saturday morning in Newark. I was too busy focusing on the young men in front of me. The service proceeded normally, until the Ark sprung open at the Cantor's push of the button. Then in keeping with my long-standing style, I began singing lustily the prayer that is said when the Torah is taken from the Ark: "For out of Zion shall come forth the Torah and the word of God from Jerusalem." Unwittingly I was singing it in my usual fervent but atonal style. I felt a strange feeling on my leg. The Cantor was standing next to me and he had put his foot on top of mine. "Kid, do me a favor – stop singing – you're throwing me off." It was the biggest compliment I had ever received about my singing. At Madison High School I had been declared a listener and prohibited from singing altogether. That Cantor Abraham Shapiro, one of the great cantors of his time, could be thrown off by little old me, was in itself quite an achievement. So I immediately shut up and it made me self-conscious for the two years that I was there at Newark with him. And beyond.

But we turned out to be good friends. I would often drive him home and he would give me hints as to how to improve my rabbinic style. In substance they were – you don't always have to come up with something novel and fresh; borrow from other people, but make sure that what you take is good stuff. I never liked borrowing other people's material and in fact always tried to come up with my own. But I have not forgotten the sincerity of his advice nor his friendship.

On one of those rides home Cantor Shapiro started telling me about his trip to La Scala in Milan. He knew Italian opera well and I guess his secret ambition was always to go to the opera like most cantors. Once when he was in Milan, he convinced the maintenance man to open up the back door for him so he could go on the stage, and in the dark he sang an aria at La Scala. It didn't seem like much to me, but it made him very happy. He taught cantors at the Hebrew Union College of Sacred Music. Those who studied with him were indeed privileged.

The other memorable event while we were living in Newark was a trial undertaken by Dr. Prinz against Conde McGinley, a well-known spouter of hate and anti-Semitism, who had issued a banner headline in the rag he promoted as a newspaper, "Three Hundred Red Rabbis In America." As Prinz's assistant that would also have me as one. This was at the beginning of the McCarthy era when red-baiting was the order of the day for those so-called Anti-Communist guardians of our freedom. McGinley accused Prinz of being a "red rabbi" and gave proof of the fact that he was expelled from Germany because the Nazis were ridding themselves of the Communists. The suit was undertaken in conjunction with the American Jewish Congress which supplied the counsel for the trial. In effect, the Congress was also being libeled because Prinz was their president. The irony was that Prinz had never been part of any Communist or Red-tinted organization. But the American Jewish Congress was cited as defending other liberals, promoting Israel, and in general, hinting at a variety of other "subversive activities."

Two lawyers undertook Prinz's case. The youngest was Phil Baum who later became the Executive Director of the AJC. I can still remember Phil excitedly gathering all the information and consulting with Prinz and collating the material. I was very impressed with him because we were more or less the same age. Later he turned out to be a member of the Jewish Center of Jackson Heights and he and his wife Betty, Ricky and I became life-long friends. Nowadays we meet and talk about the good old days as two retired people who still have not come to terms with retirement.

The case came before a Federal judge in Newark, a stolid impressive man who stood for no nonsense.

The trial gave me an opportunity to see American justice first-hand. The judge was serious and solemn. The jury looked confused by all of the allegations that McGinley's lawyer was making. The lawyer, whose name was Dilling, a well-known anti-Semite.

For five or six days, I sat in the courtroom transfixed. McGinley's lawyer made the outlandish claim that Prinz had been expelled from Germany because of his Red leanings. McGinley was a Holocaust denier before it ever became popular. While we have not heard from him lately, I'm sure he would persist in his absurdity.

But the main shock was saved for the fourth day when McGinley's lawyer dramatically rolled in the library cart with a dozen thick books on the shelves. I understood immediately what he was about. It was not good. It proceeded to unfold. I was growing progressively uncomfortable.

What the lawyer had done was to collect a number of fragmented statements from the Talmud, which had been edited by the early censors, that were alleged to point in deprecation to Jesus of Nazareth by the Jews.

It is true that the Talmud does refer to Jesus as "oto ha' ish" – that man, which could be taken with a sense of slight. But the long history of anti-Jewish activity subsequent to Jesus' time had to be taken into account. What this unsavory lawyer was now attempting was an appeal to the jury's raw Christian instincts, thereby hoping to pre-judge Prinz as one of those slighting the very foundation of their faith. That, of course, would be tantamount to subversive activity, at least by his accounting. The fact is that the Talmud never engaged Christianity in debate over the merits of the various religions, nor did it ever slur the founder of Christianity. Later Maimonides wrote that both Judaism and Christianity are destined to bring redemption to the world. Together.

Meanwhile, McGinley was attempting, in one fell swoop, to erase the hundred years of growing mutual respect, of understanding the human values of the American Judeo-Christian tradition based on the God-given principles of the sacredness of every human personality. He was also attempting to erase Vatican II, every interfaith activity ever undertaken this last half-century; the entire powerful tradition of the mosaic of faiths that America had patiently cultivated.

It was a dastardly move. Was he going to get away with it?

Prinz' lawyer tried nobly to point out that this should not be turned into a medieval disputation between Judaism and Christianity; both their representatives in Newark had the greatest respect for each other. (The local Bishop had appeared as a character witness for Prinz, as had the former governor of the state). But I couldn't suppress the sinking feeling that strong points had been scored, touching very sensitive spots in the minds of the jury. Once the spectre of insult is ignited, mutual respect is out the window. Especially in the McCarthy era.

The next day, unexpectedly, the entire case was broken wide open. The questioning of the defendant was desultory, when suddenly Prinz' lawyer asked about General Eisenhower's visit to the concentration camp after the war. McGinley's face reddened as he broke through the veils of rationality: "Eisenhower was too strongly influenced by the Reds – " he blurted out. The judge banged the gavel down hard, his face reddened as well: "We will have none of that in this court." Later I learned that the judge had been appointed by Eisenhower. The case was over.

Prinz won a sum but he was never able to collect. There had been tense moments, but justice prevailed. Unfortunately, Holocaust deniers still live.

For more than a week I was filled with the adverse undercurrents against Prinz. It was overflowing. That night, I went home and wrote "Courtroom Diary" which appeared in the next issue of The Reconstructionist Magazine. Little did I realize then that Holocaust deniers and paranoic people who see Jews as a threat to their world would persist and proliferate in the future. They persist to this day and who knows if we will ever be rid of them.

So Prinz was always a reminder to me of classic European anti-semitism, while McGinley was a flagship for the American brand. Both were reminders of the imperfections of our world.

The deeper sadness was that I saw often the effects of this invidious disaster on the Jews themselves. Instead of fighting unseen prejudices, they bought into it. At times I would hear Jews blame each other and go inward with insult, and in extreme forms some even developed a self-hatred.

All of that was noticed. But my personal experience and my faith in America withstood the negatives. At its heart and in its history America is strong for diversity and democracy. As the Jews are God's stake in history, so is America. I still believe that.

OUT ON OUR OWN

As AN ASSISTANT rabbi at Temple Bnai Abraham in Newark for two years, I felt that I had gained invaluable experience. I had come from Mt. Kisco where I felt the range of my involvement would be limited, due to the size of the congregation. The sanctuary at Temple Bnai Abraham was huge and tastefully appointed. And I was given many opportunities. I felt akin to the prophet Amos, who came from the "outer borough" to the big city.

As reparations with Germany were being negotiated, Konrad Adenauer wanted Nahum Goldman and Prinz and other German-speaking Jews to be present. When he was away, I was in charge.

But after two years I felt ready to move on, a strong desire to be out on my own. It was then that the congregation advanced me to associate rabbi. But in those roles I felt that the decisions and the responsibility were not mine. I was ready to come out of partial hiding and face the music.

We arrived in Jackson Heights, Queens, in 1955. It was a populous middle-class community; a huge number of apartment houses, not yet suburban, in the shadow of Manhattan. Ricky and I moved into a narrow three-story row house, which suited us fine. The world seemed open before us. Our fourth, Danny, was born there joining two brothers and his older sister.

The congregation had a distinguished history, but landed up on the wrong side of town. We realized at once that we would have to work to fix that. It took five years, but it was accomplished. The congregation grew. The building was new and spacious, ready to be filled.

At my installation, Joachim Prinz gave one of his fiery, dramatic speeches. Warning American Jews of the danger of Marjorie Morningstar becoming a stereotype, Herman Wolk had written a best-seller highlighting the shallow, materialistic, pleasure-seeking people of suburbia. Though Jackson Heights was not yet suburbia, there was always the danger of settling into a middle-class comfort and almost – affluence. The President of the Rabbinical Assembly, Edward Sandrow, also spoke. He too was an accomplished and persuasive speaker, and a friend.

At that point, I was neither accomplished nor dramatic. But I spoke from my heart and promised to do my best to bring spirituality and learning to what was in essence my first real challenge as a Rabbi.

The kids were young, Ricky and I were in our twenties, with more energy than we knew what to do with, and a burning vision if not to save Judaism, then at least to save the Jews.

There is no doubt that during the Holocaust, I felt deeply the humiliating powerlessness of my father's family, all of whom were trapped in Poland. He had tried, with no success, to transfer them to America. They were doomed to an ignominious death. Hearing his soul-rending cries into the night seared its way into my heart.

Our people had to be strong and together. It was my primary stimulus to a life in the rabbinate. I was convinced that passion in prayer and ritual, strongly applied study of texts, concerned social activism drawn from religious impulse and sense of community solidarity, were the ingredients we needed.

Mt. Kisco had been my training ground which Ricky and I took to immediately. That continued in Newark under the tutelage of Joachim Prinz and his lovely wife Hilde. We both had learned a great deal. We were ready for a real congregation in prime time. We found it in Jackson Heights. We were there for eleven years by which time Elissa and Jonathan were in high school and Jeremy and Daniel were moving right along.

Just last week, in 2008, Jonathan reported a visit to the old neighborhood, now a polyglot urban sprawl. But he still finds touches of the tree shaded streets and homes we knew back in the 50's and they are still quite appealing. And though it is Queens, which some people put down as outer-borough, you can be in Manhattan with a skip and a jump. Our family has many fond memories of that time and place.

CAPACITY FOR EXPERIENCE

OUR TRANSFER TO Jackson Heights was tenuous. I was interviewed in the old Jewish Center building on 73rd Street, adjacent to the railroad tracks, on the third floor. The three present were all veterans of long standing in the synagogue, J. P. Ostreicher, Maurice Shefferman and Alfred Rothschild, all warm and welcoming. We hit it off immediately. They were all a generation or more older than me.

After an hour or so of interview, they outlined for me two steps before I could be confirmed as the rabbi of Jackson Heights Jewish Center. The first was that I would have to come for a weekend, to speak on both Friday night and Shabbat morning, and conduct the service. That was fine with me, I was expecting and, in fact, I was happy because it showed that I was a finalist in their search. I prepared thoroughly for the occasion and felt I was ready to go.

On Friday night just immediately prior to the service, I entered the office of the Cantor, William Z. Glueck. His greeting: "They will never take you, you're too young." It didn't make for reassurance, but I just let it go by. Next question was equally daunting: "Do you drink schnaps?" Up to that point in my life I rarely had imbibed. This time I did answer, "No, but if you want to teach me I'm willing to learn."

The Cantor apparently had this mystical, long-standing belief that at the end of every service he had to have a schnaps or two, and would love for the rabbi to join him. In short order, I learned how to do that and the Cantor and I became fast friends for the eleven years that we were together.

Three decades later I chanced upon him on one of our brief visits to my in-laws who were living then in Hallandale, Florida. We embraced warmly and, of course, he invited me over so that we could have a schnaps together. I guess I would have to list him as a very special kind of mentor who certainly did not enrich my mind, but did offer a lot for my spirit.

But first the congregation had to be convened and approve. That was less simple. I was asked to make a brief presentation, outlining some of my plans and hopes for involving the congregation. Question and answer period.

A hand shot up, an older gentleman felt he had spotted a problem. "Rabbi, you seem like a pleasant young man. But are you aware that you are following a very well known rabbi, probably twice your age. Do you think you have the experience and the know-how to do this? It is quite a task you are undertaking."

I wasn't stumped but I was taken aback. How to answer calmly and respectfully! One of the veterans of the interviewing group jumped up. Later I was to learn that he was a Shakespearean scholar and a student of English literature. "May I remind my friend here – what George Bernard Shaw once said: 'It is not experience that counts – but the capacity for experience that counts.' We believe this young man has that capacity." That settled it. We were approved. It wasn't even close.

In the meantime a new synagogue was built on 82nd Street, in the heart of the overflowing apartment house population. Jeremy, who was then only four, remembers the excitement of the groundbreaking.

My mentor, Rabbi Ben Zion Bokser, spoke at the Dedication. We had a large three-story house on 86th Street with an intercom in the kitchen so that we could be in touch with the top floor where the kids romped.

The congregation was sizable. A few hundred were in synagogue each week. Life looked good. We were young. They were heady years.

All of this was brought to an abrupt halt on November 22, 1962, the day President John Kennedy was assassinated. It was a Friday with services set for that night and the next day.

I was totally unprepared for what happened. Throngs of mourners turned out for that Shabbat, both Friday and Saturday morning. I tried to give voice to the rupture in our lives, to the promise abruptly ended. Kennedy represented the new generation and brought eloquence, ideas and grace to his office. There was much sadness and disillusion that had to be countered.

I called upon one of my congregants and friends, Ben Rosenthal to join me on the pulpit. Ben was a dedicated congressman who had worked closely with JFK. He told of his loss and ours.

That Shabbat was amongst the most dramatic I have ever known. In times of trouble, people still turned to the synagogue.

After that first interview, the next stop was to spend a Shabbat at the Jewish Center, speaking both on Friday night and Saturday morning. Truth be told, I have no memory of what I said on either of those occasions. Nor of being nervous or anxious. It was a congregation with a proud history, but in its present location could be seen to have its glorious past behind it. For me, it would be perfect. Perhaps together we could plan a glorious future.

That Shabbat we spent with the Sheffermans, who were later to become dear friends. There were no glitches.

Jackson Heights was a good choice for our family, for growing in social concern and integrity for the future.

And while I was there, totally unexpected vistas opened, our sojourn to Haifa, involvement in the civil rights movement and the Soviet Jewry protest phenomena.

Another avenue that opened to me, while in Queens, were the older colleagues who became friends and mentors. Ben Zion Bokser, Arthur Neulander, Israel Mowshowitz, Josiah Derby.

One day out of the blue, Bokser called. "Myron, I want you to join the Editorial Board of the High holiday prayer book I'm working on." I felt as if I had been chosen to the President's Cabinet. Bokser was rabbi at the Forest Hills Jewish Center, then the largest synagogue in Queens.

We would meet weekly in Forest Hills, but we had reached a point when, with a good spurt of time, the machzor would be ready for publication. Bokser decided that we would meet for a few days at the Pennsylvania Hotel, opposite Penn Station, for our marathon.

One huge problem. It was winter, late December. A huge snow storm developed blanketing New York City with six or more inches. It was Sunday, I was supposed to get to the subway station into the city.

We started digging out our car on Northern Boulevard, something I had very little experience doing. Before long I was ready to give up, even though, no surprise, Ricky was prepared to continue. I decided to walk to the subway, ordinarily an easy lope. It was heavy underfoot but after a half hour or so, we were there and our meeting proceeded at the Hotel. Surprisingly, eight of us showed.

I remember a powerful experience ensued as we were reviewing a translation of the Avodah, the ritual performed by the high Priest in the Temple on Yom Kippur. We weren't just reading the text. We, at least speaking for myself, were the text. Here we were, with a storm all around us, huddled over a passage, a couple of thousand years old, moved by it and feeling it deeply. It reminded me once again, that some of those old texts can still have a marked impact.

HOTEL THERESA

IT WAS NOT long into our stay in Jackson Heights when I received a call on a Friday afternoon to ask if I would represent the American Jewish Congress, of which I was a member of the Executive Committee, at an outdoor rally on Sunday in Harlem in front of the Hotel Theresa. New Yorkers remembered the Hotel Theresa from the time when Fidel Castro was staying there on one of his early visits to New York and was histrionically seen plucking chickens on the top floor and having the feathers float casually toward the earth.

Friday afternoons for a rabbi are always busy and somewhat tense times. In most synagogues there are two sermons that are going to be said on the Sabbath, one on Friday night and one on Saturday morning, in addition to teaching from the Scriptures. While this begins early in the week it all has to be finalized on Friday. I didn't have much time to inquire as to the details before I agreed to go.

That Sunday was one that I shall never forget. It began an hour or so before the outdoor rally for civil rights with a march through Harlem. Leading the march was Bayard Rustin, one of the great organizers of the Civil Rights Movement and an associate of the Rev. Martin Luther King, Jr. Ossie Davis was the Master of Ceremonies. It was said that Dr. King was going to be the featured speaker. All of this was at a time when the Civil Rights Movement was gearing up in the 60's. It was early in the struggle of what became a mighty force in American life. No one knew what was coming. But it felt good to be there.

I can recall vividly Rustin walking through the streets of Harlem and reviewing with the assistant who was tagging alongside, the details that had to be prepared for the rally itself. I couldn't help overhearing, since Rustin was alongside. There was the microphone that had to be checked, there were the guests in the front rows that had to be welcomed, there was a whole horde of other things. Calmly, Rustin reviewed them all. He was a very special person, committed, open, and thoroughly organized.

On the march I was chatting pleasantly with Ossie Davis and his wife Ruby Dee, who were very cordial and welcoming. When Ossie Davis introduced me to the rally it was with a special flourish, "that I admire a rabbi who takes his religion into the streets." It was a simple phrase, well turned, but it summarized a good deal of what I believed in. A good introduction, not overly done, is always appreciated.

When I finished, the moment for the main speaker had come. Once again Ossie Davis: "We had hoped that today the Rev. Martin Luther King, Jr. would be with us. But he is unable to free himself from his involvement in Atlanta. Instead he has sent a young man, a clergyman, whose name you may not yet have heard. But you will because I predict a great future for him as a leader of America. His name is Andrew Young."

Young, in his reasoned but forceful way, spoke what had to be said to remind all of us that "we were at the beginning of a Movement that seeks to bring decent housing and jobs and equal education to the children of Harlem. The journey will be long" he said, "but we will proceed and we will prevail." Despite all the worry to the contrary the rally was peaceful and productive and I left that day feeling that I had participated in something bigger than any of us, that was going to make a difference in the America of the future.

Some of the congregation joined with me that day. I had announced that I would be going up to Harlem on Sunday. I deeply appreciated their participation. It felt good to see some familiar faces among the throng. But there was no problem even though, as I recall it, I was the only non-black speaker.

I attempted that day to give voice to long-standing values: the Biblical tradition that calls us to action on behalf of our brothers and sisters, without regard to color, religion or sex. And that tied as we are to Scripture, we dare not turn away from that call. "This is a test for America, to bring forth our best selves and fulfill our promise. We must remove the mark of Cain from all those who unfairly bear it. In the Bible, God gave Cain the mark to save him. We must remove that mark to save our fellow and sister citizens. We need renewal and reconciliation in America – Christian and Jew, black and white. The blacks in America have been the recipient of pain, not its progenitor. We need a new start, a fresh beginning. The civil rights movement is the place to start."

By then, somehow or another, I had acquired a reputation as a social activist. Time Magazine called and wanted a quote. Newsday was on my trail followed closely by the New York Post. Truth be told, I was never caught up in that whole process to the extent that I was willing to neglect my own study, which I always tried to maintain daily, and my involvement with the congregation. I'd like to think of myself as a thoughtful activist and not a reflexive one.

When I was asked by Midstream Magazine in 1966 to contribute to their issue of December on the subject "Negro-Jewish Relations in America: A symposium" I readily agreed. Some of the others who participated were well known activists in the field like Floyd B. McKissick, C. Eric Lincoln and Gus Tyler – in addition to Lucy Davidowicz, Maurice Samuel, Leslie Fiedler, and others. As far as I could tell I was the only rabbi who was negotiating my way within the congregation while at the same time involving myself actively with Black-Jewish relations. It's interesting that in 1966 they were called Negro-Jewish relations, terms which later became obsolete. But they reflected the temper of the 60's.

This magazine was later published in book form and as I read my statement many years later I am totally in agreement with it to this day. What I tried to do was to connect my religious outlook with social concerns. It was not isolated or separate but intertwined and a part of our tradition as I understand it.

I would quote a few paragraphs because it indicates what my thinking was then and what my thinking is still today.

"By no reason of disillusionment can we exonerate our disengagement. But there are other voices of caution that would entice us and to which we must at least give ear. One is that we Jews endanger our own security by concern for and involvement in the struggle. That the backlashed Christian resents it and therefore the Jew will pay for it."

"This fear has been flaunted in our faces before and constantly. In the wake of its paralysis, the only response possible would be to roll over and die. By virtue of such fears Jews place themselves into a class of disembodied citizens, forever shivering in the face of Gentilism, outside the stream of American aspirations and events."

"Let me admit to feeling sad and cheated when some marvelously idealistic college kid is ready to lay down his young life to inch along the Negro struggle but would not lift a pinky to save the whole Jewish enterprise from oblivion. Some Jewish college kids have used the civil rights struggle in a diversionary way, as some have used the peace movement. Limelight-drawing issues always run that risk though it neither negates nor validates the issue which should be judged on its own merit. But the activists who fail to acknowledge the Jewish social idealism from which their convictions were nurtured and grew are not new either. Nor would they be likely to be in *shul* next Saturday in any case. Civil rights may not have saved souls for Judaism but it has not lost any either."

"At the risk of exercising preachment, the view that Judaism is not an heirloom to be lauded in rhetoric or paraded in passive reverential piety must be asserted. We see it standing relevant to this hour, its demands, judgments and texts not as decoration but as charges. Reading admonitions in sacred books to remember the stranger, not to stand idly by the blood of the neighbor, to sense the indignity of the worker not paid on time, or the feeling of the man from whom a pledge is to be collected, is to focus unconditionally on those in our midst who have not had their fair share of the blessings so many of us enjoy."

"Who can turn away from the thousand daily slashes the Negro experiences? His manhood has been shattered and his hopes destroyed. In the South, they sometimes do it with hoses and dogs, in the North more subtly but no less painfully, by moving out when they move in, by refusing to send kids where they are, by getting scared near to death when anyone moves down the street. Do we think that all of these things go unnoticed without welling up anger, hostility and extremism?"

"The Negro is caught today in the middle of a dilemma not of his own making. It can't come as any surprise in this post-Freudian era that people often become what we say they are. Tell a kid everyday that he is illegitimate and before long, like Edmund, he will be musing on bastardy. We want a responsible Negro community while we deny those conditions which alone can bring it into being."

"We can't go on charging the Negro more for less, getting him deeper into garnisheed debt, let rats nibble at his kids' feet, send him to segregated schools – and if someone sells a house, worry, worry, start a rumor – a *schvartze* is coming – give him a job as a porter, make her always and only into a housemaid and then wonder why we can't have peace on our streets and in our homes."

Of course not everyone hearkened to my view as if it were the last word on the subject. By the time the article appeared I was already living in Roslyn. There was no black population there. It was a comfortable Jewish – Italian – WASP enclave. Some people ridiculed the fact that I would write in the manner in which I did while sitting in a lily-white circumstance. But it was related to our experience and I did not, or do not now, back down from any of it.

It is interesting to me how much has changed in the thirty-eight years that we have lived in Roslyn. Many of the Jews of that time have moved on elsewhere. Today our community and a good many of my neighbors are Korean, Japanese, Indian and Chinese. They make wonderful neighbors and I enjoy very much the opportunity to interact with them. One of the neighbors on my street is a Chinese doctor whose practice was actually in Chinatown. When he took ill and I heard about it, I was strongly motivated to go visit with him. He was overjoyed that I came. To me it didn't seem like such a big deal, because I knew his wife and children and I admired their industry and devotion. He practically kissed my hand in gratitude.

One day some years ago, our next-door neighbor, a Korean teenager rang my bell. She later graduated from Herricks High School as one of the top students, now a lovely, brilliant woman. She wanted to write about the Holocaust for a school assignment. But she didn't have enough reference books although she had already consulted some. She wanted to know if I could help her. By the time she left our house her arms were piled high and I'm sure that she produced a work of scholarship and imagination and identity. All of these incidents reminded me that the theory and the practice had actually come together. Integration is not only a high minded idea, it has become a reality, at least in my neighborhood.

TEL AVIV

BEFORE LONG, THE first opportunity presented itself in Jackson Heights for what was a long anticipated experience. It opened up a whole new vista to my understanding of American Jewish life. It was also a harbinger of my future.

In the summer of 1957, I became aware of a three-week subsidized seminar for rabbis and teachers that was being offered by the Jewish Agency in Israel. I latched on to it. It was surely going to be a high adventure: Ricky, God bless her, agreed to be home with the kids. To my surprise, no glitches appeared. The path was open and I took it.

I was not looking forward to my first flight, a dozen hours with a stopover in Amsterdam. The road, it turned out, was rocky. Over Newfoundland we had to return to New York when one engine was shut down by fire. The next day we boarded again.

Since we were flying KLM this time we stopped at Amsterdam. We were taken to a seaside resort a half-hour from the city for overnight rest. This was the first foreign city I had ever seen. It was fascinating: I was like a hick let loose on the world. "Oh, my God, the people are wearing wooden shoes." Looking at the clothes, the awesome boulevards and majestic apartment houses, all of us were silent.

Finally we pulled up at our hotel. When it was bult, probably a half century before, it must have been a castle. It had seen better days, but for me it represented that Old World charm I had heard so much about.

Each of us was given our own room. Mine was large with a spacious bathroom, a tub, another smaller tub, a large marble sink. I couldn't figure out what the small tub was about. For the dog perhaps, or the children.

Anyway, I called home to New York to report after our aborted arrival the day before. It was wonderful talking to Ricky and each one of the kids. I felt like an international traveler.

I described the bathroom to Ricky. I asked for an explanation of the small tub. Don't try to get into it she explained, if I were with you it would be more for me than for you. I was overjoyed to take a luxurious bath in the larger receptacle.

Finally, late Friday afternoon, we arrived at what was then Lod Airport, now Ben Gurion. Not enough time before Shabbat to reach Jerusalem. They took us to Ramat Aviv for the night: a close-by suburb, a short distance from the airport. The hotel was made up of a series of small bungalows, neat, clean, just fine. We were exhausted from the double trip, so we made Shabbat together, ate, sang some, conversed lightly and went to bed.

The next morning I awoke as if still in a dream. The sun was shining, and I was in Tel Aviv. Eretz Yisroel! One problem: we were a few miles out of the center of the town, with only a makeshift Shabbat service as a prospect. It would not do. I was anticipating the real thing for too long.

Speaking to no one, I started walking toward center city. I realized that by the time I would get there, services would be over. I didn't hesitate: within a minute I had put up my thumb and was on my way to Tel Aviv. Once there it was easy to find the Great Synagogue on Allenby and to catch the remainder of the service. I was taking it all in! Thoroughly enjoyable!

I decided to go see my father's relatives on Keren Kayemet. I had their address. I think my father had written of my coming, but I wasn't sure.

As I was walking the streets, there was an overwhelming sense of serenity and joy in that moment. It was as if I were drunk with it. Every store had a surprise, some so sophisticated as to be miraculous – dresses, shoes, pocketbooks, men's clothing; some so simple as to have just arrived from the stet1 – bookstores, small groceries, juice stands, falafel, shwarma. The streets were filled with a dazzling diversity. I took it all in – all the sights. Even though it was Shabbat and the stores were closed, it was still an overwhelming experience.

Suddenly, I heard a young man speaking Hebrew to his dog. I hadn't reckoned with that. I was still struggling to get my Yeshiva of Flatbush Hebrew up to speed, and here this dog was ahead of me. What a country!

Do I ring the bell or knock? I am at the door of distant cousins who all lived in Strelisk, the fabled stet1 40 years ago. What language do we speak, how do we communicate?

All unnecessary. They realized in a moment who I was. They had gathered – all ten of them – for a festive Sabbath meal at Moshe and Wanda's house. The Szolds, the Goldsteins and the kids. I didn't need language. Wanda, in particular, kept hugging and kissing me – "Uri's a zin" – she pronounced my father's name in the old Yiddish way, looking at me with disbelief. They hadn't seen each other in forty years when they were in Strelisk. They were both nineteen years old. She had gotten caught up in the Holocaust and had fortunately survived. The Szolds came to Israel immediately after leaving Europe and spent years building roads and living on a kibbutz. They had done well and had raised a family as well. What an introduction to Israel! Our pasts merged.

Wanda could not take her eyes off me, as if my father had risen from the dead. She must have been a beautiful woman in her youth and bore her age gracefully. Couldn't help the libidinous interjection; wondered if there had been more to it than larger family interests.

We ate and drank and talked – I stayed till late in the afternoon. A real homecoming! I was buoyed up by the experience. Despite the jet lag, I slept blissfully that night.

From there it was on to Jerusalem and the rest of the seminar, study, travel, synagogues and a variety of new experiences. I kept saying to myself at every stop, Ricky and the family should be here with me. Next time. But when and how? Little did I know, that it was not to be very long after.

HAIFA 1962

THROUGHOUT MY LIFE I have always felt pain deeply.

The Bible speaks of caring for the stranger, the widow, the child, the blind, the deaf and the underdog. Its application has always come naturally. Sensitivity to the impaired, physically or emotionally, has always gotten to me. Over and over again the biblical admonition comes to us. "Remember the heart of the stranger, for you were strangers in the Land of Egypt." Almost pleadingly the Bible has God saying, "When the poor man cries unto Me, will I not hear him?" If someone standing next to me is struck, I feel part of the injury. I will always carry with me the trauma of my earliest days. Every time I am in the midst of trying to comfort someone on a loss they have suffered, memory touches my insides.

One of the things that has intrigued me most about being a rabbi was my ability to become involved in controversial but important aspects of social activism. In October of 1962 my friend Wolfe Kelman approached me and asked if I would be ready to be sent by The Rabbinical Assembly, the organization of Conservative Rabbis of which I am a part, to Haifa in Israel. I would be a Visiting Rabbi there for one year. The Rabbinical Assembly had never sent an official representative to Israel before. When I first heard about it, the responsibility seemed awesome. But I welcomed it heartily. We were then the disenfranchised in Israel. Something had to be done.

Israel was then a more peaceful place than it is today and Haifa is an especially beautiful city, right on the azure-blue Mediterranean. We were to live on Mt. Carmel in the Ahuza section, one of the nicest in the country. It was a marvelous opportunity. A great adventure awaited us.

The congregation agreed to my ten month sabbatical. I think they felt honored that I had been selected.

There was one problem. I would have to go home and tell Ricky and our already four children that we would be packing up and going away, that our kids would have to be in Israeli schools for the year and that altogether we would be living in a new and unknown environment.

To their credit our family was excited and even thrilled by the news, but they were somewhat scared as well. Our youngest son Daniel was not yet ready for school. Elisa, Jonathan and Jeremy were. An unforgettable memory was the first day I took them to school in Haifa. We were waiting in the principal's office; suddenly all three of the kids were crying. At that particular moment their enthusiasm had waned. So had mine. They were all what my mother used to call, "good scouts." They rolled with the punches and all three did well.

Before going home to speak to the family there is no question that I had a considerable hesitancy to take the Haifa assignment. Since I would be the first of my rabbinical organization, which is allied with the Jewish Theological Seminary, a world class school for the ordaining of Conservative Rabbis, the hesitancy was quite appropriate. I just wasn't sure that sending me to represent the entire movement was the best choice. Wasn't I too young and inexperienced for such a vast undertaking? The Conservative Movement, as yet unrecognized in Israel, needed a strong statement from a powerful personality. How in the world would I be able to provide it?

At this point my colleague Rabbi Wolfe Kelman stepped in. I suspect that it was his idea from the beginning to send me. He was the same fellow who had recommended me to Mt. Kisco thirteen years before. But this was different. I had the experience of being a rabbi in a congregation in New York, but navigating a similar congregation in Israel seemed infinitely more difficult to me. According to Kelman, I would be a footnote to history, the first to inaugurate my movement in Israel. Apparently he was correct. A footnote.

This time he didn't undertake the job of buoying me up by himself. He recommended that I go speak to my mentor, Dr. Abraham Joshua Heschel, whom he said wanted to speak to me about it.

Being summoned by A. J. Heschel was in itself an experience. His office at JTS was small and stacked with books and papers. He had in a short time in America achieved widespread respect and admiration for his popular and yet scholarly works. One of the books that he wrote was a powerful reminiscence of eastern European Jewry called "The Earth is the Lord's." By now it has become a classic. There have been articles about him in Time Magazine and he had received wide coverage for marching with Martin Luther King from Selma to Montgomery. He was the closest person I know to being a prophet in America.

In his study Heschel was the bearded sage, sharp of mind and of tongue and yet soft, speaking slowly while deeply in thought. Heschel was in fact a rebbe of the old school. He knew why I had come. He wasted little time. In fact whenever I entered his office I always had the feeling that I was interrupting him in the middle of some very profound thought. Now he came right to the point.

"Fenster, I know of your doubts. I also know your abilities. Let me tell you about my grandfather in Europe, the Apter Rebbe. Everyone who met him or came under his influence was in awe of him. The sense of holiness surrounded him. Personally I was most deeply animated whenever I was in the presence of my grandfather." Heschel stopped for a moment to take me in. He offered me a piece of apple that he had begun to carve in the European fashion, peeling it slowly and then cutting it into pieces. I was hardly breathing. Swallowing would be impossible. I politely refused. Heschel proceeded. "The world that produced my grandfather is no more. It is now up to us. When I think of him I am embarrassed to bear his title and his name. But I look around and there is no one else to do it. So I am the Heschel of this generation."

"Now to you. Are there others who could conceivably do the job better than you? No doubt. But you are the one who we are pointing to. Perhaps it is not the ideal, but it is the possible. Go."

To this day I have never quite figured out if what he was offering was a compliment or a challenge, or maybe a bit of both. But in any case, we went.

On the eve of our departure an intense international furor broke out in the form of the Cuban missile crisis. I recall vividly President Kennedy speaking on TV explaining that the Cubans had placed Soviet missiles ninety miles away, pointing to America, and that such a condition was unacceptable to the United States. He demanded that Kruschev remove them immediately and would be sending American forces to see that they were removed.

It was anticipated that it would happen at exactly the moment we would be leaving for Haifa by ship. It did not bode well for us or the world. Adding to all of the stress of packing up our four kids and enough belongings for a year and taking a car with us, we had the additional baggage of worrying what would be happening on the high seas.

Later on the American Secretary of State Dean Rusk described the memorable moment when, "We stood eyeball to eyeball with the Soviet Union and they blinked." The Soviets backed down. There were no newspapers aboard the SS Zion, but of course there were telephone reports which circulated rapidly among the passengers. It was October 30th when we became aware of it, a goodly moment – my birthday. We were heading for a new adventure and an open sea.

The trip over was the ultimate adventure, two weeks on a ship that inevitably hit some bad storms. Someone that we had never met, who heard that we would be going on that ship, arranged for us to eat in the first-class dining room, which was not a big deal, but it enabled us to partake of the tea hour at 4 p.m. every day.

The picture as I look back upon it is still humorous. There were very few people actually in first class. At four o'clock we would be the first on line to enter. The violins would be playing, the petit-fours would already be out, the waiters and the butlers omnipresent, and our kids would burst in like onto a basketball court. But we would all sit quietly while being served, "I'll take one of these, one of those – who cares about dinner, this is much more fun." So whoever it was that arranged for that perk, he has our everlasting gratitude, though I am not sure that the waiters of the special tea hour would share that view.

I didn't realize at first that I had become somewhat of a celebrity. The captain of the ship, a wonderful young man in his early forties who had already served in the Israeli Navy, invited us to his table and we became friendly. Part of the attraction was that I was the first Conservative Rabbi being sent to Israel, a country which did not recognize any but the Orthodox rabbinate. This, of course, was many years ago though the status of rabbis like myself is still being tested in the country. The strange thing is that most of the people in Israel are secularly oriented but the religious establishment is Orthodox nonetheless. It did not make my task easier. Quite unlike America, in Israel we were struggling to be recognized. We wanted Israel to fulfill its democratic impulse. We were determined to begin from the position of the underdog.

Yet, one of the most attractive aspects of being a congregational rabbi rose immediately to the surface. We were connected from the very first day to a congregation of a hundred families. The Congregation Moriah on the Carmel Mountain, took in our family instantly.

In fact, a delegation of three of the leading officials of the congregation boarded our ship in the port of Haifa, even before we disembarked. They helped us to our apartment in Ahuza and as we drove up the mountain for the first time, enjoyed the sighs of pleasure from all of our family looking back at the beautiful harbor sights. Haifa was, and is still, a wonder.

For us, those were heady days. We were young, our kids were healthy, and we were on a mission in one of the most beautiful cities in the world.

It was my luck that the Haifa correspondent of the daily newspaper Ha'Aretz was a member of the congregation I was sent to serve. He was not a regular worshiper but rather one of those people who came on the Holidays. He immediately sought me out and came to visit our family. Subsequently he wrote an article about us and about the congregation which appeared in the Friday edition of his newspaper, which could accurately be compared to the Sunday New York Times. All that was very heady because our family in Israel and practically everybody else that I met recalled the line he used as description, "They sent this rabbi from America. He looks more like a baseball player than like a rabbi." That one sentence finished me off for good.

Later I said to him, "Aryeh, did you ever see an American baseball player?" Of course the answer was "No." But my reputation preceded me.

Altogether it was a marvelous experience. On the way home after the year, we took the car with us that we had brought to Haifa, landed in Italy and then drove across the country for a week. It was an exciting family excursion with stops for sightseeing, in Venice, Bologna, Pisa, Rome and Naples. And best of all, three days in Florence.

I learned a great deal about being a rabbi in Israel. It is that the people you serve are more or less the same all over the world. There are those who are intellectually alert and curious, and those who are not. There are those who are warm and folksy, and those who are not. But above all the inner apparatus of working in a congregation is basically the same – budgetary problems, too many meetings, and the many problems people have that you are expected to be able to resolve. You try hard but it doesn't always quite work.

HAIFA 'Ha-ADUMAH"

O UR YEAR IN Haifa was an exercise in diversity. It called forth all of our resources. I met many young Jews who told me, proudly, that they do not go to synagogue. Perhaps once or twice a year on the holidays, they bring their kids to sit for a few minutes with their father in the old Orthodox synagogue of their youth. That's it.

Then, when I would tell them that synagogues had changed, with more contemporary explanations, page announcements and a more congenial atmosphere for young people, at first they would seem interested. But the reality set in. "Truth is" an Israeli friend confided, "the once or twice a year visit suits me fine; I don't need anything more. If I am going already, I might as well go to be with my family, in my father's synagogue."

On occasion, my announcement that the Conservative synagogue would be a new experience for them, drew a confrontational response. "We don't need an American import." I understood the implication. We depend on America enough, we don't need it for religious life. Religion is a home-grown product. I readily agreed that imports are problematical in Israel. But I felt compelled to point out that they had not yet developed a native Israel style of religious expression and in the meantime almost all of their religious leaders were European imports. "Why not import the latest?"

The lovely city of Haifa was not renown for excessive piety. It was unofficially referred to as Haifa Ha-Aduma, Haifa the Red. It was a city of laborers. Its mayor Abba Khoushy, was renowned for being on the street at 5:30 a.m. to insure proper collection of garbage, municipal activity, get the city going in the morning.

How did this impact on us? An additional obstacle to overcome. We understood it better on May Day when there were still, in 1963, parades with a red flag on the main street, right past our synagogue. These were pure socialists, kibbutz people, wage earners looking for better working conditions, and higher wages. They were not looking to overturn anything.

My logic was impeccable. But I scored few points in Haifa. They did not flock to our service. We decided to take the family for a Shabbat in Jerusalem.

Back then Jerusalem was quite different than today. It was a divided city, half Israel, half Jordanian. From the balcony of the King David Hotel, you could see the Jordanian soldiers with their guns fixed on you. Crossing the line could be dangerous and worse.

On Shabbat morning, wandering around the area of the Old Moriah Hotel, we came across the Kelmans, also on a sabbatical. They invited us to join them in looking for Reb Arele's synagogue in Meah Shearim. We all set out together.

Meah Shearim was more legendary than real. We thought of it only as anti-Zionist, anti-modernist, anti-everything. Who knew?

At Reb Arele's they welcomed us warmly. The women, of course, had to be seated separately, and in my mind's eye I can still see Ricky and Elisa and Jacqy Kelman and her daughters, all climbing the outdoor staircase to the women's gallery. The staircase seemed flimsy, as did our presence there.

What was taking place in the synagogue on the main floor drew our attention, fascination and disbelief. Such ecstatic prayer I had never before seen. It had never happened that way in Flatbush. It is called "shukeling," rocking back and forth in rapid movement, eyes glazed, mind focused. These hasidim were the champion "shukelers" of the world. The Shema, the central prayer, seemed like it went on for twenty minutes, beginning with the opening exclamation of God's Oneness, declared loudly and faithfully. I would not have been surprised if the roof rose skyward. The whole experience was at once enthralling and mystifying. And moving.

After an hour and a half, it was past noon and we were ready to go. Not before we were invited to a huge pot in the courtyard, filled with steaming cholent, a special Sabbath dish. In 1963, who knew from cholent? We were a dozen people and we had reservations elsewhere for lunch, so we politely declined. But the memory of that fervency and dedication of the Arele chassidim, I believe, it's a permanent part of all of us. We did not imitate it, but we also never forgot it.

Incidentally, two of the Kelman's children – Levi and Naomi are today rabbis in Jerusalem. Not exactly of the Arele variety, but extremely dedicated nonetheless. I am sure it is in their memory bank as well.

Wolfe Kelman came to visit us in Haifa in July of 63. It was to make an offer, that we stay at Congegation Moriah beyond the time originally set; that I become the permanent rabbi there. In other words, aliyah, official residence in Israel. The Rabbinical Assembly would pay my salary.

It was quite an attractive offer. One we could almost not refuse. But after long discussion, we did.

The reasons are complex and not completely clear even now. First, I was on sabbatical leave from Jackson Heights, with the implied promise to return. Second, our family was all in the U. S. Our parents, all four of them, were getting on in years and would no doubt need support in their declining years. Not monetary support, thank goodness, but navigating their ebbing strength and health. And, of course, in those next years we were needed. Ironically, when Ricky's mother died we were in Israel – the day of Binyamin's bris. And some years later when my mother died, we were also on a short visit. But we had been there for them.

The most powerful of all the feelings was that whatever strength and talents I had to offer the Jewish community, would best be served in America. I was already serving a large and growing synagogue – we had built a new building in the livelier part of town, our kids were doing well in school – it had all come together. We decided to keep it together and return.

Still, at the end of our stay in Haifa we did have that intuitive feeling that we would be back in one form or another. And our intuition was accurate. Since then we have returned, for a short or long period, no less that sixty times.

Perhaps that was the time when our son Jeremy planted the seeds in his own mind for his ultimate return. By now, he has been in Israel thirty-two years. Jonathan and Elisa both spent long periods studying or working in Israel, and Dan and Jan's son Zachary is now part of a year-long program as well. Also, Gabe from Newton, Mass. who even speaks of being a rabbi. Israel is part of us, organic and integral. But we returned to our life in America.

Looking back on the year in Haifa we see it as an endless wonder. It presented a great ancillary benefit, a vast unifying force within the family. Oftentimes when we come together we still talk about the two weeks on the ship going there, the near-idyllic time we spent on Mount Carmel, which seemed like a land of eternal sunshine. There was, in fact, very little rain during the course of our stay on Ehud Street in Ahuza, on the Carmel. The winter was mild. And we were mellow.

There were a number of quaint touches that always come to mind. Our apartment which was quite comfortable, did not provide central heating. In those days you stayed warm in the wintertime with kerosene (neft) burners. Since our apartment, like all others, had stone floors, it could get quite cold on a wintry day. The joy of finding some neft before Shabbat is still quite vivid. Nowadays all of those apartments probably have central heating and air conditioning. But they had not made it there then.

A vivid memory of Friday afternoon that Jeremy and I share was getting into the Peugeot we had brought with us from America, and going out looking for the horse and buggy dealer of neft, so that we could warm up for the oncoming Sabbath.

At the last minute we managed to find him some blocks away. In retrospect the picture of the horse carriage and driver was right out of the world of Tevye. The joy of finding some neft before Shabbat is still quite strong. It was a warm Sabbath.

The problem with the kerosene was that if you set it up and left it on throughout the night, you would wake up in the morning with your head filled with the smell and the stuffiness of it. And so there was a bitter choice: freeze or wake up with a headache. We tried both without ever having reached a successful conclusion. Personally, I preferred the cold, until I had to get out of bed in the morning.

There were other homey touches. Our oldest son Jonathan, with his younger brother Jeremy, would leave our mountain-top enclave to go down to the lower rung of the city called the Hadar. They were then saving stamps and they had a particular store that they were fond of visiting. One day without realizing it, they spent all their money on the stamps and so they started the long tramp up the hill from the middle of the Carmel to its top. They arrived an hour and a half later, hungry and exhausted. But they both slept very well that night.

I also recall fondly the many trips I made to a local library – to prepare remarks for the synagogue on Saturday morning, or to do some research, and to find a quiet space. Often Jonathan would accompany me. He could sit and read for a long time without murmur or protest. In fact, he would often hum softly as he read. They were beautiful moments and I still savor them.

In Haifa there was a strengthening of family ties that could not be duplicated. We felt close to our past, to Jewish history. Everywhere there were reminders of days gone by. Our postman used to walk up the flight of outer stairs to deliver our mail. I can still visualize his sad but serene face. He looked like he had just been released from Auschwitz, perhaps a half year ago. Well, it was longer than that, but once I saw the number on his arm, I understood where he was coming from. He never spoke very much and we tried to respect his silence, but his appearance made for a disturbing presence. He never engaged us; he never smiled.

On another occasion we made our way to a religious kibbutz in the Beit Shean Valley area for Shabbat. We drove up in our Peugeot. We were greeted by Shelley Gursky, a dynamic young woman from Jamaica, New York, who had spent some time at our house in Jackson Heights. At Tirat Tzvi, the kibbutz where she was living, she was already a formidable presence. Later she was to become a mother and grandmother, and to this day forty years later, still lives on the kibbutz. And is still, a formidable presence.

Our experience was a very pleasant one except for the fact that it was the middle of the summer and we were as hot and sweaty as I have ever been in my life. Trying to take a nap on Shabbat afternoon proved to be impossible. The sheets stuck to your body. The atmosphere of the kibbutz on Shabbat was a sacred one. The prayer services were spiritual and satisfying. The food was fabulous. But the heat was oppressive.

The meeting of the kibbutz on Saturday night was memorable. I was allowed to be present. People there spoke without inhibitions. Under discussion was the question of using a swimming pool on this religious kibbutz on the Sabbath. The kibbutz had just completed a beautiful pool which was already open for use, but had thus far been closed down on Shabbat. This was no theoretical question. And both sides were eloquent and passionate.

I admired the way both sides let their view be known with as much persuasion as they could muster and with respect. They were not making bland statements. In fact, they were quite provocative. Those in favor of opening the pool on Shabbat agreed that it should be closed during the morning period of prayer. But immediately after that it should be open for the rest of the day. Otherwise, they pointed out, why did we bother to build it? The rest of the week they were busy. Shabbat is for joy. Open it up!

The opponents to that view, who appeared to be fewer in number and seemed to be among the older folks on the kibbutz, made the point that as a community of religious people, they should be presenting this question to the Chief Rabbinate. The implication was that the establishment Chief Rabbinate, which represented a more conservative point of view, would surely not approve. I guess they saw this as a way of dampening down the enthusiasm of the younger folks. Their argument was that this is not in the spirit of Shabbat.

This brought an immediate response from one of the "young Turks." He jumped up and excitedly proclaimed, "Listen, we have not approached the Chief Rabbinate on any other question, why should we start now. The strength of this kibbutz is that we have come together as religious people who know the law and want to follow it. We know what is permitted and what is not. Let's just do it."

Very often in these religious matters the conservative element, which may not always be the majority, seems to prevail. The result of the meeting that night was unclear. But I am sure that by this time they have long ago worked it out. One of the features of the swimming pool on that kibbutz was that there were members who wanted separate hours of swimming for men and women. And I am sure that such an arrangement prevails to this day.

In many ways the religious kibbutz seemed like an ideal setting. In fact, one of the old-timers at Tirat Tsvi suggested that there would be a place for me there if I wanted to say. "Come and be our rabbi" he offered. Of course if I had accepted it a major storm of controversy would have broken out. I would have been the first one in the pool after services. That would not sit well with the old-timers. But I always appreciated the offer nonetheless. Conservative rabbis on religious kibbutzim would have been a good match. Too bad!

Once many years later I brought a group from Shelter Rock to the kibbutz and we received a first-rate tour with Shelley. The outstanding feature of that kibbutz is a factory for bolognas, frankfurters and other specialty meats. The products can be found all over Israel. As a matter of fact, there are many supermarkets in the New York area that carry Tirat Tsvi products as well. I thoroughly enjoy their bologna even though it always reminds me of that sultry Shabbos we spent there.

It is interesting to note the many crises the kibbutz movement has gone through since then. Back in the 60's it seemed like the ideal place to live if you pined to get away from an interminably competitive society and constant economic challenges. All your needs were cared for including clothing, food, housing, health care for the young and middle-aged and protection for the elderly. Rare it was to send an old or sick person to a permanent home outside the kibbutz. In it, they provided tender, loving care.

The chronicle of their fall has often been told. People wanted more space, more independence to choose their own way. But in the summer of '63 the kibbutz seemed perfect. Even more so later on when air conditioning was installed.

Times have changed. The banks overextended themselves to the kibbutzim to the tune of billions in the 80's. It resulted in a first-rate crisis.

The children's home was given up long before and the kids would come home to sleep. Accommodations were made. But through the 90's the kibbutz movement was in a funk. High tech had taken over. Now it seems to be making a comeback with the younger generation. As Koheleth long ago observed, "One generation comes – another goes . . . ."

And I am sure that Tirat Tzvi's hot dogs are still fabulous. And air conditioning helps. As does that sense that you are building something for the future.

On the kibbutz it is indispensable to have a sense of community and that you are building something worthwhile and enduring for yourself and the country.

Another memory of our time in Haifa was when I was contacted by the late Geoffrey Wigoder, one of the editors of The Jerusalem Post, who asked if I would come to Jerusalem to participate in a dialogue with a long-time friend. Rabbi Herb Weiner was a colleague serving a Reform congregation in South Orange, New Jersey, while I was at Newark. Herb was a traditionalist within the Reform Movement and I always enjoyed being with him. He too was spending a sabbatical year in Jerusalem.

Our thoughts were often compatible and he once gave me a description of our relative situations that I have never forgotten. It was that he was better off as a Reform rabbi than I was as a Conservative one. Because he put on tefillin every morning and observed kashruth, his congregants treated him as if he were the Lubavitcher Rebbe. At a dinner in his synagogue his meal would always be brought in on a special tray, having been cooked in a special oven, after having been ordered from a special place. On the other hand, when you are a Conservative rabbi, which includes many more people of traditional orientation, there are always some quiet whisperings that the rabbi is not quite religious enough. And so he considered himself better off.

But Herb had spent a year or more in Israel at the Hebrew University and was totally conversant with Jewish sources. He had a strong spiritual bent which later manifested itself in two books that have become renowned:

"The Wild Goats of Ein Gedi" and "8 1/2 Mystics." He referred to himself as half of a mystic. Some of the earlier chapters of the book had appeared in Commentary Magazine. I remember reading one of them, "A Mystic Philosopher on East Broadway" on Shabbat afternoon lying on my couch in Mt. Kisco. It made me sit up straight. It was absolutely fascinating. And one of these days I must go back to it, or maybe I should leave it alone because it occupies such an indelible spot in my memory. It is a reminder that there is a textured spiritual world out there, for those who take the time to discover it. Herb had taken the time.

Our coming together now in Jerusalem was of a different sort. Herb Weiner was there representing the Reform Movement and I was there representing the Conservative Movement. Wigoder who was a very bright and witty Englishman thought it would be interesting and provocative to the readers to hear our differing views about the future of our movements in Israel. At that time, of course, both were on the fringe, neither of them being officially acceptable. But the point of his inquiry was whether we were on the same page or there were differences among us on how to proceed to gain acceptance. Generally the conventional wisdom had it that the Reform and Conservative were in the same boat and, therefore, should be working together to overcome all the obstacles that had been placed in front of us. This was the view that Weiner presented. I certainly felt a bond of kinship with him and what he represented.

The article, which appeared on the eve of Passover, caused a bit of a stir in the circles in which we moved. There was a picture of both Herb and myself on the page devoted to the subject. I took a less politically correct view. My point was that while we shared a great deal in terms of fate and future, our approaches were not exactly the same. The Conservative Movement was more halachically oriented toward Jewish law, while the Reform Movement depended more on the individual's conscience. I reported respect for that view, but I could not share it.

The framework of ritual practice was a necessary element of a viable Judaism. There would be times when it would have to be extended and refined but I could not see then, as I do not see now, how the parameters of halacha can be so blurred as to be left to individual conscience only. People look to and need stability in law as in life. This is one of the main divisions between the various groupings in modern Judaism. The view that I represent wants to carry on the tradition, but it makes room for contemporary life and circumstance. It accepts the challenge of modernity as being a real one and is prepared to make a positive accommodation to it.

The best in our culture today is not foreign to us. The art, the literature, the music can all be authentic and appealing. But following the ancient biblical law, we do not remove the landmarks on the terrain. They are there and should be respected. The search for spirituality needs to be enlivened by ritual practice and legal boundaries. We do not serve that search by their elimination.

And so while we agreed that recognition of our movements was a central point we would like to see corrected, there would have to remain differences in the varying approaches. But one of the central points that we wanted to present was that we had high regard for each other's integrity and that our differences were mutually respected. This was obviously not the case with the approach of other elements in the community toward us. And not too much has changed from then to now. In recent years Reform Judaism has begun to reevaluate its stance on tradition. As far as I am concerned, that is a most salutary development.

For example, the Reform Movement, under Rabbi Alexander Schindler, instituted the acceptance of patrilineal descent for determining a child's Jewishness; that is that the father no less than the mother, can be the barometer of the child's religious identity. This goes against the traditional formula and was rejected by both the Conservative Movement and the Orthodox. But it proved a boon for Reform; thousands of young people, boys and girls, now became eligible for Bar or Bat Mitzvah. It could well be responsible for the increasing number of Reform Jews reported in recent surveys in America.

From my point of view, it is still a problem. Young men and women have started to come and asked to be married in our synagogue. They are Jewish by patrilineal descent, which is not a Halachic standard. By our definition, a child of such a union is only acceptable in a Conservative or Orthodox wedding once he or she has converted to Judaism. As a result, a rift has been created. Rabbis like myself have to start checking into the background and have to reject many weddings. We do not like that role. We try to resolve the problem without deep scrutiny. But it doesn't work.

On the other hand, there is no doubt that Reform Judaism has gained many new adherents through patrilineal descent. We certainly do not wish to turn anyone away who is sincere, ready to learn, ready to practice the Jewish way, and prepared to throw his or her lot in with the Jewish People. I have known dozens of such people over the years. They have added much to our community. May their numbers increase! Any yet, the problem remains because conversion is not an easy solution, and many are not ready for it.

So on ideological matters there is often disagreement and controversy. When we do come together it is on an emergency basis, when Israel's future is on the line, when Jews are being attacked in Crown Heights, Buenos Aires or in the Muslim areas of London. Unity brings us together. Too bad it has not yet become a regular feature of our existence.

The tensions from Anti-Semitism have not gone away. In fact, in Europe and in many other parts of the world they have increased, on college campuses in America, in government, and in life. The Netherlands, United Kingdom and France are all dealing today with outbreaks. Under Putin in Russia, for example. Despite the appointment recently of a Moscow-born Chief Rabbi, who knows how much of the native Ukrainian and Soviet reflexive antipathy toward Jews remains? Nobody can predict.

The rise of Islam extremism in Arab countries, and elsewhere, is an international problem. A seemingly benign blind cleric, Abdul Rahman, plotted the destruction of 9/11. In jail for life, he is no doubt still plotting. And then there is Osama Bin Ladin. And what of the others: Hezbollah, Hamas, Iranian crazies led by their obsessive heads and hotheads, in a dozen and more countries in the Middle East, Asia and around the world.

This approach that you can respect and honor those who differ from you is central not only in religious life but in democratic society. It is the basis of the authenticity of pluralism. Kennedy put it stunningly when he said, "We have to make the world safe for diversity." Diversity is often difficult, to grant an opponent the same right which you demand and the same opportunity to express themselves and to listen to their point of view. For some, if you really believe, that's got to be the only way. Fortunately, not everyone sees it that way.

A surprise visitor while we were in Haifa was my Professor of Job at the Jewish Theological Seminary and his wife, Dr. and Mrs. Robert Gordis. They spent a few days in Haifa and Dr. Gordis gave a magnificent talk in Hebrew to the Moriah Congregation on the subject of Ezra, in the Bible, returning to Jerusalem. Gordis was intuitively brilliant and spoke in both Hebrew and English in a torrent of aphoristic prose, but I am not sure that the people of the congregation understood it all. But they were impressed enough to know that he was a very learned man.

Gordis and his wife were staying at a hotel downtown and after the lecture when I was driving him back, he expressed an interest in seeing Tiberius, and especially the situation of the Golan Heights. In those days the Golan Heights were in the hands of the Syrians, who were occupying the high ground and there would often be difficulty when they would aim their ammunition down on Kibbutz Ein Gev below. You never knew beforehand when shooting would start. I told all of this to Gordis who was undeterred and said, "Let's drive."

So we started out in our small Peugeot, Jonathan and I sitting in the front and the Gordis' in the rear. As we were leaving the city, Gordis suddenly said, "Stop the car." He jumped out and returned a few moments later with an ice cream pop for Jonathan which, of course, was most welcome. Once again we were on our way.

Less than an hour later as we were approaching the area. I thought I heard shots in the air. It did not bode well for our visit but I said nothing. As we got closer, I saw roadblocks. It was the habit of the Border Police not to let civilians anywhere near the area if shooting was going on or was suspected. Strangely enough when they stopped us they did not say anything about shooting. They simply said that no one is being allowed through because they discovered an outbreak of foot and mouth disease in the area. Well, it had been a nice trip to that point at which time Gordis said, "You know what – let's head back to Haifa" which we did.

Many people all over the world have taken up the Syrian cry for the return of the Golan Heights. It would be nice if some arrangements could be made where the prior situation would not return, which was totally unacceptable. The one positive aspect is that the Syrians have always adhered to their commitments, once they make them, As of this writing there are rumors always of an impending deal, but as yet nothing has happened. After the Six Day War, the Golan Heights was taken back and we have been all through it a number of times. Nowadays they produce fine wines up there in the Golan Heights, all of which can be negotiated in the future. We live in hope.

JOB OFFERING

R ETURNING TO THE states, I was offered a job which I turned down on the spot.

I wasn't quite Saul Bellow's Herzog, but I was always responding inwardly, in those days, to events, both written and oral, around me. It had been building up for a long time so I wrote an open letter to Mordecai Kaplan, my teacher, of my disappointment and unhappiness with his theology which I found wanting in his "concept of God" which I proceeded to analyze and dissect. It was not the first time Kaplan heard a rejection of his naturalistic theology, "Judaism without Supernaturalism," but I had been a student, even a disciple, and Kaplan did not relish disagreement.

He printed my piece in The Reconstructionist and later included it in his volume, Questions Jews Ask, with a muscular rejoinder. After that Harold Schulweis, a west coast rabbi, wrote an article in the naturalistic style of Kaplan, using the same theological set of formulas. I responded to that as well, critically. Biblical and modern theology was my main interest in those days. But I was more drawn to Buber and Rosenzeig, the Europeans, than to my own teachers. (Those were the days before Heschel.) I held firm opinions and was not shy about expressing them.

One day I got a call from Wolfe Kelman who already then, in the 1950's, was a Seminary intimate. The Chancellor wished to speak to me. "What's it about?" No idea.

It was about becoming a member of the Seminary faculty. Not exactly a full professorship, but rather a lecturer in Theology. Not full time teaching, but with administrative responsibilities. Louis Finkelstein was speaking to me like a kindly mentor offering a comfortable stroll in the park. He had liked what he had read.

I was surprised. Actually, I was stunned. We were in the first years at Jackson Heights, in our own house with young kids going to the Solomon Schechter School of Queens and Camp Ramah in the summer. I didn't see how that could be improved upon. I had the congregation to teach and lead and I couldn't see giving that all up to move to Morningside Heights or elsewhere, to chase a fantasy, however enticing it might be. Acknowledging that I was delighted to be asked, I respectfully declined, explaining that I was enjoying the congregational experience where I saw my future.

Subsequently Kelman told me that the Chancellor was taken aback that I declined immediately without going home to talk to my wife or considering it more fully.

In retrospect, I am grateful for having made that decision, but still find it hard to believe that I was not tempted to pursue it further. Intuition had triumphed.

Not that a spot on the Seminary faculty is a small honor. Actually, I did happily accept an adjunct position years later but in "Professional Skills" not in theology. Back then I already sensed my destiny was linked to a congregation. It was special for me and my family to be tied to a community. Being a "parish priest" has much going for it, serving the people amongst whom you live. And I have never regretted that approach. To me, it was the highest calling. Through the congregation I could indulge whatever interests I wished to pursue, in religious studies, philosophy, literature or whatever. And then enjoy teaching them to whoever would listen. One of my proudest moments was the first week I was teaching at the Seminary. They have long had the tradition of the Rosh Chodesh breakfast with the Chancellor. Once a month, at its beginning, the Rabbinical School would come together, whoever could make it by 8:30 a.m., all one hundred and twenty of us, at times, to hear a message relevant to our studies and to Jewish life. I remember those breakfasts from my own student days, because I had a special problem getting there from Mt. Kisco so early in the day.

That first week of my joining the faculty fell on Rosh Chodesh. I made sure to be present. Chancellor Gershon Cohen welcomed a half dozen of us, new to the faculty. When it was over Professor. H. L. Ginsburg, the one who tendered my Bible exam on Martha's Vineyard some decades before, came over, shook my hand and with a smile added, "Welcome home!" It was a special moment! H. L. was not known as effusive or sentimental; that made it even more special.

PRINCETON PLAN

O UR STAY IN Haifa concluded in August of 1963. We returned home the day after the monumental March on Washington, at which time the Reverend Martin Luther King Jr. delivered the most memorable speech of a clergymen in the Twentieth Century.

That next day we arrived in New York and I heard immediately what was happening in my own community of Jackson Heights. The Princeton Plan was being recommended for two schools in our area. These schools were on either side of Junction Blvd. which was later to be called the Mason-Dixon Line in the borough of Queens in New York. One school was totally white and on the other side in neighboring Corona there was a totally black school. There was this early fumbling attempt on the part of the Board of Education to integrate both schools. The procedure was that in one there would be all children kindergarten to fourth grade. That would be on the Corona side. In the Jackson Heights part, all students from fifth through eighth grade would attend. The schools were only ten blocks from each other but as you might expect they represented the sparks out of which a deep controversy ensued.

I learned of all this the first day I was home and the next day a meeting had been called for in one of the large cooperative apartment houses not far from Junction Blvd. The meeting was attended mostly by whites and I recognized many faces from my congregation among those who had gathered. It was a raucous uproarious meeting. Barely no one could get through any kind of a statement without being repeatedly interrupted. A number of well-known civil rights activists were there. Since I didn't know all the facts, I held my peace. But it was obvious to me that the opponents of the plan were being motivated more by fear and lack of understanding than by anything else.

A short time later I publicly supported the Princeton Plan. Some people from that housing cooperative decided to picket the synagogue I was serving as rabbi. But to the eternal credit of the officers of my congregation, they stood solidly behind me. They were not intimidated by the threats of a few people that they would receive. I remember the remark of my friend Maurice Schefferman who told one such protester, "We accept your resignation and we will gladly return your dues. People like you we don't want in this congregation." He has always had our eternal gratitude.

There was an additional call to my late friend Mike Schwartz. He was the head of the Forest Park Funeral Chapel on Queens Blvd. which was popularly known as Schwartz Bros. In keeping with the usual style, he had taken out a small ad in our synagogue bulletin which appeared once a month. It made it handy for those who, unfortunately, would need him, to find the telephone number in an emergency. The caller did not give his name but shouted into the receiver, "You should take your ad out of that Jewish Center Bulletin. Do you know what their Rabbi is doing? He is supporting the Princeton Plan which would mean that I would have to send my son five blocks from my house to school. We don't want it. We don't want him to continue."

Mike Schwartz was a constant friend. Undisturbed by the whole squawk. "Listen fella, I don't know anything about Princeton. I went to NYU."

Subsequently I wrote a number of articles on the evolving crisis and its resolution. Unfortunately the plan was never put into effect and the tensions spiraled downward, sprouting in all parts of New York City. I often think of what would have happened if this plan had been given a chance to work and all the pain and turmoil that it could possibly have avoided. My first real plunge in social activism had not been totally successful but I felt good about it. I felt that as a young rabbi I had done what I could to help bring people to a higher level. Perhaps from this experience I learned that you cannot move so fast so as to leave the people behind. And it takes abundant patience and constant reaffirmation to bring a community forward.

MORDECAI KAPLAN COMES TO CAMP

G EORGE GERSHWIN'S "SUMMERTIME and the Livin

is Easy" surely applies to the rabbinic world as well. It's family time, vacation time, opportunity to go out into the countryside. For many years going back to the 60's, I was part of a faculty to train leaders for the Jewish community, which took place in July until the middle of August. The setting was Camp Bnai Brith in Starlight, Pa., a lovely area in the Pocono Mountains with sky and lakes and a totally different focus from the rest of the year. We were given our own bungalow on the camp property and we ate our meals in the dining room so we had a user-friendly set up. Our students were teen-age campers from all over the United States and Canada.

I remember meeting young people from places I had never heard of before, like Regina, Saskatchawan, small towns in California and the mid-west. These were specially designated young people from the Bnai Brith Youth Organization who had been selected because of their promise for the future as leaders. It was a pleasure being involved and to this day I still meet some, now no longer young people, who had been part of the program.

The man who designed and ran the program, Dr. Dan Thursz, liked to bring outstanding people to speak. He asked me if I could arrange for Dr. Kaplan to come. Kaplan did the same kind of work at Cejwin camps near

Port Jervis. Contacting him he said he would be glad to be present, if we would send a car to pick him up and take him back. At camp there were always many drivers and cars available so I was able to seek help. But I decided instead to take our son Jonathan with me and do the job ourselves. It's a very scenic run down along the Delaware River and before you knew it we were at Cejwin and Kaplan was ready and waiting.

One of the main reasons, I wanted to give Jonathan an opportunity to be exposed to Mordecai Kaplan, who was arguably the outstanding thinker and teacher of his day with profound impact on every segment of American Jewry. Anticipating a vivid running account with Dr. Kaplan sitting alongside me in the front seat, I asked a number of leading questions to enable him to talk about his earlier life. Kaplan was an exciting personality who would open up at the drop of a hat. I had heard all the stories before in one context or another of how his daughter Judith became the first Bat Mitzvah in America, despite the opposition of both his mother and his mother-in-law, who were much more traditionally grounded than he. There were many stories of similar content that he told on this trip.

Dr. Kaplan had been the founder of the Reconstructionist Movement, indicating his desire to reformulate Judaism for modern times. He was a rebel but had a clear picture of what he had in mind, to update the Jewish religion, removing all archaisms, miracles, transcendentalisms and sense of superiority, from the mentality of modern Jews. Jonathan, as a bright and searching young man, knew what Kaplan stood for. But I figured it would be impressive to hear it from the master. Though no longer young, Kaplan was still vigorous past eighty. And he did not like when his outlook was challenged. But the future leaders took to him thoroughly. In spirit, he was still a young and feisty rebel.

Much to my dismay, when we finally got to Camp Bnai Brith and we were alone, I asked Jonathan what he thought of all those stories. Jonathan always had a problem with motion sickness and the way he overcame it was by closing his eyes and falling asleep, and so he had not heard even one of Kaplan's ripostes. But Dr. Kaplan's appearance was a major event of our leadership training program of that summer.

As was the time when Elie Wiesel came to speak to our youth organization. This was still in the early 60's before Wiesel became world-famous and a major platform speaker. He was still suffering the after effects of the traumatic events of the Holocaust and did not easily engage in dialogue with either the staff or our students. But, of course, his impact was enormous and his book "Night" was read avidly by all of us.

KAPLAN'S INFLUENCE

T HESE EXPERIENCES OF social activism often took up my days and occupied my nights. The concern for civil and human rights and their denial, especially for Jews after the Holocaust, was something I always responded to and pained me deeply. I see it as all being related to the frustration that I had as a youngster sitting on Ocean Avenue, realizing the world was collapsing around me, and not having the foggiest notion of what to do about it. Later on the pain was no less great, but at least I felt there were avenues of expression.

At the same time there was always the search for God's larger purpose in the universe, the theological question of why terrible things often happen to good people. From my earliest days as a rabbinical student I had come into contact with Dr. Mordecai M. Kaplan, who was the founder of the Reconstructionist Movement in American Judaism. Reconstructionism felt the necessity to cut away religious beliefs that were no longer tenable, to update Judaism and to bring it into a contemporary mode. Dr. Kaplan had studied with John Dewey, his fondest hope being to bring pragmatism to Judaism. Kaplan rejected super-nationalism, asceticism, and obscurantism. "What do you mean by God, by Torah and by the Jewish People?" He would probe and push and often verbally tie up his perplexed students.

Dr. Kaplan was a profound influence upon me. I appreciated his probing mind and his total dedication to finding the solution that would lead to a positive continuity to American Jewish life. In my mind was like a modern Socrates, often asking disturbing questions, often ready to upset our complacency. But I did have the feeling that he was preparing us to serve our congregations. He would often say that the people that we would see in American life today were mostly college graduates and they would not be ready to accept the miraculous, other-worldly, unclear concepts that have been passed along to us. He urged total clarity and definition. God he defined like Matthew Arnold as, "God, the Power, not ourselves, that makes for human fulfillment."

I was always unhappy with that formulation. It seemed to cut away a good deal of the biblical tradition and of the prompting of the human heart. There was no room in it for the personal sense of God's sustaining presence, which had meant so much to me.

Now there are some who hold that a belief in a personal God is wide-eyed mysticism. I have always been an advocate that what one of my other teachers, Dr. Max Kadushin, wrote about biblical and rabbinic religion. He referred to it as "normal mysticism." Kadushin meant that you would not be able to communicate your religious and spiritual feelings completely because they are very often deeply personal and private, but that does not mean that they are not there. It is that aspect of religious belief, that of experience rather than of formulation, that I have come to know and accept myself. I may not be able to define it, but religious experience is real.

But I was always wary and am still today of religious and spiritual formulations that stop at the border of involvement and activism. A traditional Jew prays each morning wearing a prayer shawl and phylacteries. When I put on my tallit and tefillin, I feel that I am connected to God. My thoughts are taken out of the ordinary realm, but I have trained myself also not to get lost in the heavens above without keeping my feet firmly on the ground. I look at the morning prayer like a plan for the day, a blueprint of what I hope to do, my marching orders. I read, for example, "To honor father and mother, to practice loving-kindness, to welcome strangers, to visit the sick, to put the bride at ease, to accompany the dead, and to bring peace between a person and their friend." I am admonished as well to continue my studies so that I may look more keenly into my practice. These formulas have enabled me, I believe, to keep my balance of not being totally absorbed in the affairs of the day so as to lose my rootage or my bearings. I hope to remain connected above as well as below.

FIRST MEETINGS
WITH SHLOMO

AFTER HE DIED, I could not help but think back to our first meeting many years before. Rabbi Shlomo, without doubt, was one of the most colorful and controversial people I have ever known. He was unique and I loved him.

My first meeting with him was most unexpected. We were running the summer program at Bnai Brith Camps and as best I can remember it was 1962. We had one hundred and fifty high school kids from all over America and Canada and we were trying to give them an intensive program which included study, and cultural activity in addition to all the other things one does at camp. I was walking on the large campus one day and someone taps me on the shoulder and says, "There is a hippie out there, says he wants to talk to you. Says his name is Shlomo. He has a guitar with him." I had no idea who he was referring to and my inclination was to dismiss it as one of the many distractions we had in running such a program. Nonetheless, I decided to go see what was up and that is how I met Rabbi Shlomo Carlebach for the first time.

At that moment he was not well known since he was just beginning his singing career. Shlomo was then and has since then been called a hippie rabbi, a Hasidic troubadour, a Jew with a guitar and a song. He was all of these. But primarily he was a warmhearted person who took traditional lines from the Bible and the prayer book and worked them in with new spirit, sometimes jazzy, sometimes plaintive melodies, always heartfelt. He followed his own beat and that often turned people away. But his melodies were memorable. You could love him or hate his songs, but Shlomo Carlebach was not to be ignored.

Nowadays, when I go to the Western Wall on Friday night in Jerusalem, I am delighted to hear Shlomo's songs, many of which have become world famous. I guess we could say he was the Jewish Bob Dylan, who started out humbly and obscurely and before you knew it everyone was singing the songs. When I hear these melodies today they are being sung by young people first discovering their religious identity, but also by older Hasidic types who never would acknowledge Shlomo in his lifetime and even now look quizzically at who and what he was.

Shlomo started out his life as an Orthodox person. But since he was unique, he bent the rules to his own service. Orthodox Jews do not touch or kiss young ladies, but no one every accused Shlomo of that. He kissed everyone in sight and hugged them and had a word of personal greeting for them, men, women and especially children. His enthusiasm overflowed his body and his spirit was pervasive, his generosity legendary. Though he was called everywhere to do concert work and probably made huge sums of money in his lifetime, he once confessed to me that he didn't have very much left. Only his musical legacy endures. That was varied and plentiful.

When I went down to the gate of camp Bnai Brith that summer day, Shlomo Carlebach was standing there alone, with his guitar. He said simply, "I have come to play for the kids here." I was not sure exactly what to make of it. I said, "Look, I don't have any budget for that so I'm not going to be able to pay you anything." He was slightly offended. "Why should we talk about money, let's talk about music."

It was not that easy for me to convince the director of the program that this would be a great experience for our young people. I couldn't speak out of personal knowledge because I had actually never heard him. But I was taking a gamble because the first song that he sang, "I Will Lift Up Mine Eyes Unto the Mountains . . . . Esaa Enay El Hahorem" I had already heard and it was new and different. Anyway I did convince the director to give him a chance.

That night one hundred fifty campers and twenty-five staff gathered in this relatively small room and Shlomo began. Perhaps because we were not expecting that much, his program was electrifying. He started singing – they joined. He started jumping up and down – they jumped up and down with him. It went on and on building in momentum until finally the director told me I had to stop it – it was time for the kids to go to bed. It was not that simple; they were having a great time. But finally we quieted it down and sent everybody back to their bunks. Shlomo had been a huge success, far beyond any expectation.

Feeling really good about what had happened, I went to breakfast the next morning and joined my colleagues at the staff table. Among them were some of the more distinguished musicologists of American Jewish life. I hesitate to mention their names. But as soon as I sat down, this is what I heard: "Myron, that was not Jewish music. That was pandering to the lowest element in our community." Looking back, I would have expected from myself a vitriolic and blistering response, like 'What the hell do you know about music.' But instead I kept my peace and stayed absolutely silent, for which I am grateful to this day. It only goes to show that when you want expert information, do not always go to the professionals. They don't always recognize the authentic article even when they brush up against it.

Over the years I would run into Shlomo in the oddest places. Once I boarded an E1 A1 plane on my way to Israel and at the last moment who came running on board, with his tzitzis – fringes – flying. And his guitar in his arms, "Man" he said, "I am beat. We were up all night with the chevra, the holy brothers. Just let me sit down here and rest." Shlomo actually was seated just a few rows in front of me. He sunk down into his seat and didn't move for the ten hours of the flight. When we landed he awoke refreshed and said, "I'm staying in the Rova, the Jewish Quarter, come and see me – but not in the morning." Shlomo was known as a night person but I never saw him further on that trip.

A SOLID WORK ETHIC

INADVERTENTLY ONE OF the things I learned from my father was a strong work ethic. It stood me in good stead, especially when I went as a young man to the Jewish Center of Jackson Heights which was then a large and thriving congregation. Often on Sundays especially I would have what our kids came to call "helicopter days." That was the designation for a day when I would have to be in five or six different places, including cemeteries, which did not often stand cheek by jowl. Our official synagogue grounds were in Pinelawn out on Long Island, but many people had their private burial grounds in the Cypress Hills area in Queens or at Beth David in Elmont where our family grounds are found as well. I remember those days as being especially trying and tiring. I would start out early in the morning and if I was lucky I would get home by three or four in the afternoon. It was not that the hours were so oppressive but that our kids would be home that day from school and I couldn't spend any time with them.

On a number of occasions I would take Jonathan and Jeremy with me if they would come, and if I had a half hour or so between what are called unveilings, we would go to a remote part of the cemetery and throw a football around until my next appointment. But most times I just remember rushing home, putting the kids in the car and often we would go under the Whitestone Bridge where there was a large grassy area and hang out there for awhile on a blanket, trying to imbibe a leisurely picnic style lunch.

Sometimes it even worked, though often the nervous tension of rushing around all day was not easy to shake off.

One early Monday morning I got a call from my father. "Where were you yesterday, I was trying to reach you all day." I tried to shrug off the annoyance but I am not sure I accomplished it. "Where was I? I was racing from one place to the next with my foot hard pressed against the accelerator. I barely made each appointment. And when I came home I had a glass of wine, something to eat and I promptly fell asleep." My father responded rapidly. "Best thing for you. Keep pushing that pedal and you'll always stay young." Well, what else would you expect from a salesman who went out every day and saw perhaps twenty or thirty customers in all parts of Brooklyn, and came home himself at the end of the day satisfied or annoyed, but brimming with a sense of accomplishment.

As important as accomplishment and success figured in my father's horizon of values, he never lost sight of the human and ethical values in which he was reared. His customers often confided in him regarding personal matters. At times he would report of his role, that it seemed more of a confidant than a supplier of bread and bakery supplies.

When I started at Yeshiva College, I came home excitedly to report that we would not have to pay tuition – it was then $300 a semester. They told me I had been given a scholarship. I believe it was related to my being a rabbinical student. They had invested in me and the others because of anticipated future service.

My father's reaction was quite unexpected. "Say thank you for the offer of the scholarship. Tell them we don't need it. Someone else who depends on it more will appreciate it I'm sure." I learned a great deal from that simple declaration. My father was a proud man and independent as well.

Ruefully, I recall in the last months before he died shortly before his birthday, that my mother reported he was having trouble finding his way home from the outer reaches of Brooklyn or Staten Island. It didn't last very long because he died shortly thereafter, but it was difficult for me to picture that. Going back decades before, on rare occasions I would accompany him. And he had these handy stops like at Bickford's for a toasted muffin and egg for lunch, or elsewhere for a slice of pizza and a coke. He had the routine down perfectly, so it was hard to see him losing it. I would not be at all surprised if somewhere he wasn't still urging us all to push the accelerator as hard as we can.

Part: 2

EARLY SHELTER ROCK

THE NEXT PERIOD in my life and in the life of our family began in a very unexpected way. The year is 1965 and I am sitting in my dentist's chair in Jackson Heights. Dr. Herbert Ostreicher is drilling. My eyes are closed and I'm feigning courage. The drill seems to be going deeper and deeper into my tooth but I'm not allowing it to interfere with our one-way conversation. He is trying to convince me that there is a synagogue in Searingtown, a section of Roslyn in Nassau County, New York that has been formed just a few years before and is now searching for a rabbi. He thinks I would be a perfect candidate.

In the chair with my mouth open I'm unable to speak. But I'm giving negative sounds. Once the cavity is filled we can talk more easily. At times we would go to the kosher deli on 37th Avenue, and over franks and beans we would discuss the nature of the world and how to cure its ills.

The question for me turned on whether I was willing to give up what was a stable, metropolitan-type situation, to head out to the suburbs which were in the process of developing but were hardly there yet. It was a risk, a gamble. It wasn't only a totally different congregation but it was an altogether dissimilar lifestyle. From Jackson Heights we could be in the city in twenty minutes, walking to the New York City subway and being transported on rapid transit trains. Out in the suburbs just to get to the city was more complicated. First you had to get to the train station which is a few miles away. Then you had to find a place to park your car. And then you had to hope the Long Island Railroad would be running on time that day. I must say that usually it did, but very often I had to go up to the Jewish Theological Seminary which required taking another train once I got to Pennsylvania Station. After awhile I learned that from the suburbs you drive – and I even found a parking garage on Broadway and 124th Street.

It was one of the most indecisive periods in my life. We were so comfortable in Jackson Heights and yet it seemed like the suburbs were calling and everyone was responding. It was the place to be if you wanted to influence the next generation.

I remember speaking to my father about it. He always had a sense of realism, of the possible. He was exalted by the prospect, the newness of the suburbs and the challenge of it. We tried to fire up excitement.

Around that time, Walter Roth and then Ernest Rothschild, leaders of Shelter Rock, came to Jackson Heights with encouraging words and welcome. I overcame my hesitation. They helped me make a good choice.

To this day our kids remember Walter who came at 5:00 p.m. one day and left at 1:00 a.m. Apparently we needed a lot of convincing. Walter and his wife Lois have remained good friends throughout the years, as did Herb Ostreicher and his wife Lola.

Full disclosure, however, requires me to elaborate further. Synagogues, after all, do not operate without committees. Herb Ostreicher could not act on his own. One Sunday morning I am giving a talk to a group from the United Synagogue Metropolitan Region Adult Education Committee. I don't remember exactly in which synagogue it took place, but it was somewhere on Long Island. There was a large group in attendance. Someway, in the middle of my remarks about the importance of adult education within the synagogue framework, I happened to spot Herb Ostreicher in the audience, with two other people that I knew vaguely, Walter Roth and Chester Gerber, all three from Shelter Rock. It was a temporary distraction which fortunately I was able to overcome. It occurred to me, when I saw them, why they were there. They were talent scouts on behalf of the Shelter Rock Jewish Center.

At the end of the meeting they said they wanted to speak to me. I told them I had an appointment to officiate at an unveiling in forty-five minutes. Their response was, "Good, we'll come along."

So what can I say, the offer to become the rabbi of Shelter Rock, where I remained for thirty-six years, was given at a cemetery in the midst of the tombstones. I accepted. Fortunately, it was not a harbinger of what was to come. The setting was strange, but the result was good.

We moved to Roslyn in the summer of '66, beds and bicycles, furniture and clothing. The weather was beastly. Ernest Rothschild, the president of the congregation, came over to see how things were going, the second day after our arrival.

"It's warm in here, why don't you put on the air conditioning?" he asked. "There is none." Ernest was aghast: "They will be putting it in on Monday morning." And so it was. Cool.

Leaving Jackson Heights also meant uprooting our kids once again from the schools they were attending. We managed to have them graduate the elementary school called the Solomon Schechter School in Queens in which they were enrolled and subsequently they went to a school very close to our home, the Herricks Senior High School. This procedure followed that of my own, attending a Jewish and then a general school. I always thought that my direction enabled me to be firmly within my own tradition and then to partake of the American life which I came to admire and appreciate.

For me, the combination worked well. By the time I attended Madison High School, I was well grounded and secure in my faith.

SIX DAYS OF WAR

N O SOONER HAD we settled in at Shelter Rock Jewish Center than the '67 War broke out in Israel. Events moved at a rapid speed. The Egyptians blocking the straits of Tiran, nighttime excursions into northern Israel, Nasser put troops in the Sinai; and sending out the UN force, and President Lyndon Johnson warning Egypt not to perpetuate the lie that American pilots destroyed the Egyptian air force.

All resulted in the eruption of war and made for a stunning victory by Israel in early June. Weeks of tension led up to it, masterfully chronicled in Michael Oren's "Six Days of War."

In our home at 6:15 a.m. that fateful morning, I was awakened as usual by my bedside radio. "The Arabs say they are bombing Tel Aviv – ." I sat straight up. Had I heard correctly? So soon after the Holocaust. Another heavy blow. How could we survive? No, not this time!

There was little moment for imaginary thoughts or fears. Our doorbell started ringing. Members of the synagogue were bringing checks to help Israel. I realized immediately that enormous effort had to be made. But where to begin? What actually was happening on the homefront? Already the broadcasts were denying the PLO's claims. How could we be sure?

I decided to get in my car and head as soon as I could for 515 Park Avenue, Manhattan, the headquarters of the Jewish Agency, a quasi-governmental Israeli body and the home of the Presidents' Conference where all the major

Jewish organizations of America were represented. I knew my mentor Joachim Prinz would surely be there – he was the chairman.

Arriving at 515, I witnessed a sight I shall never forget. It couldn't have been later than 10:00 a.m., just a few hours after the news had broken. The building was besieged by young people volunteering to fight for Israel's survival. I could barely get in but when I did, one of the first persons I saw was Prinz. He must have seen the expression of deep anxiety on my face: "Myron, don't worry, 'Od lo ovda tikvotenu' – our hope is not yet lost."

He invited me to sit in on the emergency meeting. The Conference was sorting out the facts as they were filtering in. It was not half as bad as first reports sounded. The battle over UN headquarters in Jerusalem was a fierce one, as well as other places, Ammunition Hill, in the Holy City. There were casualties, but we were holding our own. And then we started making advances.

I saw clearly what had to be done. Our people had to be rallied. We needed a huge demonstration at Shelter Rock. It had to be organized today for tomorrow. No time to lose.

Within the next hours, every organization in our community had been called. Every single one responded cooperatively; Hadassah, ORT, National Council of Jewish Women, all the Men's Clubs, Senior Citizens, Youth groups – all were invited to Shelter Rock the next night. It turned out to be the largest gathering in the history of Shelter Rock and in the shortest time possible.

The next night Israeli representatives were present for reassurance, but also to remind us that the war effort was costly, in lives and in keeping the equipment coming. It was a time to show that the American-Israeli partnership was real. "If not now, when?"

The crowd was so large the fire marshal showed up and closed the doors. No one else could enter. We set up loudspeakers in the parking lot. Hundreds heard there.

The speeches went off predictably. Even mine. You didn't have to summon histrionics or false drama. It all came pouring out, the hope and fear, the reality of war and the prayers for an end to it, the faith of Jewish survival. Pieties were invoked: "We shall not die, but live – and go on to speak of God's help."

But the essence of the evening, its most memorable moment, came at the end. The crowd was huge. Small card tables had been set up at the front of the hall, manned by volunteers for U.J.A., Israel Bonds Emergency Appeal. They were overwhelmed with people and gifts. There was no way to keep track of who was giving what. I saw people tired of waiting on line, take fistfuls of cash, throw them on the table and leave.

Never in my days had I seen such a spontaneous outpouring. I closed my eyes for a moment to savor the scene. American Jews! The fire was surely still burning! Don't tell me they're falling apart.

PLYING THE "TRADE"

C OMING TO THE Shelter Rock Jewish Center in Roslyn in 1966, especially from the well-established synagogue that I had been serving, was a daunting challenge. It had a great potential but at that time it was still in the early process of growth. Its membership was small, around three hundred families, the building was inadequate for all the activities that were taking place there, the religious school was one floor down below the street level, which made it neither convenient nor very attractive. What was available was a large auditorium where practically everything was held – services on the Sabbath and holidays, meetings and assemblies, and social affairs. It was what we call a kolbo or all-purpose room, not very inspiring, but I was to discover that inspiration comes from the content rather than the physical size.

My agenda had not been explicitly set down, but if it had, it would have gone something like this: vitalize the religious services by engaging the mind and the heart of those who come. Intellectually I hoped it would be stimulating, as I have always striven to do more than comment on the affairs of the day, or read some passage from Scripture, and give some commentary upon it. In fact, I always saw the purpose of a service to combine the contemporary with the Scriptural. To the degree that they fused together it was a successful service.

For example, before elections I would comment on both major candidates and the major issues. My position was never a partisan one. During all the years of my active rabbinate and even subsequently, I refrained from registering as either a Democrat or a Republican. I took a degree of pride in my independent status which gave the independence I needed to make whatever comment I felt was appropriate. On a personal level I have voted for Republicans and Democrats without resort to the party, but rather focusing on the individual.

During the Viet Nam War this position got me into some hot water with those avowed partisans of loyalty to the United States and its foreign policy no matter how far off they were. Early on I spoke about the mess in Viet Nam and how we did not seem to be able to extricate ourselves, and in the end what were we doing there? The domino theory was always thrown at me. I tried to maintain a strong degree of loyalty to our troops which I have always felt, while at the same time criticizing the foreign policy which in this case seemed like it was getting us into a quagmire. Many years later I was startled, but not surprised, when Robert McNamara, who had been the Secretary of Defense during that period, admitted that we made major mistakes and that every time we did, we put more troops in there. Many people think the same process is being followed now in Iraq. To my mind, that is a totally different matter.

In any case, at times like that you often hear, "The rabbi ought to stay out of politics and stick to religion." Others say: "the rabbi's opinion on the war in Viet Nam is no better than mine. He is not a military analyst and neither am I. That is why we have a President and a Cabinet and a Congress." These arguments always carried some weight with me, but they paled into lesser significance with the continuing numbers of war dead that were being sent back to the United States. In those days they used to show pictures of the soldiers, who had been killed, arriving back home. So what do you do in a time like that, when people are pointing at you and suggesting that you are doing the wrong thing? If you are smart, you take the hits and keep doing it. Looking back, that is exactly what I was able to do and I am very satisfied that it was correct.

Of course another factor was present, the issues of Soviet Jewry, and civil rights, were engaging Americans at the same time. Especially with regard to the Jews in the Soviet Union, we were very much involved. I remember mornings gathering at 6:30 a.m. in front of our synagogue, boarding a bus with another thirty or so shivering participants and heading for the United Nations, carrying banners for Sharansky, Begun, Schlepak and Ida Nudel. On one of our journeys to the United Nations a very interesting thing occurred. We would go there to pray and on occasion would even take a Torah with us to read on a Monday morning. This particular wintry morning, which has been preserved for us in photograph and newspaper, there must have been fifty or so people present. The service was winding down at about 7:30 or so in the morning when a lanky young figure approached me and said, "You're Rabbi Fenster, aren't you? I'm John LeBoutillier, your Congressman. I heard you were having a protest here and I would like to join with you." LeBoutillier had just been elected and decided to present himself at that moment. In the end he proved to be a one-term congressman who got himself into a lot of verbal trouble, but I must say at that particular moment I embraced him with great enthusiasm. I admired very much what he had done by joining us.

Meanwhile, the numbers increased; the congregation grew. It was obvious that we needed to build larger facilities. Plans were drawn; money was raised – not easily but enough to begin.

We had wonderful leadership and we managed to stay focused. Abe Magid and Ed Albom were builders; Carl Rosenbleuth, Jack Rosenthal and Walter Bernstein pounded the bushes with me for the cash to flow. We were on our way.

Building began, a new sanctuary, offices, a chapel, and other auxiliary space. The problem was that I had previously committed to the Leadership Training program at Camp Bnai Brith for five weeks in the summer. They could have managed without me, but I was responsible for the rabbinical staff of five and had been part of the program from its inception. With some reluctance we headed up to Camp. Lisa and Jonathan were at Camp Ramah, Jeremy and Dan came with us. At night at camp the air is brisk and the stars shine. It is a fabulous breather for the year ahead.

Returning in late August, I was happily surprised to see the progress of the new building. Miracle of miracles, the money had not run out. We were going to be able to finish without heart-rending appeals to the congregation. We had sown, ready to reap.

The biggest surprise was when Abe, Carl and Jack told me to follow them to the lower floor. An auditorium had been built, which made the building infinitely more usable, for assemblies, meetings, carnivals, songfests and the like. I had not known that it was coming and it was a delight. "What do you think?" I was asked. I was stymied so I blurted out, "Fabulous! You should have made it bigger!" What a response. We all had a good laugh. But we now had the space we needed. And we immediately put it to work.

In order to reach that point there were many evenings when Walter Bernstein would ask me to accompany him to help solicit a member of the congregation. It wasn't exactly my cup of tea, but how could I refuse? So he would pick me up and we would start our rounds.

Walter was an interesting guy. He had lost a leg in the Battle of the Bulge, but that added to his determination to build a new life for himself. He did – with Rita and three children, while he started a dress business which he called Whippets after the dog. For quite a while the business flourished. He and his partner came up with the idea of a paper dress, which was then featured in Life Magazine. Walter was a creative salesman.

Our forays together never failed – we always got some pledge. But this one night we visited a member who Walter knew, but I didn't, a wealthy man known to be generous. Within ten minutes he promised us $25,000. It may not seem like much nowadays, but then in the '60's – it was awesome! We were thrilled. It enlivened the campaign. The building was built!

So to come back to my agenda, in 1966 when I arrived at Shelter Rock it was to bring a new spirit of joy, enthusiasm and content into religious services. More than that, I wanted to teach classes for adults and later on ended up with a Bat Mitzvah class, for women who had never gone through the ceremony, thirty-six women who were my pride and joy as we taught them over a period of two years. I used to call them my 'lamed vovniks' which is the Hebrew equivalent of thirty six but which stands in the Jewish tradition for especially sainted people who sustain the world with their piety. It was one of the most deeply exhilarating experiences of my rabbinic life.

In addition, we started a High School department of our Hebrew School which had not existed before. I made it my business to get to know every Bar and Bat Mitzvah candidate at Shelter Rock, most often with their families, and visit many people at home, the sick in the hospitals, the mourners sitting shiva, as I possibly could.

I now recall fondly a visit to the home of Chad Blank, whose family were members of our congregation. Chad was always an exceptional young man, smart, respectful and just a plain nice kid. So I decided to visit the family at home before the Bar Mitzvah because I did not know them quite as well as I wanted to. It turned out that I had officiated at the marriage of Chad's parents, David and Pam, years before at Shelter Rock. We spent a lovely hour or so around their table talking and sipping coffee, and I felt really bonded to the family. It was one of those moments that make being a rabbi worthwhile.

Little did I know that many years later I would be sent to Dr. David Blank, an oral surgeon, so that he could extract some wisdom teeth for me.

As I always tell him, he practices painless dentistry. He cannot prevent you from spitting out some blood at the end, but the truth is there was virtually no pain at all, even when I received the novocaine shot at the beginning. Without detracting any other oral surgeon, I must say that David is a star.

That story could be repeated many times over with young people of our congregation, men and women, who have now gone out into the world. Whenever I meet them and whatever circumstance, there is a special feeling of kinship that I have. Not too long ago a young man stopped us in Manhattan, Ricky and I. He was wearing a week growth of beard, looked okay, but not ready for a ball at the Waldorf. He told me who he was and there was immediate recognition. He added that he is an artist, doing quite well, living in Soho, painting and selling his works, and is quite happy.

In addition to all those other activities there were many weddings at Shelter Rock, too many funerals, and loads of unveilings, most of which took place on the weekends. I made it a point never to turn down anybody if I could accommodate them. This meant a great deal of hustle maneuvering for time, and on occasion delaying family opportunities. There were moments when family life had to be put on the side burner. But as far as I was concerned, it was never put on the back. When our kids were young I made it a point to be home every night between 6:00 and 8:00 p.m. I tried always to be there not only physically but having shucked off the day's activities at least temporarily. It is true that in the evening I often had to go out to meetings, on many occasions more than one. But at least those moments were sacred.

Meantime, the congregation was growing and that was a source of deep satisfaction. Hundreds and even thousands of people passed through its doors, even on a weekly basis. Over a Saturday and Sunday there could be two or even three weddings, where we would gather people from all over. Often the synagogue was filled on Saturday morning with people celebrating a Bar or Bat Mitzvah, an aufuf, an anniversary, or the remembrance of someone who had died. There were baby namings, where I would take the baby in my hands (and hope there were waterproof diapers) show her to the congregation and offer a blessing, after which we would all sing Siman Tov and Mazel Tov, dance a little, and clap. In the midst of all of this it must be admitted that a rabbi, or at least me, often finds it difficult for personal time, for friends with whom you can let your hair down, and for opportunities of total relaxation and absorption in other matters.

Many rabbis do not deliberately mix with their congregations on a social level. I understand the perils of doing that, of appearing to pick out some people to be close to, to the exclusion of others. To the rabbi, that is fine. He learns to live with it. But for the family that presents a problem, for they are part of the community. Your wife and kids need sociability and support in the long hours that you are away from home. To balance the competing elements is not always easy. I would say that one has to keep a number of factors in mind, but the middle way is discoverable. How to stand aside from the congregation and yet be part of it is often a delicate balance. It is what Martin Buber called, "the narrow bridge." If you go too far on one side, you will be considered an appendage of one segment of the congregation, but if you stay totally aloof people will look at you as if you are an elitist. In this, as in all other things, I was helped by the good sense and smart insight of Ricky.

So when we came to Shelter Rock I immediately started teaching. My adult courses at the beginning focused on the biblical Book of Job, for which I have always had strong attachment, and the Book of Koheleth, both of which are part of the wisdom literature of the Bible. Unfortunately, they are an unknown element in the minds of most Jews and Christians, though they both contain very important messages for life and its meaning and direction. Concerning Koheleth, for example, most people regard him as a cynical misanthrope, which I believe is way off the mark. I always made my students consider the following passages from Koheleth.

"Go eat your bread in gladness, and drink your wine with a merry heart, for God has accepted your ways. Let your garments be always white and let your head not lack oil. Live joyfully with the woman whom you love all the days of your life – for that is your good portion in life and in the labor which you have done under the sun. All which your hand has accomplished to do, do it with vigor for there is neither wisdom nor learning in the grave to which we all are going."

That passage is from the Ninth Chapter of Koheleth, but later on he says, "In the morning sow thy seed and the evening of your life withhold not your hand – make sure your light is sweet and that your eyes enjoy the sun. For if a man live for many years, let him rejoice in them all, and let him remember the days of darkness for they shall be many."

What many people most vividly remember about Koheleth is his statement, "Vanity of vanity, all is vanity." In that verse he is talking about most of us, men women, rabbis, rock stars, Hollywood, and so on. There is a certain glitz about our time and presenting it in a kind of press agent way to feature its bright and outstanding parts. Koheleth wants us to emphasize the positive and the joyful in our life but to remember we have to account for everything before our Maker. What most people remember are the passages when he seems most pessimistic. Personally, I regard them as intuitive and brilliant and pointing to a realistic appraisal of what we are about. "I looked again and saw that in life the race is not always to the swift, nor the battle to the strong, nor bread to the wise, nor riches to the people of understanding, or favor to the person of skill, but time and chance happens to them all." Such teachings always gave me stimulation and I hope imparted knowledge to others. Most people fail to realize that Koheleth is a diary of many moods, some contradictory, but all real and honest. The lives of most of us exhibit a variety of emotional ups and downs.

There were many others as well. The biblical books of Ezra and Nehemiah each detailed the importance of the framework of tradition and how vital it is to keep that intact. That law, that is to say the rules and regulations, are as important as the Kavannah, that is the spirit of the law and the direction of where it is going. There are many people who talk about the intricacies of the law and uphold that. But we need more people who are prepared to dedicate themselves to both, to what we call tradition and the contemporary and to bring equal fervor and passion to the continuity of both.

This was the substance and what I tried to teach all those years at Shelter Rock and elsewhere, a passion for the framework and a passion for the goal.

IT TURNED INTO A VERY GOOD YEAR

THE BIG CHANGE in our lives with regard to Israel came in 1977 when our son Jeremy went to Israel and called us excitedly one day to say that he had just gotten engaged to this lovely young lady from Kansas City, Missouri who was studying in Israel. Ellen Gibian was a Phi Beta Kappa graduate from Washington University in St. Louis. She and Jeremy would become the parents of nine children over the next years and of course that was a drawing card for us to often return to Israel. Now that they have added seventeen great-grandchildren to the retinue, the attraction becomes even stronger.

But here too the beginnings were quite humble. Ellen was studying in Jerusalem though we had already read the signals that things were warming up between them. By then Jeremy had become Orthodox in his practice and by that standard of course there are no premarital relationships. Nonetheless Ricky and I went to Israel that summer on vacation to see what was happening. We had met Ellen at our home when she came for a visit. But we had no real idea as to what was happening. After a two-week stay, Jeremy rented a car and drove us to the airport. We had some time so we were sipping espresso at a lovely outdoor area at the airport. "Jeremy, do you have something to say to Mom and I before we leave?" "Dad, Mom, have a nice trip home." Five days later Jeremy called to say that he had been engaged and that he wanted the wedding, if possible, to take place at the Shelter Rock Jewish Center.

Jeremy was then a rabbinic student and many of the people at Shelter Rock had seen him grow up. By then we were living in Roslyn more than a decade. So we invited the entire congregation and five hundred people showed up for the wedding. Ellen's parents were there as well as a delegation of friends from Shawnee Mission, Kansas, which is really where they come from. Elissa and Bill had been married a short time before in the same place but in a much less crowded atmosphere. People who were there at Jeremy and Ellen's wedding still remember it as an exuberant, dancing-well-into-the-night, affair. It was highlighted when at the last moment after the bride and the groom were already under the wedding canopy, one of Jeremy's friends who had just arrived from Jerusalem came running down the aisle. According to an old tradition if you hand a bride and groom a prayer or a petition, it has special potency under the chuppah. He handed Jeremy a bagful of prayers and petitions.

There were some memorable moments at the wedding itself. It could have been the first time at Shelter Rock that there was what is called a, "chassan tisch." Before the groom goes to help bedeck the bride before the ceremony, they sit in separate rooms, the groom with his entourage and the bride with hers.

Jeremy's tisch was uproarious and memorable. There were dozens of friends and family singing, clapping, dancing, drinking and just hanging out. When the time came to accompany him to meet Ellen, his brothers took him by the hands, Jonathan on one side – and Danny on the other.

It was quite a dramatic sight. Dan, the Younger, was smoking a cigar and smiling happily. Jonathan on the other hand, was green with tension. We were led into the bride's room by a trumpeter and a violinist, through the lobby of the synagogue crowded with people, into the bride's area, also crowded. The bride and groom had been apart for the full week before the wedding. Now their eyes met. There was a brief silence as we were all onlookers. No time for passivity, however, – we were already being swept toward the synagogue sanctuary for the ceremony itself. It was about to begin and everyone had to find their place. The energy of the moment took over.

The day after the wedding the young couple boarded an El Al plane for Israel, their new permanent home. They had already taken an apartment in the Old City of Jerusalem, the area in which they were to live for the next thirty-plus years. As a wedding gift, we had arranged for a few days at the King David Hotel in Jerusalem, just as our parents had arranged for the Waldorf Astoria for us. They were looking forward to it with great anticipation and we too were excited awaiting the call afterward describing a cool weekend.

Too bad it never happened. Unbeknown to us, that was the exact weekend Anwar Sadat decided to appear in Jerusalem, speak before the Knesset, and begin the peace process with Golda Meir. Jeremy and Ellen never came closer than two blocks before the King David. The roadblocks were up, the police were out, and no one was going through – "we don't care who you are and what reservations you have."

Well, they had the apartment; only problem was there was no furniture in it except the mattress, and no food prepared for the Shabbat which was oncoming even thought a table was there with two chairs.

Later Jeremy and Ellen were to tell that they had the best time. Their friends invited them over and they made last minute comfortable arrangements. As far as I know, they never collected that King David weekend; but it certainly was a memorable honeymoon nonetheless.

Jeremy and Ellen are Orthodox and observant, what the media often refers to as right-wing extremists. Of course since Jeremy had been a Viet Nam protestor as well and had spent the early college years as a secularist with long hair, we didn't quite see the extremism of his new religious belief. We were just happy and proud that it gave him direction and faith and made him extremely happy. While we didn't share every aspect of his belief and still don't, we have worked out a modus vivendi. Certain delicate subjects we just don't touch upon. While we often study texts together, we avoid the broader implications of theology since there are aspects of his traditional pattern which I personally cannot accept. They have to do with my earlier experience and my inability to say that whatever happens in this world happens for the best. I wish I could say that, but I cannot. And I don't expect that I ever will. I still don't think that Elliot died for the best. Or that the Holocaust took place for the best.

Then there are some stereotypes to dispel. One of them is that all of the religious people are painted by the same brush. Jeremy and Ellen's family grew up in the Jewish Quarter of the Old City of Jerusalem. It has become a religious enclave though there are many variations. We have rented apartments there at one time or another and felt totally comfortable. Most people think I am exaggerating when I say that each one of our grandchildren is different from the other. They each have their own unique personality and style and it is not a matter of one-size-fits-all. Most of them are very studious but not all. Most of them are very careful about nutrition, but not all. But they are all observant, respectful of their parents and grandparents and as far as we are concerned they are all delightful. But when we think of them, we think of viva la difference.

One of the most repeated stereotypes about what are called 'haredim' is related to their marriage procedures. They are called "shiduchim" or arranged marriages. Now that five of our grandchildren are married we have much deeper insight, into how it takes place, than before.

I must start by saying that all the spouses of our grandchildren seem perfectly suited to them. Having officiated myself at hundreds of weddings here in America, I long ago gave up the phrase a "marriage made in heaven." With the divorce rate approaching fifty percent, that is a dangerous term. But as far as they are concerned, each one of our adopted grandchildren is also different but seems marvelously suited to his or her mate. And the idea that they meet under the wedding canopy for the first time is totally false. While the contact between them is set down and proscribed, they do spend a number of evenings sitting and talking and learning about each other. There is no physical contact between them and these meetings always take place in a public place, usually with a coke bottle between them. But you'd be surprised how much you can learn about each other when you spend some eight to ten, or more, hours just talking about backgrounds and aspirations. And potential suitors are sometimes rejected and sometimes accepted. But there is no pre-described pattern and there is no guarantee. The only thing that seems to be set in stone is that if you continue to go out after the fourth time and you are not ready to make a commitment, then it should be cut off.

I am not going to say that this arrangement is much better than what we have in other parts of the world. There are some nasty divorces in the Orthodox community in Israel as well, but not to the degree nor to the percentage that generally takes place nowadays. The father of the young man or woman is crucial to the whole process. He meets the young male suitor before his daughter. He has a strong vote and may exercise a veto. But he never acts alone.

I remember when Bracha, our eldest granddaughter, who married Moshe Krohn and who now are getting ready for their fifth child, called excitedly from Tel Aviv to say that she and Moshe had just decided to become engaged after walking on the beach. For some unknown reason Burt Lancaster and Deborah Kerr suddenly popped into my mind with that famous scene on the beach. Of course, nothing like that had happened and whenever I see them I am still revved up by the joy which they have within themselves and the energy as well. If you ask me, it was a match made in heaven, as well as Sarah and Huddy, Binyamin and Rachel, Kyla and Yacov, and recently Chani and Dovie. The only thing I am really suggesting is that stereotypes are not always accurate. Life defies categorization.

So it is obvious why we have continued to visit Israel regularly. Our family has proliferated. We now have seventeen great grandchildren. Often we would manage to go twice a year and stay anywhere up to a month each time. During the summer visit I would often visit Rabbi David Hartman, for a rabbinic seminar with colleagues, which always stimulated my mind and prepared me for the High Holiday period when I would return to the congregation. David Hartman is a spirited teacher of texts and their interpretation. He is also an exuberant person whom I have had the opportunity to bring to congregations in America on a number of occasions. Once in the summer of 2002 we were invited to his home for Shabbat lunch. There were fifteen or so colleagues and family present. The lunch began at approximately 12:30 in the afternoon and we didn't get up from the table until 5:00. When you were with David and his wife Bobbie time melted away. Whenever I don't manage to get to the seminar for the summer I can truly say, "My body is in the west but my heart is in the east."

In 1991 after a short stint in Israel, I returned to America in preparation for the coming year. I visited with my physician for my annual checkup. Looking me over he spotted something on my abdomen. "What is that? How long have you had it?" I had, in fact, noticed it and had been watching it in my shower every morning. It didn't seem to be getting any bigger but on the other hand it wasn't disappearing either. "I want you to visit the dermatologist right now."

A day or so later the dermatologist was looking at it intently and told me to lie back. I barely felt anything at all and he told me to sit up, that it was out. He said he didn't like the looks of it either, but he couldn't tell for sure. Well, it was a melanoma, but fortunately it was only on the surface. It had to be cut out twice, the second time so that the cells around it could be looked at. Needless to say, since it was right before Yom Kippur, it focused my mind on the transitory and tentative nature of life. Waiting for the result of the biopsy was not pleasant, nor were the early visits every three months to check me over again.

I became powerfully aware of the inevitability of decay, of change and even of death. Suddenly everything around me took on deep meaning. I came across Robert Frost's poem,

"Nothing gold can stay: Nature's first green is gold/
Her early leaves a flower, but only so an hour/
Then leaf subsides to leaf/ So Eden sank to grief/
So dawn goes down today/
Nothing gold can stay."

Was all of this new to me? Not really. I had long been a student of the Book of Job and was powerfully impressed with the opening of Chapter 14.

"Man that is born of woman is short-lived and sated with trouble/
He blossoms like a flower and withers/ He vanishes like a shadow and does not endure/

His days are determined/ As are the numbers of his months/

You have set limits that he cannot pass/ Turn away from him that he may be at ease/ Until, like a hireling, he finishes out his day."

In the prayer book for Yom Kippur the liturgy contains the following dramatic reminder: "Our origin is dust and our end is dust. We are as a fragile vessel, as the grass that withers, the shadow that passes and the dream that flies away." Very often looking back, life does seem like a dream that has passed away.

So on that Yom Kippur I had to confront my mortality directly. I realized once again that none of us are going to be able to fool the Angel of Death forever and we would have to face up to it. My physician had called it a freckle and it certainly was feckless. Once it was removed I learned that, in fact, it could have been deadly, but thank God it was gone, goodbye, good riddance. Do me a favor, I said, don't come back again!

The procedure took a couple of weeks from discovery to dismissal. There were difficult days, even terrifying at times and dotted by sleepless nights. I had to stare down the Malach Ha-Maves and come to terms with my not being around. I had trouble picturing it. I remembered the story of King Hezekiah who took deathly ill, who prayed to God sincerely and wholeheartedly and had the Prophet Isaiah do so as well. In response he was told that God had heard his prayer and seen his tears and so was going to add fifteen years to his life. Hezekiah is brought to his senses by the terrible experience, changes direction and brings his people along with him as he becomes more humble and more penitent.

The whole story can be read in the Second Book of Kings, Chapter 18.

For me too, the world suddenly took on a new meaning. Had I ever really smelled the early morning dew on the flower, or looked at the low-slung moon on a clear night? Had I ever fully appreciated the dimension of love with my wife and family? At that time we had thirteen grandchildren and I decided that I had to spend more time with them. Did I ever fully appreciate the joys of mellow contemplation at the end of the day, or the power of an inner religious experience, of sensing God's presence in my life? Did I ever fully savor the full impact kindled by music or literature or fantasy? I didn't, but I promised to try harder.

And I began to realize how fortunate you have to be even with sickness and how much support we should be giving to those who are not that lucky, how much pain can be concentrated in one life, and how fortunate those of us are who are free to move around and to experience good health and a contented spirit.

So on that occasion, unlike the death of my brother Elliott, it occurred to me that perhaps it was all for some higher purpose, to turn pain into power and to bring out our humanity. All of that is what is meant when the rabbis of the Talmud spoke of the afflictions that turn into love. I was attempting to turn my pain into the power of love.

In addition, I began to ask myself why melanomas are now more frequent than ever before. This led to a more intensive interest in the early detection of heart disease and cancer. I developed a deeper interest in how our ozone layer had been depleted so that the sun is ever more dangerous upon our bodies. And I was aghast when I learned that acid rain from the mid-west was being dumped on New York. I became deeply concerned with the water and air quality and cleaning up our toxic waste dumps, and of those terrible people who are oblivious to all of these things.

And I became more interested in car emissions and air pollutants, and more healthy foods, and calories, and cholesterol, and fiber and figs. And I told my congregation that year that I wanted them to become more interested as well. Together we must choose life if we want to be written and sealed in the Book of Life. Of course there are never any guarantees.

There is an old traditional story of how in the Garden of Eden God led Adam around showing him the beauty of the place. God said to Adam: "See My works. Look how beautiful they are. All of this was created for your sake. Think of it and do not corrupt or destroy My world. For if you corrupt it, there will be no way to set it right after you."

So after the darkness of that night-like experience, I was hoping for joy in the morning. I loved when Louie Armstrong would sing, "What a beautiful world." Its lines spoke immediately to me. I found it once again in our tradition: "How precious is Your kindness, Oh God, the children of earth take shelter under Your wings. God, we pray, give us shelter. Draw us to each other in Thy grace."

Of course all of this will not help evaporate disaster and darkness. That is why in one of our most popular hymns, with which we conclude the service, we sing out with great force: "My life is ever in His hand/With Him there is no fear/ When I sleep and when I wake. May we sense that He is near."(B.Z. Bokser)

Two years later we had reason for great rejoicing. Ricky and I were going to Israel to celebrate the Bar Mitzvah of our grandson Binyamin. It was a cold morning in January at 5:45 a.m., with our cab hurtling rapidly toward the Western Wall of Jerusalem. The sun was just beginning to rise and it was casting a haunting purple mystical glow over the surrounding mountain. It is a totally bewitching color like the prayer shawl we wear, it is the essence of Jerusalem itself.

The plaza in front of what is called the Kotel is empty at that hour except for Binyamin and his father (Jeremy our son, the Rabbi) setting up the reading table and chairs. Binyamin is dressed up in his newest and best clothes, proudly sporting the crown of a shiny new black fedora, which religious boys begin to wear at the age of thirteen. His is perched tenderly on the top of his head. When I first spied Binyamin decked out in his black hat, my eyes filmed over when I realized how far he had come. Many years later in June 2004 I had the same feeling when he called excitedly from Jerusalem to tell us that his wife Rochel had given birth to their second child. Now there are five.

Binyamin is putting on his tefillin, boxes containing verses from Scripture that are used to help connect us to God and our people. His parchment has been carefully written by Ezra, expert scribe of the Cardo in the Jewish Quarter.

Friends from the Jewish Quarter have begun to arrive. Then from the Yishuv, a Judean Hill settlement fifteen miles outside of Jerusalem. These are all associates of Jeremy and Ellen for many years. We have known most of them for a long time, and while they are still young by our standards, gray has begun to show on the beards of many. Almost all of them are expatriates from all parts of America who are now devoting their lives to religious and spiritual matters. Their daily prayer is, "to find grace and good wisdom in the eyes of God and Humankind."

When we finish reading from the Torah and are returning it to the ark, we sing, "May God bless you from Zion and may you see children unto your children and may there be peace to Israel."

Afterward a dozen or so close friends are sitting in Jeremy and Ellen's living room enjoying a simple breakfast fueled by a strong "L'Chaim." After the early morning cold, the schnappes and hot coffee have made our toes operational once again. And so the sentences begin to flow as during the next seventy-five minutes a multi-dimensional celebration proceeds. There is singing, laughing, crying, all centered on Binyamin's young life and future. Each person has something personal to tell regarding his learning, his good deeds, or in my case, drawing on family history and summoning up the memory of those who are no longer with us. I cannot escape the feeling of how far we have come. I guess it is indigenous to all grandparents who are grateful, "for having been kept alive and been preserved to reach a great milestone in their lives."

By the time we leave to return to the world, the sun is shining high and the day has fully begun. We are filled with a grateful glow of seeing our eldest grandson join the ranks of our people as we pray for him that he will always be a caring and compassionate person.

THE ADMOR OFFERS FISH

B INYAMIN WAS ALSO a part of another intriguing segment that spun out in Jerusalem. I always loved to go into the Geulah section of the town, which is filled with the religious folks, and especially on Friday when they are all bustling around getting ready for Shabbat. Actually, when he was young it was always my practice when I came with Ricky to spend some time buying Binyamin a pair of shoes or whatever, before the High Holiday period. We would go to Geulah.

But this time we were bent on a different mission. We were going to see one of the venerable rabbis of Israel, the Lelover Rebbe, whose school and court were on Zephanya Street. This would be the first meeting we were to have and that actually took place shortly before Binyamin's Bar Mitzvah. Our Cantor Avi Albrecht, from Shelter Rock at that time, was very close to this rebbe as had been Avi's mother before him. And as Jeremy, Binyamin and I walked up the worn stairs to his second floor study, I realized that I had never been with an admor – Chasidic sage – before. I knocked on the door lightly, hardly expecting the admor to appear himself. But I was wrong.

An admor is a honorific title usually given to a Chasidic rabbi, the descendents of other distinguished rabbis, what many used to call a "Grand Rabbi." His leadership is generally charismatic, containing a court and followers who believe in his special powers in prayer, in healing and in his insight into all matter of life. Most people over the last years have become familiar with the name of the Lubavitcher rebbe and all the extravagant claims that have been made about his leadership and even Messiahship.

This particular admor seemed to belie all such advance billing. He sat alone in the room, smoking and studying a volume of Maimonides. He always seemed preoccupied. His look was traditional, heavily bearded and wearing the long dark silky clothing that one associates with a man of his position. He was short of stature and the outstanding memory I have of him is that he looked into your eyes deeply, but his eyes were always slightly dreamy. You knew that he heard what you were saying, but he also could be inhabiting another world while he spoke to you.

When we went up to his office that first time unannounced, he nonetheless greeted us warmly. I saw no irritation whatever that we had interrupted him. We had come inquiring to the study hall and were told it was perfectly all right to go up the stairs and knock on the door. All of this was very unusual for an admor, some of whom ensconced themselves in all kinds of preventative trappings.

The Lelover Rebbe proved to be a reserved but an engaging host. Before we departed he blessed Binyamin, Jeremy and myself. His blessing was fervent and direct and we felt good about it.

I tell this story now as further demonstration of how the stereotype of the Chasidic rabbi is often misleading. The Lelover Rebbe was most approachable and down to earth. Some years later when I met him in Borough Park, I told him I was thinking of retiring. His answer was immediate: "Don't do it, you are not ready for it."

This confidence had come from being a descendant of a long line of distinguished spiritual leaders going back to Rabbi David of Lelov in the Nineteenth Century. Subsequent members of the family inherited the dynasty. This Lelover Rebbe, whose real name was Abraham Biederman, was the son of a well-known figure around Jerusalem who had occupied his role for many years. Lelov was the town from which they were derived in Russia. I happened to be in Jerusalem some years before when the former rabbi died. I recall the pictures in the newspaper the next day of many thousands of people who had turned out to do him honor. This rebbe was an introspective man and, unlike the fabled reputation of others, he did not speak very much. When he taught a word of Torah it was brief. It was not often repeatable. This struck me as unusual, but every rebbe is known to have his own style. This Lelover Rebbe was broodingly reticent.

In essence, that was his fascination. He inhabited the title, the court, the soup kitchen provided to the poor, the students and the school. He administered to all of the needs with enthusiasm, but he was not into promotion. He excelled in one-on-one situations in the arena of private conversation, of listening to individuals and their problems, of offering advice, blessings, and an optimistic word. He was a good model for those of us who were younger and more modern.

One thing he was not, was modern. One evening he conducted a memorial service to his father's memory in the Jewish Quarter of the Old City of Jerusalem. We were invited to attend. It was to take place at a neighbor's home. Jeremy was invited as well as Binyamin and myself, but not Ricky because there were never any women present at these occasions.

It worked out that I alone ascended the three stories to the open roof where this memorial service was to take place. There were no more than twenty people present. There was a service of prayer, brief but fervent, the memorial kaddish prayer was recited, and then we were invited to sit down to a festive meal in memory of the departed. Since it was after my own dinner, I was a participant but not a partaker. This proved to be a problem. A large and delicious looking fish came out whole on a platter. It was well known that the Chasidim did not often follow the ways of western etiquette. The fish having been placed on the table, the rebbe scooped out some of it with his bare hand, uttered a blessing, and ate. He had taken a minimal portion. The plate was then placed on the table at which point the other Chasidim dove into the nearly whole fish with their fingers, and proceeded to demolish it. Licking one's fingers from the food of the Rebbe apparently had special significance. The Rebbe was obviously enjoying the appetite of his disciples.

It was a sight to behold, but in all honesty it triggered no yearning in me. Lo and behold, the Rebbe is now pointing what remained of the fish and looking at me askance, as if to say, "Nu?" Refusal would have seemed to indicate an elitist distaste. After the briefest moment of hesitancy, I also dug in, came up with something and put in into my mouth. The salmon was tasty, but for the rest of the evening I couldn't get rid of the smell on my fingers. If there was anything charming about the whole experience, it was the complete unselfconscious way in which it was done. Chasidic custom had prevailed over contemporary habit.

Coming back home, months later Avi Albrecht called to say that the Rebbe wanted to come visit me at home. Remembering the scene I had witnessed in Jerusalem, I was slightly unsure of how to proceed. Avi assured me that the Rebbe doesn't eat anywhere except in his own surroundings and all he would do would be to make a L'Chayim with me. The Rebbe drank from the kiddush cup deeply after which his face flushed, and his eyes sparkled before turning dreamy again. It was altogether a pleasant and even a memorable experience. Who would ever expect an admor in Roslyn?

There is in Chasidic literature the tradition of the Nistar, the hidden one, who has not yet revealed himself. But by this time the Lelover Rebbe was no longer young. I wondered whether he was one of those who preferred to remain in the hidden rather than in the revealed. It was a beguiling circumstance and so I began to search in some of the literature.

The story is told of a young disciple who was upset by an aspect of his relationship with his wife. While it did not apply particularly to himself, he felt sorry for the way in which she treated the servants of the family. So he went to his teacher, Rabbi David of Lelov, and asked him if he should oppose his wife.

The admor answered: "Why do you speak to me? Speak to yourself." Later the disciple wrote and understood what his teacher had meant to convey. "Do not depend on others, everything depends on yourself."

Further, I discovered that the same Rabbi David of Lelov, who died in 1813, did not want the title Tzaddik, or thoroughly righteous person, to adorn him. He did not feel that he had yet attained such a high stature. Once he taught his Chasidim: "A man cannot be redeemed until he recognizes the flaws in his own soul and tries to mend them. A nation cannot be redeemed until it recognizes its flaws and tries to mend them. Whoever does not recognize his own failures, be it human or nation, will never be redeemed. The first thing we must do is come to terms with ourselves." Perhaps this explains the humility of the man I knew and came to respect and admire.

Once the admor of Lelov invited us to a Friday evening gathering. It turned out that he was staying that summer in the Old City. When we concluded our family dinner, my son Jeremy and I decided to go and visit. It was just a few houses down. With a group of his most devoted disciples, the Lelover Rebbe was on the roof enjoying the splendor of the moon and of the Sabbath. Once again he did not speak very much. But I shall never forget the way he tilted his face toward the moon, his eyes half closed, and began rolling his head gently from side to side. "Shabbos kodesh, Shabbos kodesh." Sabbath was indeed holy. As he repeated the phrase over and over again it seemed that the words became more deeply etched upon his soul. It was as if they had a magnetic impact upon him and upon all those who experienced it with him. That was a special holy and memorable Sabbath in Jerusalem.

As a souvenir of those days I have recently found a picture that was taken at the wedding of Moshe and Bracha in the late 1990's. The wedding, a festive occasion, was held in Jerusalem. I had extended an invitation to the Lelover Rebbe and, lo and behold, he and his entourage showed up. It caused quite a stir and immediately a circle formed around him as we slowly and methodically danced in a circle, clapping hands. Everyone, except the groom, Danny and I, had beards. Black hats are flashing everywhere. But I especially enjoyed the imperturbable look on the Rebbe's face, his full white beard, his eyes wide open, savoring the moment. He is holding onto Jeremy, the father of the bride, who is marrying off his oldest child. His eyes on the other hand, are closed, also savoring the moment, holding his brother who seems to be smiling, as am I. It was a special moment and if you are inclined towards symbols, they could be called, 'the Chasidic and modern joining together.' I particularly enjoy it nowadays when Bracha and Moishe have five children.

BINYAMIN AND THE
ARI HA-KODOSH

S HORTLY AFTER BINYAMIN'S
Bar Mitzvah in Jerusalem, we
decided to take a trip together to the city of Tsfat (Safed) in the north.
Going back to when our grandchildren began to arrive on the scene, Ricky
and I always had this idea to spend time with each of them separately
to get to know them better. Whenever anybody asks me nowadays can
I remember the names of our nine grandchildren in Israel, my standard
answer is that I not only know their names but I know what each one likes
to eat for breakfast.

From his earliest days Binyamin was always a serious student. When
he was quite young, ten or eleven years old, Ricky and I took him to a
vegetarian restaurant in downtown Jerusalem for dinner. Looking back I
guess it was not such a smart question, but since I had some indication what
the answer would be, I asked it nonetheless. "Binyamin, what do you think
you would like to be when you grow up?" He answered within a minute.
"If I could I would like to be a teacher or a Rosh Yeshiva." My response was
almost immediate. "That's beautiful, Binyamin, if you could do it we would
be very proud." But then I added the kicker. "Binyamin, how does a Rosh
Yeshiva make a living?" Binyamin was undaunted. "Zayde, you know that
passage in Pirke Avot which tells you what you have to be prepared to do
if you want to be a Talmudic scholar. Remember how it says: 'a dry slice of

bread, water in measure and be prepared to lie on the ground to sleep.' At first blush I thought he was joshing me but looking carefully at him I saw he was deadly serious. I won't claim that I snapped, but apparently I did become slightly agitated. "Binyamin, no grandson of mine is going to sleep on the floor and eat a dry crust of bread. That's how we started out in this family a long time ago in Europe. I have no plans to see it repeated."

The next day our son Jeremy told me that Binyamin was quite upset that I had become so agitated. Jeremy, who knows me better than his son, reminded me that I cannot kid around with him too much because he is such a sincere and dedicated young man. I told him I was not kidding, that it just came out.

In the light of all of this, I was looking forward to our trip northward. We were both seeing a renewal of our love for each other in a meaningful surrounding. No place more powerful than Safed.

Binyamin had been there before so he served as the guide. We go immediately to the grave of Shlomo Halevi Alkabetz, author of the L'Cha Dodi prayer sung by Jews around the world on Friday night to welcome in the Sabbath. In it Sabbath is pictured as a Bride and Queen, so that each Sabbath in the mystical community of Safed there would be both a wedding and a coronation. The Sabbath Bride would reign supreme and it has through this mystical masterpiece composed five hundred years ago.

Next to Alkabetz is buried one of the most powerful of pre-modern sages, Isaac Luria. He is referred to as Ari Ha-Kodosh. They were all part of that very special community in the hills of Safed in the Sixteenth Century. Luria, the Sacred Lion, was a charismatic rabbi and teacher who is often called the father of modern Kabbalah. As such his grave is a magnet for people from all over who come to spend some time reflecting on his life and his work. While I myself am far from a kabbalist, more mainstream in my religious outlook than esoteric, many of the insights of Lurianic Kabbalah have become part of the modern religious outlook. And I guess everyone in the world now knows that the singer Madonna pledges loyalty to Kabbalah.

We were not in Safed very long when Binyamin comes up with a boldly unexpected suggestion. He is, of course, deeply of the culture that produces people like Isaac Luria, Moses Cordovera, Alkabetz and the rest, and he now proposes that we climb a few hundred yards up the hill to the mikveh, or ritual bath, which was used by the Ari himself in preparation for the Sabbath and holy days. According to the lore, this mikveh and its bracing waters revitalized not only the physical, but also the spiritual being. Since the day was Friday what would be more appropriate for preparation for the Sabbath than to immerse ourselves?

One major problem. In the past, I have often accompanied both men and women to the mikveh because immersion is part of the conversion process. But personally I have never actually been in a mikveh. Time apparently was to change all of that. Binyamin is insistent.

A very special experience ensued. Fed by natural cold and clear running spring water, the mikveh now produces a tingling refreshment to the exertion of the climb. Now I begin to understand what many who have converted to Judaism have reported, the sense as they emerge of a new beginning to their spiritual life through the embracing effect of water.

I now recall that a fresh start is a keynote to Luria's Kabbalistic system. To "sing before the Lord a new song" was his daily prayer. It meant a constant striving for a deeper piety and higher goals. Each day, he writes, is a spark (nizotz) of God given to us to fulfill our purpose in prayer and deed. A good year is a collection of fully fulfilled days. When a day is complete, the spark burns.

Amazingly, Luria who died at the age of thirty-eight, only spent his last three years in Safed. Yet his name will always be identified with the hill city, and with the synagogue that bears his name, and with the mikveh. It was from there that his student Hayyim Vital took his teaching to Italy where it spread to all of Europe.

I have always been in admiration of Isaac Luria's basic doctrine, with Tikkun. Luria's teacher Cordovero had stressed in his works the olam hatohu, the world of confusion from which we must always struggle to extricate ourselves. So fragmented is our world that only God can provide us with the unity of soul and the purpose that we need. To accomplish that we leave the travail and disaster of this world which otherwise would envelop all of us. Not so, teaches the Ari Ha-Kodosh. The world of blemish can be repaired by the olam hattikun, by the order of elevated thoughts and deeds which can become the focus of our life. According to him, restoration and redemption await us by our cleaving to God in the performance of the commandments given to us and by attachment to our people. A tikkun, a step up the ladder of holiness, is possible at any moment. God's presence awaits our invitation to enter our life for, "the whole world is filled with God's glory." True, at this moment the world is unredeemed. But given intense kavannah, directed prayer, we can change all of that. To the Ari Ha-Kodosh the reality of God's presence was as certain as his own self, not an eerie evanescence but an exalted spiritual fact. He had experienced God directly; he felt after that, he needed no further corroboration.

Personally, I have always been inspired by the works of Isaac Luria, though the full comprehension and impact of them I would have to admit sometimes escapes me. But it is valuable to affirm the possibility of tikkun olam, of the personal and collective correction that leads to fulfillment. He points to the need to proceed tenderly up the ladder of piety towards holiness. That is exactly what Messianic stirring represents. A community collectively embracing the olam ha-tikkun and a reordering of our present priorities.

Of course not all of these musings came to me on that hot summer day in Safed. But I have gone back to the works of Isaac Luria many times. And while I still would not pretend to understand it all, aspects of his teaching do prod and inspire.

And I hope the same is true for Binyamin. That day still represents a memorable one, I hope, for both of us.

"And they both walked together."

SOVIET JEWRY RALLIES IN JERUSALEM, WASHINGTON AND NEW YORK

I T IS ONLY a short hop and a jump from civil rights for blacks to protest on behalf of Soviet Jewry. Suddenly it became a burning issue of the American Jewish community. The two comingle in my mind, a coin of two sides.

Not everyone agrees with this progression but I firmly believe that the Jewish involvement in integrating bus and restaurant and restrooms and water fountain facilities in the south gave us all the heady sense that we dare not let our people down in the time of trial. Rosa Parks and those students sitting in at lunch room counter, and those children attempting to integrate schools and being blocked, had all touched the heart of America and its Jews. In the Soviet Union they were being denied, imprisoned, beaten up and for nothing more serious than teaching a few lines of Hebrew to students or having a Bar Mitzvah in some back room. We had learned the hard way during the Holocaust to get beyond helplessness. We could not afford it again.

Soviet Jews were not being burned alive. But what we know now from Stalin's reign, from the Doctors' Plot, from Malenkov, Kruschev, and the rest of them, bitter pills were being fed the Jews through arrest, interrogation and denial of fundamental rights.

We decided to see for ourselves. A week in the Soviet Union was in the offing. Before leaving for the USSR, I received a tense call from my father. "I hear you are going to Lwow. Why? Don't you know that our family's name must still be on one of their lists? They could kill you. Why take that chance?"

"Dad," I responded, "you don't understand. I have my American passport. At the first sign of trouble, I whip it out and hold it up. They will evaporate." It was only half in jest. I honestly believed that the Russians didn't want to mess up cold war détente, which was then developing, over piffling matters. And I was right.

While we were visiting with my friend and traveling companion, Jack Rosenthal, in Leningrad in the late '70s, we came upon a small group of Jews in the park. They were pensioners and they were conversing in Yiddish. Of course that language was considered far too ethnic for the Soviet authorities. We asked these elderly gentlemen how come they were speaking Yiddish. One of them answered boldly, "Listen, let them cut off my head, it will still be speaking Yiddish."

By that time the Soviets were favoring the Arab countries. Though the Soviet Union voted to bring Israel into existence in 1948, they were now turning away from it in favor of oil and influence.

That day in the park was a Friday so we asked where we could go to synagogue that night. We had already been to the main synagogue of the town, but everybody was warning us that on Friday night and Saturday it would be crawling with KGB agents. They gave us the name of a private home where a service would be held and to make sure nobody was following us.

My friend Jack is a bold sort. He is a Holocaust survivor who has looked death directly in the face and has long ago transcended it. The prospect of going to that apartment did not scare him at all. On the other hand, seeing that I had been brought up in the padded precincts of Flatbush under the watchful eye of my parents, I was a little less comfortable with the prospect. But of course we went. Truth be told we went twice, once in the 70's and then later in the 80's.

And we didn't look at ourselves as exceptional or heroic. We were activists, like many others, on behalf of Soviet Jewry. And we were part of a group called The Long Island Conference of Soviet Jewry. It was begun by

Lynn Singer, an audaciously outspoken organizer of the Conference who had direct contact with many who had been refused exit visas in the Soviet Union. She was in constant touch with them.

Though we did not see ourselves as anything exceptional, we did take with us jeans and jackets, kosher salamis and warm pajamas – articles we knew would be useful to the Jews of the Soviet Union.

Once, when we came to Leningrad and proceeded to the main synagogue, we saw a small number of Jews assembled. It was impossible to make contact. There was a huge barrier. They were suspicious. KGB agents were all over. I said to the elderly sexton "Lynn Singer sent us." Jack dropped a salami on the table. It disappeared in a second.

All barriers dropped. Within fifteen minutes a tall bearded Jew appeared. He was the Lubavitch shochet who continued to work through the tense time. Later he came to Israel. He and others like him were the real heroes of that time.

As we got back to our hotel that day, getting ready to go to the synagogue, Jack suddenly blurted out. (Of course it was done with the realization that all the rooms of the tourists were bugged.) "I don't know why people talk against the Soviet Union. It is a wonderful place here. It is a workers' paradise." I collapsed in laughter. Of course Jack is a wealthy owner of apartments and real estate in New York and had no problem at all coming out with that.

The synagogue we visited that night was in a small apartment on the third floor of one of those nondescript Soviet houses. As we climbed the stairs, a number of doors opened and then shut rapidly. Was this the welcoming committee? Or other Jews happy to see us? Or someone looking to score some points by reporting us to the KGB?

At that time I for one was unaware that just talking to a foreigner, be they American or whatever, was already cause for suspicion and interrogation in the Soviet system. One of the comforting aspects of the Jewish religion is that Friday night services are pretty much the same all around the world. Everyone welcomes the Sabbath Bride with song and music. The custom is to turn toward the door at the last verse while saying, "Come Sabbath Bride, come Sabbath Bride." Turning that night, I hoped there would be no unexpected guest in the small synagogue. And there was none. Relax, I told myself for the hundredth time. Enjoy the peace of the Sabbath.

And we did. There were only a handful of worshipers present but they greeted us with a warm and welcome hand.

By the end of the service we were feeling quite mellow. Again down the stairs. More doors opening and again closing. By this time we figured it was a Soviet custom.

The next morning, however, it all changed. We were told by the woman in whose house the service was taking place that she had been visited by the KGB. They just wanted to tell her that they were watching. The neighbors had already scored their points.

At the service on Saturday morning my friend Jack, always looking to push the envelope, told the leader of the group that he had brought a rabbi from America with him who, of course, would be happy to offer a short mini-type sermon. The people's response was very polite. "We are sure that we would enjoy it. We know that he would enjoy it. But the KGB would not. And if they are not happy, we will suffer." The sermon that day went unspoken.

Having seen all of those restrictions imposed on Soviet citizens, in direct violation of their constitution, only sharpened our desire to become more deeply involved when we returned home.

Yet, denial of rights persisted.

Looking back, I just became aware of the paranoia, narrowness and insecurity of The Soviet system going back to our first visit in 1976. The Rosenthals, Jack and Elizabeth, Ricky and I landed in Vienna with the hope of driving a car into the Soviet Union, It was, of course, Jack's idea, who was not afraid of the bold gesture as far out as that might seem. In those days people did not just drive into the Soviet Union. Crossing the border and passing through customs required a major effort. We were detained for a number of hours. Of great interest to us were the border guards themselves. Heavily armed, dressed in the Soviet uniforms, with boots, they methodically went through our belongings. Out came the American magazines which they confiscated and which we saw them looking through. Apparently the pictures of the fashions intrigued them.

But the major memory of that day was that they put the car up on a lift and began examining its underpinnings, piece by piece. They were tapping everywhere, opening, looking, as if examining for some contraband or drugs. Before putting it up on the lift, they already had taken out the upholstery, searching, looking. They did put it back neatly, but all this took lots of time. They were not rushing, even though they saw us standing by getting more nervous and impatient by the minute.

Finally, I decided to go for it and I said to one of the officers, "could you tell me what you are looking for? Maybe I can help you." "Beebles." I thought he was kidding me. I had no idea what he was talking about until it occurred to me that he meant "bibles." We each had a few which we were claiming were for personal use. Then, as I remember it, he said something which I have never forgotten: "You Americans like to bring 'beebles' into this country. It is not allowed."

That memory has always stayed with me, especially in the light of the Soviet collapse sometime later. Here was the mighty Soviet empire instilling fear and awe around the world, causing revolutions and disruptions, and they were shaken by the possibility of the Bible being brought into their country. It was an awesome realization, sobering and yet enlightening It was a manifestation of what the rabbis had said many centuries before: "The Book is stronger than the Sword." And so it was!

So how does all of this relate to the American civil rights struggle? In 1964 millions of Americans and I among them, were witness to the televised beating of nonviolent protesters on the Pettus Bridge in Selma. John Lewis who had a strong commitment to non-violence, remembered later sensing, "We are only flesh. Black capacity to believe that a white person would really open his heart, open his life, to nonviolent appeal was running out. The reaction was instantaneous throughout America. This was obviously such a flagrant violation of all decency and justice that people poured out to Birmingham from all over the country. And it was very effective. Bull Connor, the city's Public Safety Commissioner, was hard pressed to justify the extreme measures that had been adopted. An electric cord of indignation shocked America into the reality of prejudice and racism."

Anyone who participated in that protest or in something similar to it sensed the reality of expressing an indignation at the corruption that needed to be addressed. I had a similar sense in Harlem in front of the Teresa Hotel, an exaltation of purpose and unity with brothers and sisters. That day in Harlem I had been the only rabbi. I certainly was there in that capacity. But it was an American problem that we were addressing. Religious Jews as much as anyone are under the imperative to "burn out the evil in your midst." Evil does not go away by itself.

Participating in those events of civil rights or Soviet Jewry was especially meaningful to me. Jews who were attached to their tradition and turned to it for motivation and courage were no longer helpless. Remembering those feelings from Ocean Avenue long ago, I sensed an invigorated strength and new hope for our future. This was social activism based on its spiritual wellsprings. It has always been a powerful combination.

Yet, denial of rights persisted.

It was getting to know people that were in difficulty and pain, because of the denial of civil rights that were coming to them, has always gotten to me. Whether it was in Birmingham or in Moscow or such as when I met Avital Sharansky in New York in the mid '70s. Her husband then called Anatoly, but now referred to as Natan Sharansky, was languishing in a Soviet jail for undesignated crimes of no account. He became the cause celebre of a worldwide protest movement on his behalf. After many years of difficulty, he was released to universal sympathetic acclaim as he crossed the bridge into freedom. At that time he revealed the most unsavory episode of his life. The Soviets had refused to release him because he knew, "state secrets." In his autobiography he writes that the greatest secret he had was that the Soviet Union had nothing to hide. They simply did not want people to know that they had nothing. That was their state secret.

In any case, Avital was a totally sympathetic person. Quiet and reserved, she had become religiously involved, thought of course that was not her background. She always wore a kerchief neatly arranged upon her hair as a sign of modesty. When I met her she was making the rounds of people who might be able to help by protesting the continued imprisonment of her husband. She became acquainted with many congressmen and senators and influential people. In the end, she met with President Ronald Reagan who spoke on behalf of her husband. Who knows but that the protests we started on the local level wound up influencing national and international policy. President Reagan spoke of being very moved by meeting her and listening to her story. I could well believe that since we had all been similarly moved.

Once in Jerusalem, with a group from our synagogue, I invited Avital to come to our hotel for breakfast to speak to our group. She was not the most forceful speaker in English but her warmth and her genuine feeling conveyed itself to our group and we were all moved by her words. On another occasion a few years after that, we were walking on a street in Jerusalem and I spotted her on the other side and went over to say hello. "You know I was just thinking about you," she said, "because Congressmen Jack Kemp and Bob Mrazek are in touch with me and want me to come to Washington for this demonstration on the steps of the Capitol. Do you think I should go?" We had been planning a similar rally at the Conservative Synagogue Moreshet Israel on Agron Street in Jerusalem which I told her about and wanted her to participate in. "But of course" I said, "going to Washington is certainly going to yield a greater and wider benefit, so I would recommend that." She went and we had our rally in Jerusalem which received wide coverage in the Israeli newspapers of those Americans who had come to protest the continued imprisonment of Natan Sharansky.

I knew what that rally in Washington would be like on the steps of the Capitol. We had participated in some such similar meeting the summer before. Washington in the summer is referred to as 'capital punishment.' It was a very hot day and as is my custom I was sweating profusely in the sun, even with my straw hat. I turned to Bob Mrazek, my congressman, who had already removed his jacket and said, "Look at Jack Kemp. He looks like he just stepped out of a shower." Much to my embarrassment, Bob turned to Kemp and said, "Jack, the rabbi thinks you look real cool." Kemp hastily responded: "It may look like that but inside here it reminds me of the locker room of the Washington Redskins."

Because of the many protests and continued involvement over a long period of time, I look back with satisfaction that when Sharansky was released, one of the first congregations he came to was the Shelter Rock Jewish Center. We had received notice that he would be coming only two days before. We gathered around as quickly as we could and something like twelve hundred people showed up on that Saturday night of Selichot to hear him. Selichot, which takes place on the Saturday night right before the New Year, is usually a quiet service at midnight. That year we held the most memorable Selichot service in our history.

The interesting aspect of Avital, his wife, has been that once Natan was released, after the spotlight being upon her for many years, she completely retreated into private life. They have children and she sees her role apparently as a wife and mother. She continues to be religiously oriented, though Natan has not gone that way. But apparently they have worked it out between them.

One of the other people that I met during the '80s was Yosef Begun, a man who was imprisoned in Siberia for a number of years. Altogether he was confined for something like twelve years. Interestingly enough, in Siberia they don't bother putting you in jail. The weather is harsh, the winter is forever, there is no place to go, and impossible to get out. One of the most dramatic aspects of Begun's incarceration in Siberia was a story he tells about his friend from Moscow one day showing up carrying two valises. The friend had traveled by train for days to reach him. The suitcases bore cheeses and meats and other delicacies. The friend had heard that Yosef was starving in Siberia. Yosef's eyes opened widely when he saw the cache. But much to his surprise, his friend refused to take a bite. He wanted

Yosef to be able to enjoy it and live on it for many weeks. Yosef still tells that story to this day with the relish of a real friendship.

In America Yosef was trying to win friends for the plight of Soviet Jewry and to continue the protests until they would be let go. One Friday, early in the morning, I received a call from Yosef who was in Manhattan. "Rabbi, I must speak with you. I can take the train out of Pennsylvania Station within an hour and will meet you. What is the name of that town again where the train stops? Is it Manhasset? I will be there by 10:15."

Friday is not a favorable day for rabbis to be receiving guests. It throws off the schedule and gets the mind out of its appointed task of getting ready for the Sabbath. But when Begun calls, it is very hard to say no. Meeting him on this cold morning we go into the coffee shop to warm up. "What would you like Yosef?" For a man who had spent so much time in jail, Yosef was in especially good condition. He had learned how to exercise even in jail. His eating habits obviously were regular. "I would like some potatoes, whatever kind they have. No coffee. Water." Not having exactly the same background, I settled on coffee and a toasted English muffin. But I always felt meeting with Begun that something was just about to happen and if it was not, he was going to make it happen. He always had that freshness of having just arrived, or beginning a new cycle in his life, replete with possibilities.

In fact, in April of 2004 I chanced upon Yosef in Jerusalem. He was all excited, a book that he had published in Russian had just appeared and there was to be an evening to celebrate and to hear from its author. Yosef invited me to the meeting which was to take place that night and asked if I would say a few words to the assemblage. As it turned out there were about fifty people present, all of whom had come from Russia during the last decade. I explained that my Russian was rather weak, so I spoke to them in Hebrew, lapsing on occasion into English, but I am sure they got my point. It was to say how happy and gratifying it was to be with them in freedom in Jerusalem. Their journey had been long and I am sure there are still many problems they faced, but looking back they have brought a great deal to the people and to the State of Israel. Israel, I said, is occupied with the problems of security and the safety of its people. That is the first duty of any government. But a Jewish state also has to be concerned with the culture, the religion and the spiritual life. Those of you who have come from Russia are much concerned about these issues. The appearance of this book is a reminder that the Holocaust is not very far away from you in history or in thought. So I mentioned that it was a great thrill for me to be there and to participate in the appearance of a book in Russian on a subject that I am very much taken up with and interested in. Begun beamed. The meeting continued in Russian. I politely excused myself and headed back for an evening with the family.

As I look back to that period of Soviet Jewry protest, my mind focuses on one extraordinary event, which did not turn out exactly as I had anticipated, but was memorable nonetheless.

The event took place on April 18, 1971 in front of the Kenilworth estate in Glen Cove, N.Y., that very spot a small number of us had been going to often to hold the morning service.

After our congregation and others had conducted that type of service for a month or more, someone came up with the idea of a joint rally on an open field facing the Soviet country estate. Our thought was that hundreds, perhaps even thousands, of people would demonstrate more eloquently than our freezing in the cold on an early morning.

The planning meeting was called to speak of publicity within the congregations and the community, as well as the program content that we would have on that morning. Someone came up with the names of the two most prominent activists on behalf of Soviet Jewry at that time. One was Dr. Abraham Joshua Heschel, my old mentor, and the other was Rabbi Shlomo Carlebach, the guitar-toting Chasidic rabbi who taught audiences to jump and dance and sing along with him. It was obvious that these two would be our best representatives for the occasion. But how would we get them since everybody turned to both of them? The vote was that I would call. It was a long shot but I accepted.

I hesitated strongly with Heschel because he had suffered a major heart attack a short time before. We had heard that he was recuperating nicely but it would be quite a drain to get him out here, have him speak and then get him back to New York. Deciding to jump in, I called. His voice sounded weak but he readily agreed. No hesitation whatsoever on his part. We were half way there.

Carlebach was not quite that easy. Shlomo was always flying off somewhere to give a concert. He was literally all over the world, as comfortable in Jerusalem as he was in London or New York with avid followers all over. Finding him was a major problem. But I left a message and lo and behold, a few days later he called back and was ready to come. We were anticipating a really enthusiastic event.

Imagine my shock and surprise a week before when I opened the pages of the New York Times one morning and saw that the mayor of Glen Cove had turned to President Richard Nixon to explain that a group of protesters had applied for a permit to come and demonstrate in front of the Soviet mission. This was unlike the daily group because we were anticipating a very large crowd. The mayor called upon the President to enlist the help of the FBI and the National Guard. I had no idea where this was coming from or why he had done it. But I did know that Heschel would be seeing the same article in the Times and was hoping concern for his health would not suggest to him to forget the whole controversy. I quickly dialed him up and when he heard who it was he said, "Yes, I have already seen the article. Don't worry, I don't get scared by things like that." Of course as a European who came to America during the Hitler regime, Heschel had seen and experienced many close calls and had, in fact, escaped from Poland shortly before the Nazi takeover on September 1, 1939.

The theory about the rally was to have it after Passover so that in all the congregations they would be announcing it. Theory worked, but the protest of thousands did not materialize. Too many people were scared away by the prospect of the National Guard and the FBI. Only a few hundred showed and at times it appeared there were more government officials present than people. I remember standing on the platform getting ready to introduce Dr. Heschel and looking up to see helicopters above. Everywhere there were suited plainclothesmen with buttons on their lapels and wires in their ear. You would think that a gang of desperadoes had descended upon that empty field. But instead, they were ordinary citizens concerned about the plight of their fellow Jews who were being denied their fundamental human rights. The rally proceeded.

When Carlebach was singing in his usual way, he was jumping up and down. The platform was shaking but the people were responding. It was a sing-along, a clap-along, there was jigging, swaying, a full identity. While he was doing this I remember Dr. Heschel turning to me and saying, "I don't understand it. His father was the most gentle and quiet scholar. I don't know if he would be able to explain it either." Nobody could explain Shlomo Carlebach. He was unique.

The rally did not produce large numbers of protestors. But the message got out.

Within the last decade culminating in 2008, two important biographical works appeared on the life of Abraham Joshua Heschel. The first was written by Edward Kaplan and Rabbi Samuel Dresner called "Prophetic Witness" which covered Heschel's early life in Europe. The second written by Edward Kaplan after Sam Dresner had died, was called "Spiritual Radical: Abraham Joshua Heschel in America, 1940-1972." I read these two books carefully, and especially the second volume, with a strong sense of identity since I had personally been involved in some of the events recorded. I had also written some memoir-style reminiscences of Heschel and was interested in seeing if I had gotten it right.

But here it was in these books spread before us, Heschel – warts and all. Having been brought up as a Hasidic "prince" he could be the warmest of persons and then switch and be indifferent and almost hostile. It was good for me to read these accounts of his monumental efforts in theology and social concern. It was a reminder that like all of us there were many human failings lurking behind the heroic visage. Heschel's heroism shone through.

Reading these books reminded me of events that had happened between us which I had long since forgotten. When I was still a student at the Seminary, I wrote a review of his book "Man's Quest for God" which I have often used in classes on Jewish theology in subsequent years. It is an excellent book with much that is incisive and contemporary even today.

This event took place on a Friday morning on a day when I did not have to go into the Seminary. The phone rang at 7:50 a.m. I was still asleep. "Hello" the voice said softly, "Fenster? This is Heschel." I stammered something and he must have sensed that I was still half asleep. "I thought I would tell you that I enjoyed your review." Click! End of conversation. Did I dream it? Or did it happen? I am convinced it happened!

Once I sent him a copy of an essay I wrote that had been published in a magazine, The Jewish Spectator. He wrote back promptly but tepidly. No comment or critique – just keep at it. It could be that is what it deserved. I kept at it.

RIDING THE LIRR WITH SENATOR TED KENNEDY

O NE DAY IN 1980, out of the blue, I received a call that Sen. Ted Kennedy wanted to meet with me and two other rabbis in Freeport. L. I. so that he could ride into New York City on the LIRR with us and have a conversation about important issues. It sounded like a hair-brained idea to me, but to the senator it made a lot of sense. He had decided to challenge President Jimmy Carter for the Democratic nomination that year. Carter had done some good things, but there was widespread disaffection even then. Kennedy bore a magical family name and had his own brand of charisma. In addition to myself, there was an Orthodox and a Reform rabbi.

Of course, a large detail of photographers and newsmen came along. And the next day, lo and behold, there was a picture in The New York Times of three obscure rabbis sitting with the aspiring candidate.

Kennedy's effort fell short and Carter was nominated. By pure chance we were at the Democratic convention the night Carter gave his acceptance speech. My long-time buddy Stanley Harwood, who was then the head of the Democratic party in Nassau County, provided the tickets for us.

What I do remember of the whole series of events was that Ted Kennedy was very well informed about what was taking place in Israel. Each of the rabbis naturally came prepared to give their own view of the situation. Ricky and I had returned a short time before from a summer visit. But Kennedy's insights were full of depth and information and I still treasure the hour or so together with him as we headed toward the city. I never knew how he had gotten my name or that of my colleagues, but I was always told that his staff work was exceptionally good. In this case, I am glad they came up with whom they did.

The whole experience was quite strange. There we sat the four of us huddling as best we could, to hear each other, with all these folks hovering over us. The whole exercise lasted an hour. We reached Penn Station, Kennedy was whisked away by his security detail, and we were immediately absorbed into the crowd. Our "fifteen minutes" were over.

DIVERSITY IN ACTION

A S IN EVERY synagogue there is always diversity of practice among its members. This came to a head at Shelter Rock during the 80's when some of our graduates of the Religious School came and asked if they could have their own service where men and women would be separated and a mechitza would be present. I was very pleased that they had come because the easier way would have been to simply bolt the synagogue altogether and meet in someone's basement. They were joined by their parents and the young people who originated this request were Eddie Roth, Michael Ripka and Alan Salzbank. And the Kormans, Abe and his sons Jerry and Billy. They had already picked out a room and promised to transform it into a beautiful small sanctuary. They wanted it to be called "The Underground Shtiebel," a catchy title which immediately caught on.

What to say, everyone liked the idea. Except that it had to be run by the Board of Directors of the synagogue before the room could be assigned. I anticipated that might not be so easy since there were members of the Board that might not take lightly to this new arrangement of offering a parallel service.

My intuition proved correct. As soon as I brought it up at the Board and indicated that it would enable many of our young people to stay within the walls of the synagogue in which they were brought up, the hand of a prominent attorney in our midst immediately flew up. "Let me remind everyone here that our constitution says that this will be a Conservative synagogue and this new arrangement is Orthodox." I felt a sudden deflation because he was citing a true fact, and in the minds of most people, if there is a separation of men and women that is the sure sign of an Orthodox synagogue. But having been associated with the Conservative Movement at that time for about thirty years, I knew not only its highways, but its byways, and I reminded the assemblage that at the Seminary itself, the flagship of the Conservative Movement, there were two services, just as had been proposed for us, one of which allowed for men and women to sit separately. This was done out of accommodation to some of the older professors who were accustomed to this style, either from Europe or from their earlier days in America. And so, I said triumphantly, "If it is good enough for the Seminary, it should be good enough for us. We can do this and it will not change our main service one iota, while we can demonstrate a much needed diversity for American Jewry."

And it is true that over the next years I received many a telephone call from rabbis who had heard about this arrangement and wanted to know how to bring it into being in their own synagogues. My answer was always the same: these were people who were part of our synagogue for a long time, young people who had been through our Religious School, who were not looking to make a statement in defiance of our Conservative practices, but they were only looking to feel comfortable within their own way.

The underground shtiebel operated for many years, but by then partisanship was becoming more pronounced and at one point its participants left to form an Orthodox synagogue very close by. And, to this day, we maintain good relations with them.

PROFESSIONAL SKILLS

D URING THE COURSE of my time at Shelter Rock beginning somewhere in the 1980's, I was asked to join a group of a half-dozen colleagues, all congregational rabbis, in fashioning and teaching a course at the Jewish Theological Seminary, from which I had graduated, to be called "Professional Skills." The Vice Chancellor who had gathered us told that the students complained that the teaching they were being offered was not adequate to what they found in the reality of congregational life. They needed more hands-on, down-to-earth reality. Actually, it was a cry that is heard in every professional school where the students feel the professors are too academic and not readying them sufficiently for the realities they are going to face day-by-day. It added a new dimension to what I had been doing and a note of contemporary excitement to my weekly work.

I found the students surprisingly bright, serious and anxious to absorb as much as they possibly could for their future careers. There were, of course, variations, but on the whole I would say that they were above average. There was, however, one area which I found on occasion hard to believe. These were ofttimes graduates of the best colleges and universities in America, they were after all, top grade students. But their writing was deplorable, filled with incomplete sentences, run-on phrases and not quite germane ideas. In fact, I once mentioned it to Dr. Gershon Cohen, then Chancellor at the Seminary, who responded that of course everybody knew that nowadays you could be a Princeton graduate without writing a straight

English sentence. In any case, I took it upon myself to try to correct some of their extremely discursive writings, believing that it was an important part of communication between a rabbi and his or her congregation.

One student in particular generally did not fit that bill. What he submitted to me was immediately recognizable as being outstanding. I didn't know anything about him so I asked him to stay after class on the second session of the year so that I could explore a bit. I asked him to tell me his story which went something like this. "I grew up in Princeton, N. J. and inevitably went to Princeton, but I was uninvolved in any Jewish activities. In addition, I had no idea when I graduated of what I wanted to do so I entered Harvard School of Education and got my PhD. there. (Parenthetically, I thought that quite a description of not knowing what to do). "In any case, I was at the end of my doctoral period and still had no Jewish connection. One day a friend said that he was going to a synagogue nearby, Temple Emanuel of Newton, Mass., and would I want to come with him. He said that they have a special Sabbath dinner for college kids and many came, young men and women, and that he had been there before and had a very nice time. The kids were good and so were the coeds. So I went. And that began a journey of meeting the rabbi, being invited back, getting involved, and lo and behold here I am today, a student at the Seminary."

In the meantime he had met and married Aliza Rubin, daughter of Rabbi Mel Rubin and Gila. Mel had been my roommate and oft-time study companion at the Seminary. I had the suspicion that he had taken my course because of the connection. His subsequent confession proved my initial appraisal to be on target.

That story stuck with me because I heard it repeated in one guise or another over and over again by many of the students who today are rabbis. Actually, the rabbinate today for men and women is a much more viable choice than back in the early '40s when I made my decision to go for it. Too bad my father is not around to see the kind of young people going into the rabbinate today. They may not be saints, but they're not schleppers either, and they are able to live their lives and do their work with dignity and ofttimes with a remarkable degree of success. When I look at these young people and talk to them, I see a confidence that I am not sure we had in my time.

People nowadays speak often about the leavening out of Jewish life, the watering down and some even speak about disappearance. And in terms of the numbers, a good case could be made to show that. But what those pessimists do not take into account is the intensity of those who have chosen to live their lives as authentic American Jews. They often serve as examples and models for those who will follow them. These are the young people who are going to the Ramah camps, the Solomon Schechter schools, the Yeshivas, getting for themselves an intense Jewish education. They may not become rabbis, but the majority of them will stay on to lead the Jewish communities of the future, and that may be even more important.

In any case, these were the young people I suddenly started to meet and teach. In addition I had during this period a whole string of Assistant Rabbis at Shelter Rock. It all started with my old friend Wolfe Kelman one day saying he wanted me to meet Michael Wasserman to consider him as an intern at the synagogue. He was followed by Lee Buckman an extraordinary, industrious and devoted young man, and then by other outstanding assistants, such as Elliot Pachter, Howard Stecker, Jeremy Wiederhorn, and David Weitzman. Their tenure at Shelter Rock varied anywhere from two to five years and I realized that if they were in any way symbolic of what was going on elsewhere, our future was going to be bright indeed. Subsequent events showed that I was correct and already they have made outstanding contributions to the emergence of the future of the American Jewish community.

FATEFUL DAYS
IN JANUARY 1991

W E HAD BEEN looking forward for a long time in 1991 to be in Israel for a few weeks. To be sure the atmosphere was tense, not only because there were incursions into Israel and even the beginnings of suicide bombings and other violence, but on the international scene it was a tense time with Iraq having invaded Kuwait. President George Herbert W. Bush warned Iraq and Saddam Hussein that if they did not retreat, the United States was going after them to force their withdrawal. It was a crucial moment in the history of the Middle East. Saddam Hussein was gassing not only his own people, but was now on a total rampage and the question was, could he, and would he be stopped, and who would be doing it. President Bush's action, to my mind, was heroic. In fact, he even announced the exact date when the United States would be attacking Baghdad.

It was in the middle of January 1991. His announcement came while we were in Israel, scheduled to leave on the 15th of the month which by chance was the exact date when he promised Saddam that his glory days were over. This announcement caused great consternation among the American tourists who were there at that time. Many immediately left the country. I remember going by the El Al building on Hillel Street in downtown Jerusalem and seeing the line around the corner for people anxious to change their tickets back to America for earlier dates.

Ricky and I decided that Saddam Hussein was not going to be our travel agent – the hell with him! We were scheduled to leave on the 15th and that is when we were going.

In the meantime, one of my former students called and asked if he could come over to talk with me about his situation. He was there with his family and his parents were calling from America urgently asking him to come back. He had little children with him and he and his wife were deeply concerned. It was an interesting problem, pitting his own desire to stay against the wishes of parents riddled with anxiety and fear. I assured him that whichever path he chose was an honorable one, and that even if he stayed no harm would be forthcoming. At least, so I hoped.

Needless to say, we were quite concerned about January 15th and how that would work out. Ricky and I were staying at our usual spot, the old Moriah Hotel, and when I approached the desk around noon time and asked for my gas mask, which was being distributed to the local population, I was told their orders were not to give them out until the signal was given by the Israeli government. This was not such good news for us because we wanted to go up to the Jewish Quarter to say goodbye to the family before leaving for America. But we thought it would be a good idea to have gas masks with us in case hostilities began before we had a chance to get back. We didn't get the gas masks, but we went to the Old City anyway.

Before we did, we received a call from El Al saying the flight that was supposed to leave at midnight was going to be leaving early so as to avoid potential danger. Much talk had been circulating about the scuds Saddam Hussein was preparing for Israel. So we ran up to the Rova, said our goodbyes, and packed up and got ready to go to the airport. The glitch was that the first three taxi drivers I approached refused to take us. Taxi drivers in Israel are of course a tough lot, but this was one moment when the tension even got to them. On my fourth try I approached a driver who used to be around the hotel often and told him I needed a lift to the airport. He was a no-nonsense type guy and said, "Of course, what's the problem? You think that momser's going to stop me?" And he didn't overcharge either – the regular rate. For years after whenever I would see this man, I would always go over, shake his hand and say thanks to him again. He never saw it as any great valor – just doing his job.

We left Israel with unusual sadness, leaving the family behind to who knew what fate. But Ellen and Jeremy had seven kids to care for. They didn't need us to make matters worse.

The flight was uneventful. Hours later as we approached the American shore our pilot announced: "I have just learned that the U. S. Air Force is attacking Baghdad." Total silence pervaded the aircraft. No cheers and no jeers.

And the predictions all proceeded to be true. That night the first scuds came into Tel Aviv. They bypassed Jerusalem for fear they might hit the Al Aksa Mosque which is just a few hundred yards away from the Jewish Quarter. And the scuds proceeded not only that night, but for the next week. After it was over, our daughter-in-law Ellen Fenster published excerpts of the diary she kept during that period in Newsday, a Long Island newspaper, in which she described in accurate detail what it was like living through those days – putting infants into a little carrier during an alert and getting her children, into their gas masks during a raid alert. She reported that her girlfriend was wearing a gas mask while she delivered a baby girl in the hospital. New life in the midst of danger!

The following is an excerpt from her article of Wednesday, January 30, 1991: "The sirens sound like nothing I have ever heard before. By the seventh air raid alert, we even took family photos of the kids – call it The Theater of the Absurd. Everything sounds like the sirens – the whistling of the tea kettle, the hum of the fridge, two jets flying overhead, my husband's snoring, the church bells in the distance, the mosque's call to prayer. At night in particular, when everyone is in their 'jamas, the silence itself rings in my ears, imitating the rise and the fall of the ominous siren. It's spooky.

"On a wintry gray day we eat dinner uninterrupted. When the sound of the kettle whistles in the kitchen, five of us jump in our chairs.

"Hooray for the Patriots! They should have called them Patriarchs. As parents we have been through a myriad of sleepless nights, nursing croup, bronchitis, upset stomachs, teething, night terrors, earaches, emotional traumas. We have even had a few nights with false labors. But nothing can compare to our night watches now. My eyelids are heavy and my shoulders ache. I am all-around weary. We are into day nine of this Gulf War. It seems so much longer. What will be? We wait and keep faith."

All that took place seventeen years ago. At this moment in time in 2008 the United States is engaged in what appears to be an interminable war in Iraq, finding insurgents and hoping to stabilize the situation. Many people curse the day that America got involved and went into Iraq. But personally, ridding the world of Saddam Hussein never brings regret to me. People rapidly forgot how he struck against the Israelis, who technically speaking were not even involved in his invasion of Kuwait nor in the war the United States was waging against him. Any excuse to hit Tel Aviv.

So when President George W. Bush decided to go after Saddam Hussein, it certainly was no disappointment to me. It is true that some bad mistakes were made, like not having an exit strategy, like not finding weapons of mass destruction. But in my mind and in the minds of many people who remember those scuds, Saddam Hussein himself was a weapon of mass destruction.

And so, personally, I have great pity for the soldiers who have been killed or wounded in Iraq, and I pray daily that it will be over soon. But to forget the insidious terror that this maniac killer foisted upon the world, is to be very short-sighted. The toll has been great, but thank God we have been rid of him.

Now, if only we could end the war!

AMERICA AND ISRAEL: THE TWO SIDES OF LOVE

M Y INTEREST IN the State of Israel no doubt goes back to the year I served as a rabbi in Haifa in 1962-63. Actually I had been in love with the country before I ever saw it.

As soon as I was old enough to hold a prayer book in my hand I had been saying, "Help us to rebuild, Oh God, Jerusalem, Thy Holy City, speedily and in our time. Blessed art Thou, Oh Lord our God, who in compassion will help us rebuild Jerusalem." In my grandparents' house, as in so many others, there was a picture of what then was called the "Wailing Wall" which was the focus of Jewish prayer around the world. The pious folk everywhere prayed in that direction. Beyond the biblical promise and the purchase of the Cave of Machepela by Abraham, there was the Balfour Declaration in the late nineteenth century emanating from the British Government and the purchases from the Arabs by many Jews privately and through the Jewish National Fund.

When I was a kid in elementary school, on the wall of our classroom there was a tree with leaves to be filled in for each child. For ten cents you were able to buy a leaf. And when the tree was finally completed, we were told that its counterpart would be planted in the Land of Israel. Every year there would be a box given to us for a two-week period to help collect monies for these trees. I remember going on the trains with my late friend Samuel

Schafler to collect money for this purpose. I learned from him the practice of taking the box and shaking it in the faces of prospective contributors. I was always slightly embarrassed to do it, but as long as he was with me I gained courage. The neighborhood we lived in was primarily a Jewish one but on more than one occasion we heard some slurring remarks. But we were strong enough in ourselves to disregard them.

In any case, like so many others I thought that each tree that we planted would have our name on it. When I first went to Israel in 1957 I expected to sit in the shade of my own trees. Looking back I could see how childish a fancy that was but at the time it was a disappointment. Subsequently, I was fortunate to participate in the planting of a whole forest together with many others and for that there are plaques and acknowledgments. By this time it doesn't matter very much, but it is a pleasure to see arid land that has become green and thriving.

When I think of the role of Israel in my life and in the life of other American Jews, I am not at all conflicted or embarrassed by it. As the son of an immigrant father I heard all of my life how badly Poland treated its Jews and what a marvelous country America is for its openness and possibilities. Our children who were growing up during the Vietnam period would often note some negative aspect of American intrusion into the life of other peoples and nations. Our son Jonathan was an honest conscientious objector to the war and received the status of "Conscientious Objector." While my father respected the status, he never could understand the sentiment that America was anything less than the best country in the world. He was joined in that sentiment by many others, including my late father-in-law Max Walfish who also had come as a youngster together with his parents and family and had similarly participated in the American dream.

So as long as I remember, I saw no contradiction between dreaming about Israel as a Jewish state and living in America as a democratic society. I know it sounds contrived, but it is true, I love America no less than I love Israel and even though we have a large segment of our family in Israel, I always look forward with anticipation to returning to America. Actually after spending the year in Haifa, we had the opportunity to remain. The guy who had gotten me into this whole thing in the beginning, Rabbi Wolfe Kelman, toward the end of our tenure in Haifa, came to visit us and we spoke one evening deep into the night. He offered us an opportunity to stay and not to worry about what the financial arrangement would be. Our American organization would provide the funds and we would be able to do the job as Rabbi of Moriah Congregation in Haifa.

For Ricky and me it was a very tempting offer. We too discussed it late into many nights. Many cups of hot tea and lemon were consumed. But we decided to turn it down. I have never been able to figure out to this day whether it was responsibility on our part or the wider sense of service that I felt calling me back to America. Actually, I had been given a sabbatical leave by my congregation in Jackson Heights; they had been paying a small part of my salary during that time and I did feel the obligation to return. There was also the personal factor that Ricky and I spoke about, which was that our parents were getting older and it just didn't make sense for us to be in Israel while they would be aging in America. Within the next years all four of our parents did pass on and it was a consolation at least to have been there for them as they began to lose their strength.

So we never moved to Israel, but because of the events we went frequently. Somehow or another I never understood the division in the soul between being an American and of being of the Jewish faith as much as I did when I was in Israel. In America I did not feel any inhibitions or hyphenation of my identity and still don't. But in Israel there was a kind of ease in Zion. This of course was in the so-called old days when the tensions between Arabs and Jews had not risen into the Intifada in 1980. But there were always incursions and incidents. I remember when I first went to Israel in 1957 my father called me a few weeks before going and said, "This is not the time to go – it is not yet totally safe." My response was, "Dad, I get the feeling it may be a long, long time before it is totally safe and I don't intend to sit around waiting for that time before visiting Israel."

TENSION IN CROWN HEIGHTS

EARLY IN THE 1990's I was asked to become the head of the New York Board of Rabbis. Truth is I shied away from those kinds of jobs, knowing they would take away from my personal involvement with the family, in the congregation and with my own reading and writing which I always enjoyed. But It was also a flattering offer to see if you can weld together rabbis from all the various stripes, from Reconstructionist to Reform to Conservative, to Orthodox and beyond. The New York Board is the face of the city's Jewish population which is, of course, considerable, to other faiths and to the Mayor and his administration of the city. Truth is I had no idea what it entailed specifically, but it seemed interesting enough to give it a shot.

To begin with, the installation. It was to be held at the Park East Synagogue on East 67th Street near Third Avenue, a central location for all concerned. I invited our congregation which responded enthusiastically. In addition, the New York Board has its own constituency made of all rabbis from New York and lay folk alike, so that the congregation was filled to capacity that day. Our family turned out, though by then my father had passed on and my mother was not quite up to it, being in her last declining years.

I was asked who I would like to install me as the President. Abraham Heschel was no longer with us and there was no other major religious figure that I really felt close to. But I had met Senator Carl Levin on a number of occasions and he had visited with us in our house in Roslyn, where we gathered many friends to introduce him. It is true he was a senator from Michigan, but he had a kind of global view of where American should be heading and how Israel could be related to, and was generally a thoughtful and kind man. Currently he is the Chairman of the Senate Armed Services Committee which with the war in Iraq has taken on a very important role. In any case, he agreed to come and to speak.

What the officials of the New York Board did not tell me was that they had planned an array of speakers prior to Senator Levin which occupied at least an hour and a half before we even got to him. So we got to listen to a parade of people, each of whom spoke well on diverse subjects of whatever happened to strike them as important. Most were giving me advice, some of which was even relevant. The other speaker that I had invited was Congressman Bob Mrazek, with whom I had formed a close working relationship since he was the congressman from our area. Bob was a giant of a man who had made a deep impression upon all of us for intelligence, candor and honesty. But he too decided to curtail his remarks due to the length of the program. From the experience I learned something. Namely, find out who else is going to be preceding you so that you can tailor your remarks accordingly. Try not to be the last speaker.

By the time my turn came, the last speaker, the audience was exhausted, as was I. But we were passionately involved that time in the plight of Soviet Jewry so I spoke of how that involvement for me and perhaps for American Jewry at large, was helping to ease some of the guilt of our Holocaust inadequacies. I added that all rabbis agreed with the Maggid of Mezeritsh who said that the air on the top of the mountains is clear and bracing, but that you have to be careful it does not make you lose your perspective or your balance. I prayed for the possibility of keeping my program focused, which was to extend to all who would take our hand, the opportunity of friendship; the Christian community, the growing Islamic presence and, of course, my fellow and sister Jews.

It didn't take long for the first crisis of my presidency to emerge. It came about with the outbreak of hostilities after a car that was accompanying the Rabbi of Lubavitch accidentally ran down a black youngster in Crown Heights and killed him. Rioting immediately broke out and before you knew it, it seemed liked the city was going to be enflamed. A few hours later Mayor Dinkins called the New York Board and asked us to host a meeting the following day on the steps of City hall. He asked that as many rabbis as possible be present, as he was asking the Black clergy and other Catholic and Protestant leaders of the city to be there as well. I was designated to be the chairman of the event. It was an event with a pressing agenda but without a program of the day. The Mayor would speak and anyone else that we felt would be appropriate.

To their credit many of my colleagues responded immediately: Rabbis Gil Rosenthal, Alvin Kass, Haskell Lookstein, Arthur Schneir and Abraham Foxman, head of the Anti-Defamation League. Many black clergy were there as well. Also, Protestant ministers and Catholic priests. But unfortunately I did not have a list of the names of people who were present. The outstanding part of the event was a negative one. The Jewish Defense League, the militant group begun by Rabbi Meir Kahane, who had already been assassinated, also heard of the meeting and they turned out thirty or so of their members. They were standing where the police placed them, one hundred yards or so beyond the steps of City Hall where the speeches took place, but their noise level was unbelievably loud. I don't remember exactly the words of their epithets but they were not singing "Happy Birthday" – that was for sure. But they kept up their stream of invective which caused great frustration amongst those who were running the meeting, which by and large was an effort to keep the lid on the rising violence in Crown Heights by appealing to the good sense of New Yorkers, that this was a stray unfortunate incident that did not speak of disrespect of any groups, neither blacks or Jews.

But by that time things had gotten so far out of hand in Crown Heights that a young Australian hasid by the name of Yankel Rosenbaum had already been killed. He had nothing to do with the event itself, but was caught on the street by a disturbed young black who proceeded to knife him. As far as I know that was the only death that occurred after the car accident, but it threw Black-Jewish relations in the city into an absolute tailspin, which took a long time to repair, if repair could ever be done.

One of the people that had been invited to the Crown Heights meeting was a friend, a Lubavitch rabbi whom I felt should be present because he was the heart of where the trouble took place in Crown Heights. Unfortunately, he did not show nor did I ever hear from him since.

One of the other results at that time was that the New York Board instituted a series of meetings with black clergy in the hope of restoring some of the earlier cooperative spirit. I remember a meeting at which one of the clergy spoke of the respect in the black community for the Jews and that this was a temporary disruption which could be overcome. The rabbi who spoke took quite a different tack, much to my embarrassment. His point was that all these kinds of meetings were to no avail until the black clergy was candid enough with their people to tell them to go out and get jobs and then many of the socio-economic strains would disappear. Instead of trying to bring our communities together this only helped to add fuel to the fire. A few black clergymen, when they heard this, got up and left the meeting. But it has always been the hope of the New York Board to work in favor of harmonious interfaith relations and to decrease racial tension.

Crown Heights was a big roadblock on the way toward racial and ethnic harmony. But the truth is that after 9/11, the focus shifted toward preventing terrorist action. And by then the columnist Tom Friedman's observation turned out to be accurate: "Not all Muslims are terrorists, but all terrorists are Muslims." Jews and Christians have lots of work to do in bringing racial and religious acceptance to American society. Most Muslims are working in America toward that goal as well.

In late 2009 we attended a tribute dinner to my long-time colleague Rabbi Jules Harlow. Jules is a talented liturgist, editor of the Conservative Movements many prayer books of recent vintage.

While there, Ricky and I were approached by Rabbi Joe Potasnik, now executive head of the New York Board. He pointed to me.

"Lifetime Achievement Award – it's just been voted." I had no idea what he was talking about.

It turns out that the award would be presented at Shelter Rock in April 2010. I was shocked and honored. Too bad my parents didn't live to see it. But for us and the family, a high honor and anticipation of a joyful reunion with old friends.

The event itself was splendid. Friends from all phases of our lives were present. Our American family did us proud. Actually, Jeremy was there as well, and spoke of his early years at Shelter Rock. I was hugely touched by Gabe's and Zach's remarks, which proved to me, that despite everything, they had been listening. But our son Danny really prepared a show-stopper, of perhaps seven or eight minutes of polished rhetoric and dramatic description. He told the story of my father coming to America following his brother's brutal killing on the street of Strelisk. He spoke of the pain of the Holocaust, and how it had affected me. And he told of my deep attachment and love for our family, the glue that has held us all together. Half-a-dozen of our grandchildren were present at that night, studding, for us, the evening with luminous stars. And at the end, Elissa led us all in a prayerful song for peace, both personal and collective. It all came together. It was a night to remember.

THE ROAD TO MOROCCO

K ING HASSAN IN the 90's had a positive view toward relations with Jews. Conditions in his country, the early beginnings of Islam militancy, prevented him from carrying out all his intentions. But he extended an invitation to the New York Board of Rabbis to send a delegation to Morocco, visit the Jewish communities in Rabat, Casablanca, Fez and Marrakesh, to meet with him in the palace. We were naturally very excited; he offered to fly us all first class, without a charge, on his airline Royal Air Morac. Kosher meals provided. We readily accepted and ran out and bought a sterling silver Kiddush cup to present to the King in gratitude.

There were eight of us in the delegation. In Rabat, at our first stop, the head of the community, a jovial Jew, received us warmly in his home, served us a delicious kosher meal punctuated by frequent alcoholic toasts.

Then, after an hour and a half, flushed, he stood up, asked us to do the same, formed a circle around the table and began to dance, Hava Nagilla, with obvious relish and enthusiasm. We happily responded.

Not every city or every head of the community repeated that precisely, but each was an approximation. We were stuffed and liquefied, but enjoying ourselves.

One of our stops included an evening at a Berber cowboy roundup, replete with prancing horses and jumping acrobatics, fire-eaters and all. The highlight was a special tent – there were many – set up for us with a kosher meal, the mashgiach arriving in person, with a note from the rav hamachshir, the presiding rabbi, attesting to the authenticity of the food.

So there we sat, eight rabbis from America, one woman journalist, with our host Jackie in an Arab country, enjoying the food and the entertainment as honored guests of the King of Morocco. How sweet it was!

The downside took place on Friday night as we were walking home from the synagogue led by our host. We were moving in pairs, the half mile or so to Jackie's house. Suddenly, we are approached by a man alone, who says something angrily in Arabic. Within a half-minute, a black sedan approaches, two people jump out and pull the interloper by the collar into the car and then speed away. We are all left puzzled. The whole event took no more than a minute.

Jackie later explained that a police car follows him home every Friday night, exactly for that purpose. He played the whole incident down, saying it happens infrequently.

But from then on we understood there is a problem of unrest in Morocco, as elsewhere, with Islamic fundamentalists. At the moment they are still under control under Hassan's son King Muhammad VI, who is also inclined to be friendly to the Jews. And of course Morocco is the best of those countries.

In the end, we were asked by the Jewish community not to visit with the King. Newspaper pictures are not to their liking. We sent the gift to the King and left with pleasant memories of the Atlas Mountains and our visit.

So Crown Heights was one big glitch on our New York scene. The anger, on both sides, of that period never fully receded. As for Islamic jihad, who knows where that will end. Presently, it is one of the major problems of our time.

The other big event of the early 90's was of international significance; the Persian Gulf oil producing countries, Israel's neighbors, Iraq, Iran, Lebanon, Egypt and Saudi Arabia. A dangerous neighborhood. It began dramatically with an invasion by Saddam Hussein followed by an American incursion. It is still a volatile situation.

Little did I visualize in the 1990's that our son Dan, the chiropractor in New York, would meet up with King Hassan's son, fifteen years later, that they would bond together and that Dan would help the Prince in matters of health. Danny explained to the Prince that their fathers almost met. The Prince liked the story. Someday I hope to have the chance to meet him. I look back at his father as a courageous man.

MEETING NELSON MANDELA

MEMORY OF THE fate of the Princeton Plan back in the Jackson Heights days had left me with an indelible impression of frustration. I guess I will never lose it but it seems so obvious that if people were only willing to take some step forward, a minimal effort, so much tension and racial rivalry could have been avoided. But of course those events took place in the '60s and that fragmentary and inconclusive time was hardly the last chapter which still has yet to be written in race relations in America.

Tensions have taken on more subtle ways in some cases but not always. Jews are deeply disturbed today by the renewal of anti-Semitism. Blacks still feel a lack of full civil and social rights. I live in a neighborhood that is open to everybody who can afford it, but I still don't see black faces on the street. Asians, South Americans, Africans, Israelis, often feel that they are not yet fully accepted as citizens, even in a polyglot America. Xenophobia is far from dead. The rise of Muslim militancy in some quarters and the war in Iraq have given new impetus to all of it.

A number of events took place in the early '90s that were dramatic reminders to me of the way we had come but still the way we had to go. In June 1990 Nelson Mandela was freed from a South African prison after twenty-seven and a half years. His coming to New York was a very special moment and brought out thousands upon thousands of people to greet him. The overwhelming fact about Nelson Mandela was how he managed to keep his strength and his sanity intact. To this day, he is still one of the more heroic and dramatic personages of the Twentieth Century.

Apartheid was crumbling when Mandela was set free and came to America. By chance, I was then the President of the New York Board of Rabbis, which is a group made up of eight hundred rabbis of all trends in American Judaism, Reform, Orthodox, Conservative and Reconstructionist. One of our primary responsibilities at the NYBR is dealing with the Mayor and the leaders of New York City to celebrate our diversity and our pluralism. At that time Mayor David Dinkins used to refer to it as a 'marvelous mosaic' that was New York.

A short time before Mandela was freed, Dinkins called for a special candlelight ceremony at the Cathedral of St. John the Divine in New York City. Six thousand people came and Mayor Dinkins delivered a stirring speech about our coming together then and the hope that we would continue that spirit into the future. I have before me a picture of the front page of the New York Post the next day which shows many of us gathered with candles on the pulpit of St. John. I am standing next to my colleague, the late Rabbi Marshall Meyer, and I see the then Attorney General of New York, Bob Abrams, and other notables, all holding the symbol of light in their hand. Emotions like that may seem in retrospect as purely ceremonial, without substance. But when you are present and the spirit of the occasion moves you and there are Christian clergy and Moslem clergy present, you do get a brief flash that maybe some day we can all work together in purpose.

At the beginning the announcement of Mandela's arrival was a source of disunity. Mandela had spoken of his friend Yasir Arafat and legitimized the Palestinian aspiration. At that moment he had not spoken much about Israel's ultimate legitimacy. His wife Winnie was an even greater problem not only within South Africa but beyond. Later they were to part, after ugly comments circled about her, and she moved on.

The Executive Committee of the NYBR convened. The question was whether we should take up Mayor Dinkins' invitation to be part of the welcome to Nelson Mandela. I had been invited to speak at the welcoming ceremony. I was to be the only Jewish representative. After debating for an hour or more we came to the conclusion that if I were to be the only Jew to be present, we simply had to go. Actually, after the long discussion I stepped out for a moment to go to the bathroom while the issue was still being debated. By the time I had returned, the conclusion had been drawn. I was going.

It represented quite a challenge. I spoke about the search for harmony in South Africa, in Israel and around the world. I spoke of the faith that we had to persist in the face of many difficulties, and to search for the will of God. We dare not yield to despair or defeat. "Some will fall and disappear, but we will stand up and be renewed in strength."

When I finished my remarks which were toward the end of the ceremony of welcome, Nelson Mandela approached the microphone to shake my hand and to thank me. It was a noble gesture on his part, since I was feeling like a distinct minority in that place and in that time. Actually, someone snapped a picture of it which appeared the next day in the newspaper. If you look carefully at the picture, you will see that Winnie Mandela looks very unhappy that Nelson was talking to me. She looked straight ahead with no hint of warmth on her face. Actually, she was pulling her husband away. But all of that was beside the point. I discovered that Nelson Mandela was a gracious and generous man even with people with whom he disagrees. I was overjoyed later on to learn that the State of Israel had extended an invitation to him to be a guest of theirs and I believe he did accept and has been there.

The TV stations carried much of the program live and by the time I had returned home we had received calls from friends and family that had seen it. But of course my day job, which was often a night job as well, had to proceed normally. That evening there was a meeting taking place at the synagogue which I attended. Thoroughly absorbed in the discussion, I barely felt a tap on my shoulder. It was the custodian who was telling me that there was a reporter on the telephone who insisted upon speaking to me. "Can't you tell him that I'm busy right now and he should call back later." He indicated that he didn't feel comfortable doing that. So I went to answer the phone.

"Rabbi Fenster, I want you to know that we are running a headline tomorrow in our paper" – this was the editor of an unsavory Anglo-Jewish newspaper, – "which says that Rabbi Fenster sold out the interests of the Jews to Mandela." I was shocked, but, knowing the newspaper, not overly surprised. "You can print whatever you want, but remember that you are subject to the laws of libel and if you don't print exactly what I said, which I am willing to FAX you right now, I no doubt will be contacting my lawyer tomorrow." The article was not printed and I never heard from them again. So much for the integrity of that paper.

Mandela's early rejection of the ideals and the reality of the State of Israel did not come as a total shock to me. I had read enough of history to know that some of the greatest forces for freedom and independence and democracy could not quite understand the national sovereign aspirations of the Jewish People. No less a personage than Mahatma Gandhi, who fought so hard for the independence and equality of people in India, was opposed to Jewish nationalism. It evoked a classic correspondence between himself and the famous Jewish thinker Martin Buber:

"For the Bible tells us that once more than three thousand years ago our entry into the land took place with the consciousness of a mission from above. The meaning was to set up a just way of life. These were not just practical laws thought out by wise men but they found them to be the set task and condition for taking possession of the land. No other nation has ever been faced at the beginning of its career with such a mission. Here is something which there is no forgetting and from which there is no release. At that time we did not carry out that which was imposed upon us; we went into exile with our task unperformed. The command has remained with us and it has become more urgent than ever. We need our own soil in order to fulfill it; we need the freedom to order our own life. No attempt can be made on foreign soil and under foreign statute. It cannot be that the soil and the freedom for fulfillment are denied us. We are not covetous, Mahatma; our one desire is that at last we may be able to obey. You who know of the connection of tradition and the future should not associate yourself with those who pass over our cause without understanding or sympathy." Despite Buber's eloquence, Gandhi remained unmoved. He no doubt was a great force for his people, but not for mine.

And so it is with many progressive people around the world. They understand the desire for national sovereignty on the part of every people. But they still fail to accept the rightful existence of the Jewish People in its ancient land. But when I think of Nelson Mandela and others like him, I have that sense that their view has expanded and brightened and hope that they understand today more than in the past.

In reading Mandela's autobiography, I was to learn the true greatness of the man. On February 9, 1990, Mr. F. W. DeKlerk, President of South Africa, summoned Mandela from his jail and told him that on the next day he would be released. Shortly before, DeKlerk had begun to dismantle the apartheid system by lifting the ban against the African National Council of which Mandela had been head. Called into deKlerk's office and told of his release, Mandela responded in a very strange and unusual way. He asked for an additional week to remain in jail, because he was afraid that chaos surrounding his coming out after twenty-seven and a half years might incite his black supporters to actions which he didn't deem advisable. DeKlerk refused his request and Mandela was let go the next day from Victor Verster.

What happened then was truly historic. After his release he was flown to Soweto, the city of black urban South Africa, of tin shanties and dirt roads. Most homes had no electricity or running water. An enormous crowd of one hundred thousand people awaited him in a stadium. The moment was rife with tension as they awaited the words of their leader.

Later he wrote about it: "I knew that people expected me to harbor anger toward whites. But I had none – we didn't want to destroy the country before we freed it. We didn't want to drive the whites away and devastate the nation. 'Whites' I said, 'are fellow South Africans and we want them to feel safe and to know that we appreciate the contribution they have made toward the development of this country. We must do everything we can to persuade our white compatriots that a new non-racial South Africa would be a better place for all.'"

This is how Nelson Mandela spoke the day after his release after spending a quarter century and more in jail. He was advocating equality instead of hostility between blacks and whites. If only other warring peoples could hear such a message and act upon it. For me, Mandela will always remain one of the heroes I have been privileged to meet in the course of a lifetime.

HIGH HOLIDAYS
AT SHELTER ROCK

LOOKING BACK IT seems to me like the years whizzed by. I am not alone in feeling that because many people tell me they can't recall where all the years went to. I guess that is Tevye singing, "When did she get to be a beauty, when did he grow so tall?" It is a universal feeling and I certainly cannot put my finger on what I did all those years, though of course I know exactly what was happening.

Already in August I was beginning to think of the High Holiday period. There were a number of summers where we spent time within walking distance of Tanglewood in the Berkshires. We loved going to the concert rehearsals on Saturday and then ofttimes to the performances on the following day.

During the week we would enjoy immensely the Tanglewood students who were there for the summer, promising young people with what they and everyone hoped would be a great career ahead of them. Once while talking to a Fellow, we discovered he was a Russian prodigy and had already made a number of solo appearances and felt extremely fortunate to have been chosen to work with some of the leading conductors of our time.

One summer while we were there we had a singular memorable experience. The house we rented was next door to a violinist in the Boston Symphony Orchestra. One Friday morning he came over to the house to tell us there was going to be a closed rehearsal later that day and Leonard Bernstein was going to be the conductor. He said that only about a half-dozen people will be admitted but that he could arrange for us to come. We jumped at the opportunity. Bernstein was already in his declining years and he died a year or so later. He had gotten heavier and could not move with the ease and grace which he formerly exhibited. But once on the podium the old fire came back. Since it was an informal session, he came out clad in a warm-up shirt with the Hebrew word "Harvard" emblazoned on it. Somewhat apologetic he mentioned that he had just received it as a birthday gift. It was quite an experience listening to him instruct the players as to exactly what he wanted, even though he did not interrupt frequently. He was direct and forceful, but he was also soft and loving. Of course when we went back the next day to hear the performance we tried to listen for those spots where he had interjected. I never left a Bernstein performance feeling unrewarded.

There were others we came to enjoy – Yo Yo Ma, Leonard Fleischer, Marin Alsop, Garrick Ohlsson. Many of these people appeared in something that Tanglewood was noted for, those "walks and talks" on a weekday afternoon. And so we heard Marin tell of her relationship to her mentor Leonard Bernstein, and how demanding and caring he was. To this day, whenever we can we try to get to Tanglewood in the summertime because it has such a fond place in our memory.

These interludes were preparatory for the High Holiday season that shortly followed them. Those holidays are an especially intense experience for the rabbi and I guess for the family as well. Our son Jeremy remembers that both he, Jonathan, and I, went right before the holidays to Shea Stadium to watch the Mets play. He claims that in between the innings I would pull out some papers and notes and start working on them for the forthcoming holiday. I cannot say I remember doing that, but I also cannot say that I did not. I may have been watching Mike Piazza, but it could be I was thinking of Rabbi Amnon of Mayence. In any case, I am happy that he remembers my taking them to Shea Stadium. My father was never able to take me because he had not the foggiest notion of what baseball was about and even less interest. He once had some business dealings with the father of Sid Luckman, the famous football player and he asked me if I had ever heard of him. These names meant nothing to him, but he was always interested in what impact they would make on me.

In any case, before the holiday season would begin, there would be many weeks of intense preparation. The service had to be gone over, again and again, and sermons had to be put together and introductory remarks to many of the prayers and melodies that are used.

During those days of preparation it seems like you are living on a different planet. You go through the mechanical part of eating and sleeping and doing whatever else you have to do, but the mind is focused on the 2,000 people that are going to be there, listening to make sure you have something worthwhile for them to hear. Early in the 1990's I remember having to be up at the Jewish Theological Seminary two or three days before Rosh Hashanah. As I was entering its big iron gate at the front, I chanced upon Ismar Schorsh then the Chancellor of the Seminary. He looked at me for a moment and said, "Myron, you look so calm right before Rosh Hashanah. How come?" That may have been the way I looked on the outside, but within the fire was burning.

But after the rigors of Yom Kippur, talking the whole day without eating or drinking, we always welcomed the holiday of Sukkot which follows immediately thereafter. The contrast could not be more stark. Sukkot with its holiday booths and fruits is a colorful comfortable time. We always had a succah on our back porch which Ricky and I decorated shortly before the holiday began. The most impressive part for me and I think for the other members of our family, was that on the first night, which for some reason or other was usually chilly in late September or early October, a thick pea soup was on the menu, with cut up frankfurters delectably spotting it. That was enough to make us look forward to the holiday for the whole year.

Then again at Passover time, we tried to bring the whole family together and often it worked. Jonathan would often bring his friends Bob and Albert and they would join right into the festivities together with the rest of us.

Looking back upon them, these were high moments which dot our calendar year, along with our twice-yearly visit to Israel to see the rest of the family which was proliferating rapidly. First there were the nine children to Jeremy and Ellen, and then their grandchildren started to arrive. There were always new faces to be learned and names to be memorized and, of course, pictures coming constantly. I always say to Ricky that is the reward for starting early and for being able to hang around. Looking back at all those years brings many happy memories to mind. One of the outstanding aspects for us was that when we decided to retire, the synagogue generously offered to make us a farewell party. I was not exactly sure how Ricky and I would handle it, but we did not offer objection. It always seemed to me that sometimes it is better to just sneak off into the night. But of course we did not have that opportunity open to us.

The actual evening was a smash. Sen. Chuck Schumer, who had been our congressman in Brooklyn and also had gone to Madison High School, was the guest speaker. Our family turned out in force and I hope a good time was had by all. In the pictures we have we see enthusiastic dancing, and great spirit, what they call in Hebrew "Ruach." Our old high school friends were there as well as people from all parts of the thirty-six years we had been at Shelter Rock. At the same time a tribute journal was printed with letters from great notables, like the President of the United States whom I had not met, but there were many people whom I knew quite well. Ricky and I still look through it with delightful enjoyment.

By then I had been contacted by Temple Israel of Great Neck the day before this great party. We were leaving for Israel shortly thereafter and while Rabbi Waxman was quite ill, he was still able to go to the synagogue on Saturday morning. We left our number in Israel in case we were needed. Ten days later we got the fateful call that he was sinking. A few weeks later we were installed at Temple Israel and I began to serve as their Interim Rabbi.

All of it seemed slightly miraculous, since all the parts came together. But I began to hear that many people at Shelter Rock thought this was all planned out before and that I retired so I could move on to Temple Israel. I was shocked when I first heard these remarks and then became angry and indignant because we never had any master plan like that in mind. It was very gratifying that it worked out that way, but who was smart enough to plan it?

As a result, despite the accolades and kudos at the farewell party, I did not feel that comfortable showing up at Shelter Rock. For many months I went only sporadically and with great hesitation. Ricky, as usual, was telling me all along to forget it and to proceed as if nothing had ever happened. I may be the rabbi, but she is the saint in the family and I found it very difficult to accept her advice, but with the passage of time it has become much easier and by now when I see many of the people whom I have known for forty or more years, I am really overjoyed to see them. That line from Henny Youngman very often comes to me as explanation: "I am happy to be here; I am happy to be anywhere."

ON MY WAY TO THE HAMPTONS

Chapter One

THE TIME RIGHT before retirement in late June 2002 was an exciting one. After a long period of service, I was looking forward to an extended vacation without the specter of responsibility. There was anticipation of rejoicing in the sense of having the weight lifted off the shoulders. Free at last, free at last!

Actually it was the day before this long awaited retirement that I received a call from Steve Markowitz. I didn't know him at the time, but he immediately identified himself as the President of Temple Israel of Great Neck, the largest Conservative congregation on Long Island. He told a sad story of their Rabbi, Mordecai Waxman, who was now desperately ill. Since the holiday period in September was inexorably upon them, they were concerned about their rabbinic leadership. He had heard of my retirement and was wondering if I would be available for their twelve-hundred-family membership. We agreed to meet briefly the day before I was to leave on vacation, and when we did I told him where I would be and how to contact me if something dramatic occurred. We left it at that.

Riding home after the meeting in Great Neck, which is only a ten minute drive from where we live, I asked myself the question: did I really want to do this? It is very flattering, but it is going to require a huge amount of energy and commitment. If I have that, than why am I retiring? And if I don't, why bother?

At the retirement dinner, I mentioned that I did not feel dried out or blown away, it was just time to move on after almost four decades. Shelter Rock had been good to me and I had seen the synagogue grow from a fledgling congregation to one that was recognized in Nassau County as a formidable institution. It had become everything I had hoped for. Besides, truth be told, I always liked the image presented by the prophet Jeremiah, of the fire that remained in his bones after a long period of involvement and even disappointment. There are fires that even disenchantment do not quell.

Little did I know it then, but that conversation in Steve's office in Great Neck, was to be a harbinger of the next years of my life. The day we returned from vacation was the day that Rabbi Waxman died. We stayed in Great Neck for a year and a half, at which time my former assistant Rabbi, Howard Stecker, became the senior rabbi of the congregation. I knew him as a brilliant young rabbi, and subsequent events have born out his great promise.

After that, it seemed that one experience turned into another, and before I knew it I had served the Holocaust Center of Nassau County in Glen Cove, Temple Shalom in Brooklyn – which happened to be very close to where my wife Ricky and I had gone to high school at James Madison: Old Westbury Hebrew Congregation, and finally to a year out in East Hampton, all the way out at the eastern-most tip of Long Island.

This last stop, proved to be an exhilarating, challenging, and ultimately rewarding experience. All five of these positions opened up an entirely new world to me. It was as if I had undergone a career change. While in fact, serving as a Rabbi in various congregations requires repeating the same pattern of behavior and involvement, each has its own uniqueness and individuality.

Someone once asked me why we say the same prayers over and over again. My answer was that the prayers are the same, but that we change everyday, and that therefore the interaction brings a new result. The same with congregations.

Before receiving the call to become Temple Israel's Interim Senior Rabbi, it had been my intention to begin a memoir of what had happened to me early in my life to propel me toward rabbinic service. The five year detour deterred me from accomplishing the writing of the memoir. Now, I am attempting to fill in that five year gap. It requires a backward glance.

The home I grew up in was not an overly religious one, though there certainly was respect for tradition. My father had come to America from a small town in Poland in 1920, and still carried the taste and flavor of the European Shtetl. He brought with him to this country a huge ambition, unbounded energy, and an insatiable desire. He also carried in steerage with him a sense of guilt that he was leaving his whole family behind.

My Dad's father was religious in the fervent European style. My father never rebelled against that, and always carried with him a great respect for learning and piety. That's where I come into the equation. Our home was not a Sabbath observing home, but the idea that his first-born son would be ignorant of Biblical and Talmudic texts, and not experience the depth of identity that he knew as a youngster of being a Jew, was something that my father could not abide. As a business man he did not have time, he felt, for regular synagogue attendance or fixed periods of study. In America, he easily segued his way into a different mode of life.

The style in which my father had been taught was one of memorization. Until the end of his life, at the ripe age of 84, he could still quote passages of the Mishnah and of the Talmud that he had learned as a youngster in the Cheder, that multi-aged one-room schoolhouse that he attended until age 13. At that point his father told him that he needed to work and that he had to assume duties at the family mill.

My mother on the other hand, born in America, spoke of my becoming a doctor from my earliest age. It was for that reason that she suggested that I take Latin when I enrolled in High School, a language for which I have no ear and even less interest. Later on in college I took Greek, which also scored absolutely nothing with me, nor me with it.

The language that I did connect to from a very early age was Hebrew. Its sounds were always mystical to me, a lilting song in my head. I can remember as a youngster speaking a clumsy Hebrew, but persisting nonetheless. The school I attended, the Yeshiva of Flatbush, had the religious subjects taught in the morning and the secular subjects taught in the afternoon. I am not sure of the theory behind this teaching methodology; however, I do know that in my mind at least the Judaic subjects were as important as those after the lunch break.

Our morning teachers encouraged us to speak Hebrew all the time and taught us without uttering a syllable of English. This was to be a tremendous help to me later on when I became a Rabbi in Haifa in the 1960's. It took a little while to get me up to speed, but the basic groundwork was already there, and since Modern Hebrew has the biblical text as its background,

I was able to construct a passable Modern Hebrew in a short time while serving the congregation.

At the Yeshiva of Flatbush they did a very smart thing to encourage our further facility in the language. There was always a "Hafsakah", or recess, every morning for twenty minutes, when we would go outdoors and run around with fervor. But we were told to speak Hebrew even during the recess. Those who did, received a special reward. It was a button the size of nickel, and on it was the Hebrew letter "Ayin" which stood for "Ivrit", which meant that you were a Hebrew speaker. All I can say is, that if you're ever at my house in Roslyn, remind me to show you my "Ayin". It is still a prized possession.

I understand fully how the mystics in Judaism declared that God created the world in Hebrew. "'Let there be light' and there was light". This early exposure to a religious environment played a crucial role in my life without my being aware of it. The truth is that I was an indifferent student, mostly sitting in class and daydreaming. Why I couldn't concentrate, I've never understood. I remember once in the fourth grade after the first or second month of class, I realized that I hadn't the faintest notion of what was happening. I made a determined effort to follow the teaching of that day, and concentrated all of my efforts to understanding what was taking place. It was a dismal failure, and after an hour or so, I decided to turn it off and go back to my daydreams.

How I got through those classes I really don't know. But I do remember my parents coming back from open school night, saying that the teachers told them that they sensed a tremendous potential for learning, but that they couldn't seem to get through. And they were right. It took me many years to figure out what I wanted to do and wanted to study, but once I came to the realization of what that was, thank God I brought unflagging devotion to it. To this day, if a whole day goes by without some amount of time spent on sacred textual pursuit, I go to bed at night frustrated and unhappy. I try to minimize the numbers of such days.

What I did gain from those years, when learning was not my forte, was the strength of the indomitable spirit of the people of which I was a part to survive. Foremost was my father's ability to survive and remain productive: He had lost his entire family at the hands of the Nazi barbarians. As my life unfolded I am in increasing awe of that ineluctable fact. The school I attended, did not emphasize ritual piety as much as they did the return to what was then Palestine, on the part of those pioneers they called Halutsim. Their songs and their stories stirred my imagination. They too were part of the survival system. Our music teacher was a man by the name of Moshe Nathanson, who filled us with the same zeal for singing these songs as he had. To this day, imbedded deep in my consciousness, are the melodies that the pilgrims sang as they brought the first fruits to the ancient temple of Jerusalem. I owe to him and to that school, my lifelong passion to see the Jewish people return to their land and to be redeemed by it. Unfortunately, he was not able to do much with my tonelessness, which has persisted to this day. But don't tell me about that because I don't want to hear it. In my mind, musical intention is more important than musical prowess.

To give a more accurate picture of what was going on in my life at that time, I have to add now a further dimension. From my earliest years, I was always attracted to playing football on the street in the fall and winter, and baseball in the park later in the spring. I lived for those moments, when I would throw my books into the house and run out to pass, block, and catch in the touch football game that was always taking place on our block. We stopped only when our mothers beseeched that it was time to come home, or when darkness fell, whichever came first.

One of the reasons why I was never much at homework was that by the time dinner was over, I must have been exhausted from the long day and its activities. But I went to bed happily every night.

In the spring, I recall vividly coming home once when we were living on Ocean Avenue in Brooklyn. In one fell swoop, I dropped my books and picked up my catcher's mitt, dashing out of the door for the local park. It bothered me that I was already late, because our school did not dismiss until 4 pm, and it was even later when I finally arrived home.

On this one spring day that sticks in my memory, I checked to make sure I had 3 cents with me, which was the stake of the game against the opposing team. I was concerned, lest I would be late and someone else would be starting in my position. Within a few minutes, however, I was behind the plate, stopping fastballs with my glove and my body. Looking back, I was never put off by the special difficulty of being a catcher. I always enjoyed the challenge. And over the years I have always followed the catchers on my favorite teams with appreciation and admiration: Bill Dickey, Ernie Lombardi, Roy Campanella, Gary Carter, and Jorge Posada. Nowadays, my leg aches even when I think about bending down behind the plate, but the glowing memories of those early days are still with me. I was not outstanding in my scholastic work in school, and truth be told, I was no star on the diamond either. I would get a hit every now and then, but there was no connection whatsoever to the legendary Babe Ruth.

Mentioning the Babe, I have a memory of our school taking us to Yankee Stadium in the waning days of the Babe's career. I was very young, but the impact of the experience was enormous. Maybe my identifying with him had something to do with our body-types, which allowed me to dream of someday being the "Sultan of Swat". It never happened.

To indicate my happiness at being at the Yeshiva of Flatbush. I am going to share one other anecdote which is slightly embarrassing. It is hard even for me to believe that as a youngster I was a picky eater, since nowadays I can barely find a food that I don't like. In Yeshiva we were supplied everyday with a hot lunch, and while I don't remember what was served, I do remember that I didn't like it. Again, I am not proud of this, but I used to take two pieces of rye bread, and put mashed potatoes with butter between them, and eat two of them for lunch. Then, surprise! I was no longer hungry. Ever since, I have been trying to shrink those fat cells that expanded during that time, but I still like mashed potatoes with butter, though nowadays I have them about once a year.

One other aspect of those early years had a tremendous impact upon me. That was the Sabbath Junior Congregation that was held each week. As I recall it, there were literally 200 or so students who would show up every Shabbat morning. No doubt there was some teacher or instructor with us, but I don't remember the supervisory aspect of it at all. What I do remember was that I had been elected *Gabbai*, to which I suppose the closest English translation would be master of religious ceremonies. Of all the titles that I have ever held in my life, to me this was the most important. I remember running to the Junior Congregation every Saturday morning. I couldn't wait to get there; it was so much fun. Not to mention gratifying. Looking back now, if you ask me where I got "the bug" to be a Rabbi – for sixty years – I would answer without equivocation by being the *Gabbai* of the Junior Congregation at the Yeshiva of Flatbush, in 1937.

The trajectory of those earlier years is what led me into long rabbinic service. There had never been a rabbi in my family before but I did feel "called" at an early age – not by any outside force but by a strong inner prompting to serve a remnant Jewry. The helplessness of my people during the Holocaust disturbed me deeply. I was resolved to try to do something about it. Thirty-six years at Shelter Rock, enjoyable, productive, but it was time to move on. By the end of 2002, I thought I was bringing the active phase of my rabbinic life to a close. Finally I would have freedom of responsibility, which meant time to study, reflect, and perhaps even write. It all sounded good to me.

The call from Steve Markowitz at the end of June changed all of that. Shortly after arriving in Israel, he called to report a worsening situation with Rabbi Waxman. We returned to America at the beginning of August, and immediately plunged into our new situation. Even though it was summer, the usual off-period of synagogues, Temple Israel had a full agenda of Bar and Bat Mitzvahs in August.

On my second or third day at Temple Israel, the phone rang with a distraught mother on the other end. Her son was to become a Bar-Mitzvah in two weeks, and he was not prepared. None of the synagogues regular tutors were available. The other Rabbis were on vacation. She apologized and explained that she understood that as the senior rabbi it was not my job but she was desperate not knowing where to turn. I told her to bring her son to my office immediately.

Temple Israel of Great Neck had a heavy load of confirmands during the year, some eighty or more. Therefore, the weekends of August were often used. Frequently the families were coming from Florida or California in any case, so it turned out to be a convenient time for them. This boys particular family was Sephardic, Persian, with roots in Iran. Large numbers of them had come as immigrants to America, and had settled in Great Neck. These family celebrations were great occasions of joy. There were four-hundred such families in the congregation, and I found them easy to connect with and warm and appreciative of anything that was done for them.

What I did with the young man studying for his Bar-Mitzvah was quite simple. We went over the biblical portion of the week together, and I pointed to two or three themes that he could possibly comment upon. They were all interesting and provocative. I asked him to go home, pick one, and write a few sentences about it. I was very fortunate; he was a bright young man. Three days later, he returned with what was almost a finished product. We touched it up a bit, and he was ready to roll.

On the day of her sons Bar-Mitzvah, the once distraught mother was now radiant. She went around telling anyone who would listen, what a brilliant Chacham – or rabbi – Temple Israel had brought. At first I tried explaining to her that I had not done anything extraordinary. But before long, I admit, I gave up the denials and let her spread her gospel of exaggeration. Of such are rabbinic legends built.

When you're the new kid on the block, however, sometime ordinary events become tense and more difficult. This is what happened that year, before the most joyous holiday of Simchat Torah. That is a time in the synagogue when all of the barriers are removed, and singing and dancing with abandon is encouraged. The youngsters will tell you that it is the most fun they have in the entire year. We circle the synagogue with all of the Torah's that we have, and jump up and down with them in joy.

That year, there was only one problem: there were hundreds of youngsters who gathered, few of whom I knew since I had just arrived at Temple Israel. I was expected to bring some order out of the chaos which the celebration usually engendered. The cantor and another rabbi withdrew to a smaller room to do similar things with the adults. I was left to fend for myself. I had no idea how I was going to be able to finesse a celebration that would at once be disorderly and fun.

I am happy to say that we found a formula by enlisting half a dozen of the Men's Club to assist and to line up the kids as we began to circle the synagogue. There were moments when is skirted close to disaster, but by the time it was over, and the kids went home happy it was pronounced a success.

The year and a half in Great Neck turned out to be challenging but fun. And I proved to myself, and to Ricky, that despite my advanced age I was up to the challenge. There was still some fire left in the bones.

At first, however, we weren't so sure. Every Saturday morning, there were from 600 to 800 people present in the synagogue, many of them visitors celebrating a special occasion. I was excited by the number, and I responded accordingly. Someone once commented to me that when I gave a formal sermon on Saturday morning, that it sounded extemporaneous. I answered that in fact it was, except that I had been preparing all week. I purposefully never memorize the material, so that it sounds fresh and I hope engaging.

On our way home from synagogue the second or third Saturday, I was walking with Ricky, and I must admit to a rush of satisfaction at the way things had gone that morning. Suddenly she turned to me, and with an abundance of sympathetic love said, "I see you're doing here the same thing that you did at Shelter Rock, a light comment with a serious religious theme. But this is a much more formal synagogue than what you're accustomed to. I don't know if they're going to take to it. I'm not sure that they are ready for humor from the pulpit."

Truthfully, I was taken aback. I hadn't thought through a mode of presentation other than the one I had always known. In advance I always had in mind where I wanted to go while speaking, and what I wanted to affirm, but times oft in the saying of it, an anecdotal comment seemed to graphically make the point. I never used a set joke to start or to finish.

Whatever humor there was had to come out of the given situation. So I answered by saying that I really only have one pitch, and that I can't do anything but keep throwing it. I hoped they would like it, but that's the good part about being a "temp", if they don't like you, move on. My tenure had been for a year, but the congregation asked me to stay on until a suitable successor was found.

Finally, in 2006, after two other interim Rabbi positions, one in Flatbush and the other in Old Westbury, we made our way to the Jewish Center of the Hamptons in East Hampton, Long Island. There I came into a situation that was much more difficult than the others. Fortunately, by then I looked at myself as a "fireman Rabbi", willing to step into a tense situation and try to bring about a transition for my successor to step into.

The Jewish Center in East Hampton turned out to be the most exciting, challenging, and ultimately rewarding of all of my rabbinic experiences. There is an old Hebrew idiomatic expression, that all beginnings are difficult. This was certainly true in East Hampton.

I knew in advance that there at been an awesome division within the congregation. The previous Rabbi had evoked the admiration of many and unfortunately the animosity of an equal number. Before he left, the tension between the two groups even spilled over into the Supreme Court of Suffolk County. By the time I came it had been legally resolved, but the inflamed passions had not yet had time to cool down.

The Search Committee of the Jewish Center that had come to our house on Reed Drive in Roslyn had made me aware of a good deal of that controversy. But I was totally unprepared for what happened the second weekend that Ricky and I were living out in the East End. Some of the leaders of the "opposition" were high profile, influential, and affluent, and therefore all the more adamant about not forgetting the past and moving forward. They were not accustomed to losing battles. To be accurate, it has also to be mentioned that they were intelligent, and in most cases kind people. So, when I was invited to sit with them on a Sunday afternoon to hear their side of the story, I eagerly accepted. I thought of it as a good way to clear the air and move forward. In fact, it was presented to me as an opportunity for a social gathering, and that if I would like to bring my wife that would be just fine. It being a Sunday afternoon in the summertime, what could be nicer, I described to Ricky, than sitting in the luxuriant backyard around the pool, sipping a tall glass of mint tea, and exchanging pleasantries with prominent people. On that basis, she agreed to come.

Imagine our surprise when entering this "McMansion", it turned out that we were never to see the backyard at all. They ushered us immediately into the living room, where around a large table, fifteen or so people were seated. I realized immediately that I had misrepresented this occasion to my wife. The people gathered were not smiling. I was told immediately not to say a word, because they wanted to tell me their own version of what had happened. For the next hour and a quarter, I said absolutely nothing, but sat there listening to a tale of anger, woe, and misfortune, at times in the midst of tears. Obviously none of them accused me of anything, this being the first time that I had met them. But I guess that they had all mistakenly assumed that I had not been told of the diversity that the Jewish Center represented. One of the women present tearfully told me that her partner did not want to come to synagogue anymore. Another expressed moral outrage at the way the synagogue had treated the former rabbi. At a later date I heard a prominent congregant say that he did not even like the former rabbi, and that he thought his sermons were much too long, but that he could not be part of any congregation that shabbily treated a rabbi that had served the congregation for eight years. The opposition clearly was strong and bitter. They did not intend to be swayed.

After biting my tongue during the long litany of complaints of those present that afternoon, I finally had a chance to speak. Fortunately, I had decided long before that I could never rehash and re-examine the events that led up to the dismissal of the Rabbi. My point was simple: this is a great congregation with an illustrious past and a brilliant future. We must go forward. However, I allowed myself so say something that had become clear to me: that some of the people present were enjoying their hostility and were not yet ready to let it go. They had latched onto what seemed a self-evident truth, and they intended to cling to it.

Despite the difficulty of those first days, we went on to enjoy many of the experiences with immense satisfaction. The very first Friday that we came to East Hampton, we proceeded to Main Beach at 6pm to join cantor Debra Stein in what is called "Tot Shabbat". This was a totally new experience. There were 150 to 200 kids, parents, and grandparents present on the beach, sitting in the sand on blankets and towels ready to welcome the Sabbath. My role was to keep the service moving, and tell a story, with the hope that it would have some relevance. Totally disarmed, I started by saying that this was my first day at Tot Shabbat, and some people know that my name is Rabbi Fenster. But not on the beach. Here I am "Rabbi Barney," we will sing Barney songs. Every service here on the beach, I am going to raise up three fingers, which stand for the Hebrew letter "Shin". "Shin stands for Shalom" I said, "or peace". I told the kids that their grandparents would remember Winston Churchill lifting up two fingers representing the "v for victory", we are going beyond that and raising three. I also told them that wherever and whenever they see me, they should flash the "Shin for Shalom" sign. I said to do this on their left shoulder, so as to keep the sign discreet. A few days later, Ricky and I were shopping in the supermarket, and I hear an excited youngster cry out, "Hey! There's Rabbi Barney! I have to give him a 'Shin'".

Many months later, in the winter, I was teaching a course in Talmud in a conference room on 5th Avenue, Ricky would often meet me and we would have a bite of lunch together. Some fellow sitting across the way, who I vaguely recalled, suddenly flashes me the "Shin" sign. Ricky and I both laughed, and we were overjoyed that we had made an impact at least on one adult. Hopefully, with the kids too.

The format of Tot Shabbat was simple; the cantor strummed the guitar, and was joined by a wonderful musician whom I named Brother Dan who also played the guitar as we sang lustily into the wind Jewish classics such as "Bim Bam" and "Hayvenu Shalom Aleychem". Then came the serious part, during which time we would light the candles if it was not too windy, Kiddush, and give out Challahs for all to make the blessings over the bread.

For me these were very special moments. When I was ordained the pledge that I made was, "to teach Torah publicly whenever I could". I never envisioned at that time this type of teaching, and especially to youngsters 3, 4, and 5 years old. But I found it very enjoyable and quite rewarding. The service was brief, but I often left there feeling that this was as significant a moment of teaching as any that I had ever done. When someone I know told me that for the first time after attending Tot Shabbat his granddaughter called him up right before the Sabbath began to wish him a Shabbat Shalom, I knew that my gratified intuition was correct. Rabbis get excited by things like that, even though the celestial spheres may not respond . . . immediately.

There were two other aspects of the year in East Hampton that were unique to me. One took place after the regular Shabbat service on Saturday morning. I liked very much that that service did not begin until 10 am, unlike what I had been accustomed to, which was to begin at 9 am. You have no idea what a tremendous bonus an extra hour can be on a Saturday morning to a rabbi. It gave me the opportunity to drink a cup of leisurely coffee in the morning, glance at the New York Times, look again at the sermon, read the Bible portion for the day, take a sip of water, and even take a little walk before the service. By the time it began at 10 o'clock, I was wondering how I ever got ready without the extra hour.

The highlight was the hour of Torah Study at the end of the service, which would oftentimes carry us to 2 pm. I don't know where the energy that it took to conduct the service and teach the class came from, but I was glad that it could be summoned. The Torah study was a regular event of the week, some forty or so people would stay, and very often we would conclude with a "niggun" or melody, to be sung by Ricky or one of the congregants. It was a most fitting end to a most satisfying day in the synagogue. On my way home walking with Ricky, I would have that enjoyable sense of satisfied fatigue, anxiously looking forward to my tomato juice cocktail, which was the signature of the day. What followed was brief lunch and a longer nap, both legislated by the Sabbath day.

Another innovative side of my tenure there, as far as I was concerned, was a class that I conducted in the Talmud of "Brachot" – or Blessings. I had always shied away from teaching Talmud, erroneously believing that it was legalistic, dry, and hard to present. I found quite the opposite to be the case. Many points that were made in the text, even though the Mishnah was codified in approximately 200 C.E. were totally relevant to the situation of the students and me today. At the beginning of our study, the major question was presented: what is more important in prayer: the fixed form or the free-floating spirit? That is to say should prayer be set into a time frame, or should we wait until the proper mood settles upon us. It is a question of great impact for all of ritual, for all of religion. Do you need a specific time, or do you get into it whenever you can? Good arguments can be made out for both sides. The Jewish tradition calls forth a difficult but possible integration of both ideas, getting into the mood at the proper time. Is it possible? Yes, it is. Is it easy? No it is not. Out of that tension of conflicting goals can come the creativity and spontaneity of prayer at a fixed time. All of this I tried to communicate.

I found it much easier to explain than I had anticipated, and extremely relevant to those who studied with me. For here was the heart of the enterprise of organized religion, which many people, including some of the great spirits of America found hard to accept: namely how do you summon piety every week at 9:30 on Sunday morning, or on Saturday? Abraham Lincoln had problems with this as did Thomas Jefferson. What I discovered is that it is not only real, but teachable. One of my mentors, Abraham

Joshua Heschel, once wrote "the Crisis of religion in our time is the Crisis of prayer". And so I discovered that Heschel was correct. But I also discovered that there is a way out of it, with patience, understanding, and spiritual piety, there can come a sense that you are talking to God, and somehow, evoking the Divine Voice within. And singing together helps. So I was very grateful to my students for sticking with me and giving me a chance to discover something that I had not realized before. I quoted to them words that took on new meaning, "I have learned much from my teachers, family, and friends, but I have learned most of all from my students".

One of the most important teachings that Abraham Joshua Heschel gave me was the idea that, "God is transcendent, but our prayer makes Him immanent." It is a crucial point in the inner spiritual life of any person who wants to sense religious experience. What it is saying, is that abstract discussion on the theoretical proposition of God's existence, can be interesting and exciting, but never decisive. A person who experiences God in prayer or in a moment of religious fervor, or in social concern, all of which is possible, can never have that sense taken from his or her life.

When people tell me, as many do, that they are agnostics or atheists, I feel badly that they have never experienced God's presence in either prayer, ritual, or life itself. I am not one of those people that go around trying to convince others to have religious experiences. But in recent years I have begun to overcome my reticence in talking about my own. It is not difficult today to for me to speak the truth that in my twenty-minute private prayer service in the morning, there are inevitably moments when I feel a divine presence surging through me, when I feel connected beyond. The words that I am saying match a sentence of the Psalms "I have set God before me always". By persistent effort, those early morning prayers give me a strong sense of connection, which stay with me throughout the day.

Chapter Two

Physically speaking, the Jewish Center in East Hampton is one of the most beautiful, jewel-like synagogues I have ever seen. Designed by the brilliant architect Norman Jaffe, it is a splendid combination of wood and glass in unusual form and pattern, which affords a startling impression when you first enter it. The acoustics are marvelous, to some extent because it is not overly large. The bima can easily be seen by any vantage point. It seats no more than 400; therefore on the High Holidays, when the congregation swells to 1500, a tent is constructed on the ample grounds of the Jewish Center.

The tent is by no-means a fly-by-night affair. It has heat and air-conditioning, depending on what the particular season brings. But best of all, I felt a strong bonding with the congregation during these High Holidays. The microphone system was perfect so I didn't feel like I had to yell or scream or rant to make a point. I could speak in a conversational tone, as I told the congregants that in our tradition Rosh Hashanah is the birthday of the world, and therefore we all have the opportunity to start over again, and to put aside the tensions and the difficulties of the past year. On *Kol Nidre* night I mentioned that while all vows are absolved on this night, we should all be taking a new vow to banish hatred, animosity and slander from our tongues and from our hearts. I believe that many people took that message seriously, and that there was a conscious effort on their behalf to start the New Year on a positive note. Unfortunately, as often happens, I was, so to speak, preaching to the choir. The people I really wanted to get to were nowhere to be seen. I hope they were in some synagogue, but they were not at the Jewish Center.

One of the problems was that over the years the synagogue had gotten the reputation of serving the "rich and the famous". They were held in high esteem by many and there were people who reported to me that the best fun of coming to the Jewish Center on the holidays was spotting the "celebs". Needless to say I am not going to extenuate the situation by naming those good folks who people hope to spot, but if you're ever at the Jewish Center, you'll see plaques in the lobby with the names of many people you'll recognize. Okay, I'll give just one: that of Steven Spielberg, who returns to California before the High Holidays every summer; so he couldn't be there, even if he wanted to.

On my very first Saturday, literally the day after we arrived, I spoke about the anomaly of a Conservative Rabbi like myself serving a Reform congregation like the Jewish Center. I invoked the pledge that I took when I became a Rabbi. It promised, "to teach Torah publicly". I spoke of being a post-denominational Rabbi, in the sense that on the particularistic side, I was ordained at the Jewish Theological Seminary, and have served only Conservative congregations during my rabbinic career. But I sense that my teachers, many of whom were European, some of who were American, but all of whom were devoted to the Jewish people and its creative continuity, all would have wanted me to say that I am a Rabbi who will teach what

I know to anyone who gives me a chance. And that includes Jews and non-Jews alike.

One of the most beautiful prayers which we say on our sacred holidays are the words of the prophet Isaiah, "And may my house be a house of prayer for all people". There is a community of the faithful, no matter who you are, as long as you believe that there is, "hope for your future". That the concept of *Tikvah* or promise, permeates any religious tradition worthy of shaping your soul. It is to that soul, and its shaping, that I attempted to speak.

This idea of a post-denominational rabbi was no sudden invention. It is legitimate. I came to it by background and experience. I attended an Orthodox seminary for five years before being ordained at the Conservative Jewish Theological Seminary. I was a Conservative rabbi for half a century. And now I was serving a Reform congregation and felt it to be no theological stretch. My personal daily and Sabbath routine did not change one whit. In addition, I was once an editor of the Reconstructionist Magazine, invited by Dr. Mordecai Kaplan. How much more post-denominational can you get? I had touched all four bases. Through it all I was in fact searching for my own spiritual and religious essence, hoping to find the core of my own being. In the end I realized it was not a denominational search, that content was more important than label. I was attempting to provide the content, and to suggest blurring the label.

The search for spirituality in life, in your community, and in the world, is an ongoing inexhaustible one. It begins with the individual, but its rays radiate to the world. That is exactly how I understand the deepest affirmation of the tradition which I represent. When a Jew says the words "Shma Yisrael", what he or she should be doing is attempting to feel the spirituality of that moment and of God deep within themselves. God is of the world, but it starts within. By tradition we cover our eyes, so that we can get a higher concentration of inner-consciousness. But that doesn't end the affirmation. It is only the first two words, the latter part, "the Lord our God the Lord is One" is meant to be what we bring to the world after we have spoken within ourselves. As I see it, a truly religious person does not experience God's presence or the spirituality of the moment and then retreat into a corner for self-meditation and self-preservation. We all have a tendency to do that, but we must resist it. Woody Allen once said that he was born Jewish, but that he rapidly converted to narcissism. Unfortunately, many Jews and many others of a variety of faiths have done exactly that.

The person who does not accept the spiritual potential of our time or of themselves is not beyond the pale of our concern. Many, perhaps most, of the people who come to the synagogue are not atheistic, but they are agnostic. They would like to have faith, but simply do not know how to find it. For them and for myself, I announced a course of study called Modern Jewish Thought. We begin with Mordecai Kaplan, a dedicated and celebrated teacher with whom it was my privilege to study. Kaplan's main point is that Judaism is a civilization and not just a religion. His vision is inclusive and embracing. By civilization, he means a culture, a land, a language, a literature of prayers and songs ancient and medieval, addressed to God, and like the Song of Songs, to another individual. Equally important to Kaplan is a concept for which he coins a new word: "peoplehood". Initially, he would mean that all Jews are bound together in time and space and history. But looking beyond that, he sees a world of ethical "nationhood", where a true experience of God would lead to a world of peace justice and truth.

It is interesting that when I studied with Kaplan in the 1950's and thereafter, his philosophy seemed woefully inadequate to the abysmal tragedy of the Holocaust. The reason I thought so was that Kaplan downplayed the individual's experience with God. He was always stressing the group and communal sides of religious life. He would remind us again and again that what we hold and know about religion was given to us through our participation in the community. He once actually wrote a book called *Judaism without Supernaturalism.* Often he would refer to his inability to accept the miracles of the Bible, especially that of the Israelites crossing the Red Sea, as it is described in the Book of Exodus. Kaplan also denounced the idea of the Jews as the chosen people, saying that he believed that it gave Jews a feeling superiority, which was resented by the non-Jewish world. Furthermore Kaplan negated the idea of Jewish law or Halachah as such, instituting instead the term "folkways of the Jews." This eliminated the sense of command, and put the law on a volunteristic basis. This, of course, could coincide with the American democratic mood, but it could be a disaster for religious life, for if there is no command or responsibility or obligation coming from the past, then everyone is left to their own devices to decide what the content of religious life is to be. The idea of "ought," of being "commanded" will always be relevant to the religious life. Not the only principle, but an important one.

A crucial period of the transition between Europe and America has always fascinated me. I sense that in my father's life, as he described in detail his own arrival in America, that he made up his mind, in transit apparently, that he was never going to join a *landsmanschaft* organization, that is to say an organization of people from the same town who come to America and establish themselves together here. He was also determined not to read a Yiddish newspaper in America, which as far as I know he never did. Immediately he enrolled in night school and started reading English newspapers. When I was a kid growing up I remember clearly that in the morning he would buy the New York Times, and in the late evening bring home the World Telegram, which had the latest stock prices in it. To this day, I am somewhat of a news wonk, and I attribute it to my father's clear pursuit of what was happening in the world, and to his daily perusal of those papers.

Kaplan told an anecdote of his own life that was illustrative of the same point. He told of his coming to America with his mother, in steerage, on a slow-boat from France. One day they announced that since it was Bastille-day, there would be fireworks later in the day on the top deck, and that everyone would be invited to attend. Naturally, as a youngster, Kaplan was very excited, and told his mother he wanted to go. She responded by saying that it was a very good idea, but that since it was Friday he would have to recite his Friday evening Sabbath prayers before he could go upstairs for the show. By the time he finished his praying and went upstairs, the fireworks were over. Kaplan then says: "this is when I learned that I had to live in two civilizations". After that, Kaplan made fireworks in lieu of watching them.

All of this was the temper of the Reconstructionist Movement which Kaplan founded. It was very attractive to young rabbis like myself, who were concerned with the daily observance and continuity of Jewish life. We were also aware of our idiomatic, American background: We were combining Bible, baseball and Beethoven with co-ed education and Milton Berle on Tuesday nights.

But to me the heart of the religion that I discovered was deeply individual and personal. God for me was not an abstraction, but the reality of my life upon which I depended to keep going after the difficulties that I faced. Martin Buber spoke of the dialogue between the individual and God. He called it the I-Thou relationship. For me it became the building-block of my faith. I had majored in philosophy in college and graduate school, so I sensed Spinoza's difficulty on how God would hear the prayers of the billions of people that would be addressed to God daily. But in the very process of prayer, in the moments that I was engaged in it, all philosophical reservations disappeared. They were replaced by the living reality of religious experience.

This search for a personal God brought me into conflict with my teacher, with whom I had publicly disagreed. It wasn't pleasant, I am not sure Dr. Kaplan ever forgave me. One of the things that he taught us was to express our inner-most feelings openly and without fear. But when I did so in an open letter in the Reconstructionist Magazine, which Kaplan later published in his book, Questions Jews Ask, I am not sure that our relationship could ever be repaired.

In fact, many years later, I was on the teaching staff of a Summer Leadership Institute that was being held in Camp Cejwin, in Port Jervis, NY. There were 150 teenagers that we were teaching. Dr. Kaplan was the most prominent figure on our staff. One Friday afternoon, in the dining room at lunch, he asked me to come down and see him on Saturday in his bungalow at 3 o'clock. We were all the way at the other end of the campus a half-mile away. But I lumbered forth Saturday afternoon as instructed.

Dr. Kaplan proceeded to expound his naturalistic philosophy, his idea of God, chosen people, folkways. I listened respectfully and quietly. Thankfully, Kaplan's wife Rivkah was present. She heard the proceedings and finally said with gentle prodding, "Mottke, Fenster no doubt would like to go back to his wife. After all, it is Shabbat afternoon, a time of rest, and not agitation". As I remember it, Kaplan slammed his fist on the table, and said, "No, I will not let him go until he gets it!" How could you not admire such persistence? But to this day, for whatever it is worth, I remain unconvinced of what I was supposed to get.

Hoping to aid those searching for their personal spiritual direction was this course that I offered at East Hampton. We looked carefully at the thinking of Franz Rosenzweig, the German born, at first highly acculturated Jew who early in life did not even know that the Sabbath begins for the Jewish people on Friday night. Rosenzweig, after a series of dramatic events, discovers powerful meaning and great spiritual purpose in the idea of God's creation, revelation, and redemption. His spiritual life becomes a discovery and an unfolding, which begins a seminal relationship with Martin Buber, one of the great philosophical thinkers of the 20th century. Anyone wishing to discover their own spiritual spark, should be looking at the works of these two men.

If you were to ask Buber to prove to you that God spoke in the days of the Bible, he would answer that he knows it for sure, because God speaks to him now. The dialogue between God and humankind is not over. We can act as if we are dumb and silent in its presence, but God will enter wherever we let him in, and whenever we do. It is this sense that I hoped to teach my students, and it culminated in the thinking of Abraham Heschel, a European scholar who escaped Hitler and his madmen at the very last moment, coming to America to teach the embodiment of the spiritual life in thought and in action. Heschel had marched with Martin Luther King, Jr. in Selma; I wanted my students to march with Heschel, a man of deep faith and social concern.

The question that I asked myself when I came to the Jewish Center was how to convey the experiential sense of religious reality without becoming partisan or doctrinaire. At the same time there is always the danger of being vacuous and vague. The prayerbook that they used at the Jewish Center was not one that I was familiar with. It was much less detailed than the one I was accustomed to. Many of the prayers of the standard service were skipped, others were abbreviated, some were non-existent. That did not bother me particularly, since I believed that prayer was to be judged not by its weight but by its quality.

There is a sound Jewish principle which speaks of "Kavanah", the consciousness of the spirit within the worshipper, so that what he or she is saying is not rote, but deeply felt. There is a further principle which says that if you only pray what is printed in the prayer book without adding your own inner-feelings of the heart, you have not fulfilled the full obligation. With that in mind, I realized again that it was not only important to emphasize what we were saying, but that of equal importance would be the manner in which we said it. Personally, I had to overcome a degree of spiritual reticence, and even of movement in the course of prayer. If I am alone, I often rock forward and back lightly as a way of getting into the motion of prayer. Usually in public I shied away from doing that, but now I realized that I could no longer be so taciturn. I liberated myself. Let it go, I commanded myself.

Singing with our wonderful cantor Deborah Stein, at times I am clapping my hands in rhythm with the songs. Some may have felt that a more austere form was required for dignified worship. All I can say in my defense is that I never exhibited any sign of enthusiasm that didn't come from within me, and that I would have had to sit still and quiet if I didn't let it out. This was especially so when we would sing on Friday night the melodies of Shlomo Carlebach to "L'cha Dodi" and "Mizmor Shir." I simply had to go along with it. Truthfully, I expected that after any service, some group would come up to me and say, "Rabbi this is not a revival meeting here. You've simply got to stop enjoying yourself so much." I am grateful that nobody with such a message ever appeared.

During the course of the year in East Hampton we ran the full gamut of the calendar. Our original agreement was that by the end of Simchat Torah, when the holiday cycle is over, I would leave and my successor would be in place. That never happened. Before I knew it, they were asking me to stay on for another nine months. They wanted to know if I would be willing to continue. I answered graphically but truthfully: "I don't walk out on congregations".

Ricky and I had been anticipating Israel for quite awhile. Actually the reason we retired from Shelter Rock in 2002 goes back to an Ulpan class Ricky was attending five years before that in Israel. One day her Ulpan assignment, which of course was in Hebrew, a language she was making her way in rapidly, was to project a dream into the future. We were working on it together. It was her idea. The dream was that we would spend six months a year in Israel, and six months a year in America. Since we have nine grandchildren in Israel and seven in America, it would be an equal and enjoyable distribution of time.

Now the possibility of not going to Israel for another year faced us. When you're getting older, the idea of losing a year with loved ones is not attractive. The kids are growing up, and you're not there to participate in the process. My condition of remaining at the Jewish Center for the additional time was that I would have a couple of weeks off so that Ricky and I could visit Israel. With great kindness, they accepted. And so there we were, after three months on the job, with a two week vacation. And man, did we enjoy it.

As far as our American family was concerned, they rapidly discovered the pleasant potential of East Hampton living. Over the holidays in the autumn and the spring they joined us. The house was alive with laughter and chatter on Rosh Hashanah and on Passover. The table was as full as our hearts.

There were times when we felt a bit out of touch, especially in the winter, out on the East End. I would at times describe our location as, "the middle of the Atlantic Ocean." But when they were with us we felt totally connected and at the center of the Universe. The year began to unfold. Kristallnacht in November. Chanukah in December. Tu'Bshvat in January. To each of these I brought the experiences of the past. And tried to pump a little bit more energy into the congregants' observance. On Tu'Bshvat, when it is said that the sap begins to rise in the trees of Israel (during the mid-winter in

America), we stuffed ourselves with bokser, olives, pomengranates, quince, dates, bread, and white wine. All of it a harbinger of spring.

Actually, the winter out at the East End was much milder than I anticipated. We were located a half a mile from the beach and the water. Apparently less snow falls in that climatic situation, and while the winds are cold the temperature does not drop precipitously. And it is quiet. Much more so than in the summer when the summer crowds are there. We survived the busy summer, but mostly enjoyed the winter.

An additional factor of winter was a course that I gave on introduction to Talmud in Manhattan, in the conference room of one of our member's offices. The number of people who attended varied. At times there were 15, at times less. But I enjoyed the teaching and the experience. The night before, we would sleep at our home in Roslyn, in the comfort of a familiar bed, and I would often take what felt like a leisurely train-ride on the Long Island Railroad into the city. And added bonus would come when Ricky and I would meet me for lunch after the class. Somehow, we were enjoying the best of both worlds: living in East Hampton and dining in Manhattan.

In the spring after Passover, with the help of our synagogue president, Linda Kamm, we came up with a novel way of remembering the Shoah, on Holocaust Memorial Day. Linda is very involved in the effort to save the hunted people of Darfur in the Sudan. We adopted her idea of walking to the town green in the heart of East Hampton, to remember the genocide of Jews and hope to prevent further genocide in Africa.

Some might have thought it inappropriate to connect the two. Personally, I considered it right on target. The Holocaust has always been a sensitive subject to me. My father lost his entire family – some fifty people. That he was able to go forward with that knowledge has always been a source of personal inspiration to me. We each have to learn how to do that. But the weather foiled our remembrance. It had to be moved to the Jewish Center because of a cloudburst of rain. Our commemoration proceeded otherwise as planned.

The weekly Sabbath Service after summer was also very relaxed. There were always fifty or more people present, but after a few months they all felt like friends, and like an intimate gathering of acquaintances for worship and sociability. For Passover, for the first time in forty years, we participated in a congregational *Seder*. Previously we had always avoided it because it sounded like a mob-scene. But this was cool. The family came to our beach home for the first Seder, a "bungalow" of nine rooms, four of which were bedrooms each of which had its own bathroom. Needless to say, we were comfy, and the camaraderie was sensational. In the synagogue, some sixty or so people turned out, and it was a time of ritual, explanation, good food, and singing late into the night. It made me revise my view of the community Seder. Nowadays, I'm all for it.

Added to these calendrical events were am array of interesting and at times exciting people who had been invited to the Jewish Center to present their points of the view on a specific subject, and to offer possibilities of discussion. On my suggestion, we brought Irshad Manji, a feminist Muslim, who criticizes the turn many interpreters of her religion have made while trying to expound on its deeper spiritual purpose. She is a highly articulate woman, and I loved her right from the start. We first met in one of our members homes, where she initiated the discussion, and then onto the Jewish Center, where she spoke for over an hour, and her large audience was held at rapt attention. The discussion took the expected turn: why the militants have taken over and robbed the true Islamic religion of its contemporary relevance. Irshad explained patiently that she often receives death threats from those who disagree with her, but she persists in America and Europe to teach. Finally, a man stood up, who was powerful looking, at 6 foot three with a long pony-tale, clean shaven, and intense, to say that he was here to subscribe to the view of Islam that Irshad was presenting, that there are many others that agree with her, but that the atmosphere is not always welcoming to this expression now. He declared what we all felt: that Irshad was speaking for many, and that her statements were needed and heroic.

A Rabbi who presented himself, Steven Greenberg, had written a book on the painful journey of the homosexual Rabbi. He tried to explain how in his interpretation of the biblical passage, Leviticus 18, what was meant did not apply to him and others like him, whose lives and circumstances were different from those of the biblical prohibition. On another occasion, Rabbi Larry Hoffman, of the faculty of the Hebrew Union College, spent a weekend with us as a scholar in residence. He is working on a project called Synagogue 300, which hopes to revitalize the liturgy, content, and congregational involvement that is currently the practice in Shuls. He makes the point that we have to be far more welcoming than we are. People who come to our synagogue should feel that we really want them, and that they are not interlopers. He wants this to apply to the hundreds of people who may come only once to a bar/bat mitzvah, but the goal is for them to feel that they are in a warm and welcoming place, in the hope that they would return, and bring their friends and family with them.

On one weekend of the summer of 2006, Sheldon Harnick brought the Apple Tree, a delightful experience of musical theatre to the Jewish Center. It had been on Broadway once, had been recast, and was now testing the waters once again. It went over very big, had a good reception, and was back on Broadway in the full season. Of such variety was our program made up. It included an evening with a klezmer music, in addition to book reviews, movies, and a very inspiring talk by Ruth Messinger, the President of the American Jewish World Service, about Jews acting as global citizens in relation to the crisis in Darfur. All in all a full menu with plenty of protein.

The social concerns of the Jewish Center were also well defined. A group of fifty of our young people and adults went out in the fall to help the local farmers glean their fall fruits and corn. We participated in a mass demonstration in Central Park in Manhattan on behalf of stopping the genocide in Darfur. It is one thing to come to the city from Roslyn, NY which is a half an hour away, and another to come from the East End, which is way out there. But our bus was filled with enthusiastic, although on the way back extremely tired, participants. We tried to make this experience a bit more palatable with a most enjoyable pit-stop at Galil, on Lexington Avenue, where we filled ourselves with chumus and falafel, to fortify us for the journey.

On the downside, in the fall of 2007, federal officials made raids of illegal immigrants of East Hamptons and its surroundings. I am sure the federal officials have sanction for what they are doing, but as reported to our clergy-group it seemed grossly unfair. The "feds" came in at 5:30 am, scaring the kids who began to cry, perhaps presented warrants for the arrest, and generally sent a shockwave throughout the community. The officials did point out, however, that they picked up not only illegal immigrants but some wanted for various crimes. I wanted our clerical group to get more involved and take a stronger stand, but I didn't push too hard because as a temp nothing you do or say is taken too seriously. I did contact, however, the recently appointed head of homeland security in New York State, Mike Balboni, an old friend, who pointed out that this was a federal and not a state matter, of which he personally had no control. I can certainly understand the need for surveillance, but like the events at Guantanamo Bay, we wonder how high the price.

One of the really enjoyable experiences in East Hampton was the opportunity to meet with a number of poets and to hear some of their works. Harvey Shapiro, formerly senior editor of the New York Times Magazine, was one poet whose work I liked very much. In East Hampton, many of the thoughts I had had throughout my life condensed into new crystalline form of idea and ideology. Perhaps it was the opportunity of quiet, or the marvelous air from the ocean. That mystical ocean that my father had crossed ninety-years before in coming to America, that gave that renewed sense of search. "Seek God's face always". And so I liked Shapiro's poem "According to the Rabbis" as an expression of where I am, if not of where I am going:

> According to the rabbis,
> when God asks Adam, Where are you?
> He's not looking for information.
> He wants Adam to consider where he is in life,
> where he is NOW and where he intends to be.
> I could say that I'm on a bus, headed for New York,
> but that would be frivolous. I could say
> that I'm in the middle of a dark wood,
> that I'm always in the middle of a dark wood.
> But that would be despair.

As far as we were concerned, despair did not come out of East Hampton. Quite the opposite. We felt renewal, and a rekindling of the fire in the bones. One other aspect of life at the Jewish Center brought that sense of renewal dramatically home. On Sunday mornings, we assembled a group to discuss what we called, "current events". After awhile, the people who came on a regular basis became close friends. They were enthusiastic students and supportive congregants. Our mode of operation was that I had an article printed out each week either from the Jerusalem Post, the Jerusalem Report, The New York Times, or any other article I thought would be provocative and interesting. No comment was considered out of bounds. They ran the full gamut, from passionately Zionist, to negative, at time abrasive critique. The Jewish Center was known for its wide variety of ideas and ideologies, opinions and values. It is what made our stay there fascinating and engaging. The truth is no other congregation that I had ever served exhibited such a diversity of thought. This was pluralism in action, not always easy to tie together, because on occasion it seemed the participants might come to verbal blows. Not wanting to side with one group or the other, it was not always easy to wind my way through the troubled waters. The amazing part of it was that when it came time to leave I realized that I was closest to this group. I knew intuitively that I was going to miss them, and our heated Sunday morning discussions. Arguing with myself was never as interesting.

Inevitably, the summer of 2007 was upon us, and we had to begin to prepare to leave. A new rabbi, Sheldon Zimmerman, was in place. Our spirits were buoyed by the prospect of spending months in Israel with the young ones climbing all over us. That seemed like more than adequate compensation. We had plans. In early June, the president of the Jewish Center told us of a farewell luncheon that was being planned before our departure. It was to take place on a Saturday afternoon following the Shabbat service. The garden at the back of the synagogue, under the tent, would serve as an informal but lovely location for the proceeding. We were looking forward to it with anticipation.

It turned out to be a special, memorable occasion. The cantor, Deborah Stein, served as the MC. Beforehand she refused to tell me who the speakers were going to be. I liked the idea of the suspense, and was only mildly apprehensive. Deborah spoke beautifully, so much so that she brought tears to my eyes. She spoke of how when I came, she was unsure if we would be able to work together, considering my background as a more traditional Rabbi. Then she said two things that I will never forget. First was that I never passed judgment on anything that the congregation was accustomed to doing. Quietly, she noted that I did try to make some changes, but without creating a fuss. I just did them, and she was cooperative every step of the way. Truth is that I enjoyed working with her as much as any cantor that I had ever had, and more than with most.

The other thing she said was that when I would come to my study in the morning, in the style of summer I would often be wearing a short-sleeved shirt. She could see on my arm the strap-marks from the tfillin, or phylacteries, that I had donned for prayer shortly before. It never occurred to me that they would still be visible. Coming as she did from a traditional background, she explained that it brought her back to the days of her grandfather, when she would see him in the morning, in prayer, with tfillin. She heard from me later, in caustic tone, for comparing me to her grandfather. I always did, however, feel a close kinship with Grandfathers and Grandmothers of the world.

She was followed by a surprise speaker, namely Zachary Fenster, our grandson. Zach is a most unusual eighteen year old, and he had just graduated the Abraham Joshua Heschel High School in Manhattan. With little advance notice, he was speaking without notes. When he began with a reference to the Biblical portion, his grandmother and I, Bubbie and Zaide, looked at each other in awe, wonderment and the questioning of where this was going.

Zachary soon showed his hand. He proceeded to blow my cover. "Zaide this is the fifth retirement party that I have attended, that's it, no more retirements. You've pushed the old sermons long enough. Most people over eighty would not have put themselves out of their comfort zone as you have." In his short remarks, he divulged three aspects of my life that I had not shared with the congregation: that this was the fifth position since I had "retired", though in truth I actually don't use old material, and my age. While we were still getting over the shock of Zach's remarks, my old friend Jack Rosenthal from Shelter Rock walked over to the podium and took the microphone. As a survivor of the Holocaust, Jack is beyond diffidence or embarrassment. His sense of gallows humor is incomparable. "Eh, so my friends, I'm going to tell you about your rabbi here. I was the President of Shelter Rock, and your Rabbi needed a new contract. He didn't want a contract at all, but we gave him a five-year arrangement. He thought we gave it to him because we loved him, but actually we tried to tie him down with a fixed sum of money. It took his coming to East Hampton to realize he was underpaid."

Jack went on to tell some episodes that we experienced together in the former Soviet Union. When he finished, I felt I wanted to repay the compliment, and so I told an unbelievable but true story, about how we came into our Intourist hotel room late at night, fully aware that our rooms were being bugged. Lying on his bed comfortably, Jack, in an exaggeratedly loud voice proclaimed "I don't know why they talk about this Soviet Union with such insults. To me it seems like a glorious workers paradise. I think I might sell my buildings in New York to come and live here. Mother Russia is beautiful."

So now, five years after retirement, I think I am ready for it. It never quite occurred to me that way, but having been for such a long time in one place, I was really curious about the world out there, and what other congregations were like and how other people related to their rabbinic leadership. I cannot truthfully say that I have satisfied all of my curiosity, but it certainly has been toned down for the time being.

Ricky and I feel very fortunate to have been given the opportunity to serve in so many different circumstances. And young Zachary was correct: there were retirement parties in Shelter Rock, Great Neck, Flatbush, Old Westbury, and East Hampton. We appreciated all of them, and participated in them with unbounded joy.

What made this occasion at East Hampton special was the feeling that this was in fact the last hurrah. Real retirement. The end. And so in truth we approached it with a bittersweet sense. But at the end of that Saturday service and the farewell luncheon we both left with a high buzz, without a drop of alcohol.

I often reflect on how fortunate we have been. Not everybody has taken to my teaching or my style. But I certainly do not leave with cynicism or bitterness towards the people I served. And my father's appraisal that I would have many bosses simply did not turn out to be true. Naturally, I always wanted to connect to the people I was with, and I didn't go out of my way to alienate them. But I also felt no sense of abnegation or buttering up to people because they were wealthy or powerful. I can honestly say I didn't try to please any one person in particular. I always took seriously the teaching of the Talmud that says that on the last day of your life you have to render an accounting to God: "Did you live your life honestly and with faith?" I always felt that I could answer that in the affirmative. And we leave extraordinary gratified that we have many dear friends in all of the congregations we served.

So, I conclude my years of service, for the time-being at least, with a sense of positive accomplishment. Others have gone further and done more. But early in my life, I came across a prescription for success written by Felix Frankfurter, the brilliant Supreme Court Justice. He wrote:

> "Ambition untainted by vanity:
> To hammer out as compact and solid
> A piece of work as one can, to make it first rate, and leave it unadvertised . . ."

I believe I have been true to that charge.

So after thirty-six years at Shelter Rock and five additional bonus years at five different synagogues, where does all of that leave me today? Each of us is the product, not just of the last years, but of our entire lives. Heschel once said that it is important to see your entire life as a unitary work of art. The wonder comes when all the daubs of form and color come together and are integrated into the whole. This is how I am hoping to see my own life based on my early history and my later experience. This is the reason that I set out to write this memoir; to get my own life in better perspective, to see lights and shadows, and what precisely the form of it would be at this point. I trust that I have set it down accurately and honestly.

What of the future? I have as much insight into that, or as little, as anyone else. We can arrange and order our past, and we can try to do so for the future as well, but there are unexpected and mysterious elements that no doubt intervene.

One of the books which I read is a pietistic work called the *Noam Elimelech*. The rabbi of Lizensk offers this comment on a verse of the psalms: "Open to me the gates of righteousness." The main attribute of the righteous is to realize that as close as he comes to the purposes of his Maker, there is yet no end (EIN SOF). And this is the central perception that the righteous person must come to, that the totality of meaning will always escape him and the end will always be elusive. That is why the psalmist prays, "Open to me the gate" for the truly pious soul understands that all he has done is just the beginning, and that other gates open to other places that he has not yet been. None of us can complete the work. All we can hope to do is go through the next door that is open to us."

I myself feel that I have passed through many doors. What the future will bring only God knows. Here's to other open doors!

SEEKING GOD

ONE OF THE passions that I have tried to sustain is my interest in Theology, the principles of faith by which we live.

After turning down the offer to be a full-time teacher and administrator at the Jewish Theological Seminary, I nonetheless retained my interest for my personal growth, At one point in the 1990's I set down my views about seeking God. As I read them now, I do not find the need to change for a different emphasis.

When Immanuel Kant was asked about God, he answered that for him, God's existence is seen in the starry heavens above and in the moral impulse within. It is a good way to begin, but will not take us far enough. When I wake up in the morning, I search to bring God's presence into my life. The same is true when I come to the Synagogue, when I am engaged in social concern and similarly, when I am visiting the sick or bereaved. Every time I am getting ready to officiate at a wedding in the Synagogue, I like to look up at the Ark. It reminds me in Whose Presence we stand. I need to be reminded. And I need to continue to search.

Every morning I pick up the siddur and I read, "Joyous are those who search for God – seek his face continually" (Bakshu panav tamid). I often hear those words in my head. The dilemma is that, according to the Biblical tradition, we cannot see God's face. I take that to mean that we can have experiences of God, but we ought to be careful about hearing God's voice directly, or seeing God's face or any other sensate or tangible form of God.

Yet what other equipment do we have to experience God? Humans need concretion and don't do well with abstraction. We need to continue the search for God-like experiences. According to the Talmud, we can find them by engaging in exactly those activities we associate with God, like feeding the hungry, clothing the poor, and trying to bring people together rather than separate them.

When I am looking for an uplifting of spirit or a sense of exaltation, a numinous moment – what some people refer to as an out-of-body experience – I do not usually turn to the philosophical masters. Although I have studied the history of philosophy, there is little in it that speaks to my soul or my spiritual life; in other words to my *neshamah*. I firmly believe that just as our body needs nourishment, so do we need periodic intake for the soul. Otherwise it becomes flaccid through under-use.

I try to nourish my soul daily in Torah study, in social concern, in song or music of a special kind, or on occasion by meeting with someone whose mere presence lifts the spirit. In religious terms, I sense God's presence.

There are two special Jewish philosophers from whom I do derive knowledge and inspiration. They are Franz Rosenzweig and Martin Buber. They each anticipated the tidal wave of collective insanity that was to break over the heads of the Jewish people. Their response was to emphasize the individual who stands before God, thus returning Jewish theology to its Biblical mode. When God confronted Adam with the haunting challenge, "*Ayekha* – where are you?" it is understood that God was not questioning his geographical presence. Also in Genesis, when God confronted Cain asking "Where is Abel, your brother?" again, this was not a geographical question. Each of us is asked that question every day.

This emphasis on the individual confronting God or being confronted by God is the foundation for both of these existentialist thinkers. As is well known, Franz Rosenzweig grew up in an assimilated home in Cassel, Germany. When doubts assailed him, he performed a strange but intuitive act. He went to the synagogue on Yom Kippur and became completely transformed by the experience. While he did not speak of it very much in personal terms, in his *magnum* opus "The Star of Redemption," Rosenzweig describes the Jew who, on the Day of Atonement,

> *confronts the eyes of his judge in utter*
> *loneliness. Then God lifts up his countenance*
> *to this united and lonely pleading of men.*
> *Everything earthly lies far behind – it is*

Difficult to imagine that a way can lead back
From here into the circuit of the year."

Further, he writes,

On these days, the individual in all his naked
Individuality stands immediately before God.
On the day of Atonement the congregation
now rises to the feeling of God's nearness as it
sees in memory the temple service of old. At
This moment the congregation visualizes
especially the moment when the priest (Kohen)
this once in all the year pronounces the
ineffable name of God. And the congregation
participates directly in the feeling of God's
nearness. It is prostrating itself before the King
of Kings.

In sensing God's nearness, Franz Rosenzweig goes from alienation to commitment. It is a powerful model for all of us. He touches a nerve, the yearning and pleasure that many of us have experienced. While this episode transformed his life, he has to deal, as we do as well, with "the way back into the year." How do you keep the flavor going, and how do you sense God's nearness on a cold and rainy day when the kids are crying and you have to go out shopping for food? I think Rosenzweig's answer to that would be that once you have tasted "eternity in the moment" it is easier to find your way back into the life cycle.

To sanctify time, we have Shabbat, a day devoted to sensing God's presence in our homes, in the Synagogue, in the food prayer and music that we experience. If we nourish the moment and sustain the flavor, some of that feeling flows into the everyday. I often recommend beginning each day with this prayer. "God, please make this day significant and satisfying for me."

I also find this feeling in the midrashic teaching that speaks of the readiness on the part of Abraham to become a servant of God and to be a blessing. Without such readiness on the part of the individual, nothing happens. It is not by accident that Heinrich Heine, the poet, once declared, "All life is readiness."

Martin Buber understands this quite well. Buber speaks of the dialogue between heaven and earth and that it is mutual and can be opened up.

Then he adds the following, in what I believe is a very important and vital understanding of Biblical literature and Judaism in general:

The great achievement of Israel is not so much that it has told mankind of the one real God, the origin of and goal of all that exist, but rather that it has taught men (and women) that they can address this God in reality. That they can say Thou to him, that we human beings can stand face to face with God, that there is communion between God and man. Every religious utterance is a vain attempt to do justice to the meaning, the overwhelming sense of God's meaningful presence. The meaning is found through the engagement of one's own person; it only reveals itself as one takes part in the revelation.

In short, what Buber is saying is that revelation is possible at any time and at any moment if you are there. Being there means searching, being ready, and hopefully finding God's presence in your life. Once you realize the channels are open, communication can flow both ways. So where do you look for the experience that we have spoken of and where do you find the presence of God? Obviously God is inscrutable, and in our tradition shrouded in mystery. Yet always, "God's presence fills the earth." It is this experience and this presence that I am pointing to. Notice that I did not speak of God with any of the three "omni's (omnipotence, omnipresence, omniscience). Purposely.

The God I pray to is the God of Biblical scripture, and the God of my experience. That is to say, I invoke the God of Abraham, Isaac and Jacob, Sarah, Rebekah, Rachel, and Leah. You may say that you find no response in praying to the God of Scripture or to the God of the human heart. To that I can only answer that I believe God is objectively there to be found and to be experienced.

According to the mystic, Rabbi Elimelekh of Lyzhansk, God concentrated his essence in the very letters of the Torah, so that whenever we read the Biblical portion, if we read it with enough understanding and concentration, we don't only understand the words, but rather we experience God. That is holiness raised to the highest level, where the very words yield the sense of the *Shekhinah*, God's presence. That is why Torah study is so important and valuable. For God can be discovered in the letters of the Torah.

The coda then, may be found in the words of Abraham Joshua Heschel.

> *Through the ecstasy of deeds, a Jew learns to*
> *be certain of the presence of God. The Divine*
> *sings in our deeds, the Divine is disclosed in*
> *our deeds. If at the moment of doing a mitzvah*
> *once perceived to be thus sublime, if you are in*
> *it with all your heart and with all your soul*
> *there is no great distance between you and*
> *God. For acts of holiness uttered by the soul*
> *disclose the holiness of God Who is hidden in*
> *every moment of time. And God's holiness and*
> *God Himself are one.*

I would say all of this is summarized in the book of Psalms, "My soul yearns for the Lord; As a young deer that pants after the water brooks, so does my heart pant after Thee, O Lord."

I firmly believe that if we thirst and if we search, we shall find.

WHY RETIREMENT?

NOWADAYS I AM sometimes asked why I decided to retire from Shelter Rock in the year 2002, especially in the light of my continuing as an Interim Rabbi in a half dozen synagogues subsequently. It is a good question and requires much probing on my part to answer it honestly.

First off, looking back now I am not sure that I would have retired had they really urged me to stay on. I did have a strong feeling that, "I had been there and done that." After all it was thirty-six years and no matter how hard you try to avoid it, inevitably you fall into a routine and a pattern.

But with my wildest imagination operating, somehow I expected a demonstration around the house the day after I announced my retirement. Placards, protesters, tying up traffic. I looked out the next morning – nothing. The announcement of my imminent withdrawal was greeted with the silence of a dead mouse.

Subsequently, I did morph into Temple Israel of Great Neck through no initiative of my own, but with great receptivity. Later on some even accused me of knowing I was going to do that and therefore retired. They even saw a great monetary advantage for me for having done so. All of that was a fiction of somebody else's fertile imagination. By the time I retired I was not so sure that was really what I wanted to do. In Hebrew they call it, Hashgacha Pratit, – God's looking out for you. That is what happened at that moment and I have been ever grateful for it since. Ricky and I have had a rich experience these last years and we have enjoyed it immensely.

Now I look back on the thirty-six years that we spent at Shelter Rock. When we came, our kids were young and I distinctly recall the moving vans pulling into the driveway at 2 Reed Drive, heavily laden with furniture and bikes, clothes and contraptions, so much so that they broke the walk in the driveway as they came in. To me it was a sign of our bursting energy, wanting to do well in our new home and looking forward to years of service.

It took awhile to get adjusted. I remember the first year as not being overly comfortable in the new setting. I did get accustomed to the fact that on certain days with the atmospheric conditions changing, the air pattern to Kennedy Airport apparently went right over our house. It was amazing how frequently the planes came and how low they flew, even though we are on the north shore and the airport is on the south. About forty years ago I stopped hearing them altogether and it seems that nowadays they use this pattern less frequently.

Also, the new setting included a whole new set of people. It seemed to me at the beginning that the people at Shelter Rock were very suspicious of me, as if I had some mysterious motive in coming here besides just being the rabbi. It is true, as I have described, that a number of the leaders really went out of their way to bring me, but I had no special feeling other than I was here to do the best job I could do. After awhile that dissipated and we became thoroughly comfortable with each other.

So now as I look back almost half a century later I ask myself what actually took up my time here at Shelter Rock, in other words, what did I do. I come up with more or less of a blank. If you ask a doctor after a long period of service how he spent his time, he also would probably shrug his shoulders. He or she looked into throats, took pulses, dispensed pills, bound wounds, set limbs. He did some of those each day, every day. Obviously each was important, but without making an outstanding impact on his mind. They were not routine, but they did have regularity. And I guess some of the analogy applies to what a rabbi does: he goes to the early morning service, stays for the breakfast with the congregants, hearing what is going on in the community; he studies a little, visits the sick, dictates letters, eats lunch, meets with people, talks to the principal of the religious school, visits classes, teaches in the high school, prepares adult education and arranges for courses to be offered, tries to be home for dinner, goes back for evening meetings, and finally after a sixteen hour day, falls into bed, exhausted, at midnight. So when you string it all together, it sounds overwhelming and it often is. But when you do it, day after day and month after month, you do not think of it as egregious or outstanding. It is just what you do.

That is not to say that there were not frequent breaks in the routine and outstanding events that dotted them. The arrangement that we worked out at Shelter Rock was most satisfying and the leadership was often extremely accommodating.

It all began with the President of the congregation, when we first came in 1966, who was Ernest Rothschild. He was of German-Jewish extraction and had actually witnessed the events of Kristallnacht as a youngster. He saw the synagogue in Frankfurt, that he was part of and sang in its choir, burned to the ground, with no intervention from anyone. It was a sight he never could get out of his mind for the rest of his life.

An undramatic aspect of being a rabbi for a long period in a congregation is the strong attachment you make with youngsters who later grow up to be young adults, parents and even grandparents. After you retire it even becomes a problem because people are kind enough to invite you to their joyous occasions and in my case, still being busy, it is painful to turn down certain people with whom you have felt special bonds of friendship over the years. And that is true with dozens of young people. I know I should not give an example, but I will. There is a youngster that we have known since the day of his birth, Max Hirsch, who is shortly going to be Bar Mitzvah. We have been invited to attend, but events out in Greenport that day will make it very difficult for us to be there. The occasion will take place during Hanukkah when in Greenport they light a public menorah at Mitchell Park, to which it is necessary for me to be present. As the Yiddish expression poses it, 'How do you dance at two weddings at the same time? Yet, the idea of missing Maxie's Bar Mitzvah is not pleasant. I always loved to watch Maxie and Mollie when they were two and three years old, holding hands during and after the services. They were and still are irresistible.

A key to our survival was the arrangement that we worked out and that was operational for the last twenty or so years I was at Shelter Rock. I would work five months and then take a month off. The months that we were usually gone, we went to Israel. It was usually one month in the summer and one month in the winter. But each time I came back it was with renewed energy and desire to go forward. I always felt that I was coming back with a fresh outlook and a new vision. Israel inspired me and still does.

In the nineties a most unexpected event took place. Avi Albrecht was then our Cantor and his wife Ahuva's brother Dudu Fisher was gaining a reputation as a popular singer in Israel. Les Miserables had already opened on Broadway and the Israeli version was now being put together. Dudu was dying to get the part of Jean Valjean. Lo and behold he made it! He invited Ricky and I to come to one of the early performances, in Hebrew, and we loved the music immediately. Dudu was a sensation.

Before long they were considering him for the same role on Broadway. It was to be a major achievement of his life because he not only played the role but, as a religious Jew, would not appear on Friday night or Saturday afternoon. We could not believe that Cameron Mackintosh, the international producer would take on the Sabbath observer for the main role of a major Broadway play. But he did.

Now a problem appeared. At one point in the play Dudu was to hold a crucifix in his hand as a sign of his religious piety after having been accused of a petty theft. But Ahuva, Dudu's sister, told me that their parents were coming and as religious people they would find such an act most offensive as, of course, would many other Orthodox Jews who the producers hoped would be anxious to come to the play. By then Dudu had acquired an extensive reputation in the Jewish community. Now the problem came to me, could I write to Mackintosh and tell him the dilemma and would it be possible to put a crucifix on the wall so that Dudu did not have to hold it in his hand. It was obviously a difficult and delicate assignment because we certainly did not want to show any disrespect to the symbol, but at the same time Dudu holding it would be offensive to many people. I wrote to Mackintosh as delicately as I could and a few days later surprise of surprises, I received a call from his assistant that an arrangement that would be satisfactory had been made. We attended on Dudu's opening night and all went smoothly! We gathered at a post-performance party at Sardi's with kosher food, and happily raised a glass of wine with Dudu to signal his great success.

To this day when I contemplate that I had something to do with changing a Broadway play, I am still in a state of amazement.

It was not every day that such dramatic events took place. But they did come from time to time. One of the amazing and surprising aspects of being a rabbi in a large congregation is that you never really know what is going to happen. Each day presents its own surprise and you have to be ready for almost anything. Our children, when they were young, used to laugh at the fact that I wore a tie to work every ay. They used to ask whether I wore it at night to bed. But in truth, I felt more comfortable being ready for whatever new event was to happen. My old boy scout motto "Be Prepared" stood me in good stead.

THE RABBI AND FUNDRAISING

I N THE MINDS of many people fundraising is a very important part of the rabbinical function. Judaism teaches that you cannot make bread without flour, you cannot have Torah without having a way to sustain yourself. As much as we might like synagogues and rabbis to be able to live on air, it just does not work that way. A synagogue today with a million dollar budget is not unusual. Depending on its size, the budget may be many times that. Fundraising is necessary to sustain synagogue life.

I have never disdained that necessary aspect of the synagogue. But I have never excelled at it either. Truth is I tried to avoid it as often as I could. When I was teaching my course of "Professional Skills" at the Seminary, my students would often ask to what degree should they be involved in the fundraising efforts of their synagogues. My answer was always the same: do it when you have to and take it seriously and succeed, but don't enjoy it. Some of my colleagues delight in that aspect of their rabbinical service and devote a great deal of time and energy to it. I cannot say I did that, or that I delighted in achieving great success at my fundraising abilities.

I was always slightly embarrassed when I had to ask a congregant or anyone for money. To my mind it would change our relationship. Prior to that, I would always feel that I could speak to someone on an equal basis and if need be, comment or even criticize some of the things they were saying. Hence, my reluctance. In my mind no rabbi should come hat-in-hand and place himself in that kind of position. The rabbinical hat should stay on the head.

There was one huge exception to my preconceived notion. That is when I used to go to visit my late friend, Capt. Leo Berger, whose offices were close-by in Lake Success. Often I would be with Cantor Avi Albrecht. Capt. Berger often greeted us at the elevator and ushered us into his office. We would be treated like honored guests. He would introduce us to everyone, and though he knew the purpose of our coming, was genuinely happy to see us. Once the business aspect of our deliberations were concluded, it was as if he would heave a sigh of relief, stand back and say "Now let's hear about your personal lives. How are you doing?"

Capt. Berger's principle residence was in Florida. He would be in New York only two or three days and then not every week. He had been a former seagoing maritime captain and, by the time we knew him, owned a fleet of commercial ships. I remember when he died the obituary in the New York Times highlighted that he was the largest private commercial carrier. He was a very socially-minded person who had received commendation from the U.S. Government for diverting one of his ships a few hundred miles to help pick up Vietnamese boat refugees who were stranded on the high seas.

He was the only person that I ever met in my life who made you feel you were really doing him a favor by taking his money. And they were not small sums.

Once I was asked by the Jewish Theological Seminary whether I would go to speak to him for a contribution to its scholarship fund. I hesitated-not liking the role. But out of loyalty to my alma mater, to which I owe a great debt, I acceded. As usual, he met me at the elevator and before anything else, said, "How much do you want?" He didn't even ask for what. I responded that I would like a hundred thousand dollars. What the hell! Might as well think big. His immediate response was, "I have already made out a check for fifty thousand dollars. Here it is." That, in fact, was what it was, but he had left blank the name of the recipient. For all he knew, I could have made it out to myself, but I was proud indeed to hand it over to the Seminary.

Avi Albrecht and I often talk about Leo Berger, of blessed memory. He was one of a kind-Unique! If there is a special section in heaven for generous, kindly, successful people, who didn't allow their vanity to get the better of them, Capt. Leo Berger surely is presiding over it. His memory is a blessing.

One of the most difficult, but in the end successful, fundraising ventures that we did at Shelter Rock took place in the 1990's when Soviet Jews suddenly had opportunity to leave Mother Russia and migrate to Israel. Prior to the '67 War Soviet Jews knew very little about Israel, nor were they involved in her fate. The Soviets had repressed as much information as they could about the dynamic quality of Israeli life, and in those years Elie Wiesel's description of them as the Jews of Silence still held sway. After '67 that whole picture had changed radically.

In any case, the collapse of the former Soviet Union gave rise to a mass migration. Close to a million over the next years came to Israel. They brought many problems, but they were anxious to work and they were by and large educated and skilled people. At that time the joke was current of three people coming down the gangplank at Ben Gurion Airport, each carrying his musical instrument; they were obviously bonded. The fourth fellow, empty-handed. "Oh, he's the pianist."

One of our members, Stanley Sanders, enlisted the Kagans-Bob and Arlene-to join in putting together a fundraising effort of $250,000 to sponsor a planeload of Soviet Jews to Israel. We were told that we would have to do it within a month because the terrain with the Soviet Union was always rocky. We made an appeal to the entire congregation to participate. They responded magnificently in a very brief period. When we put it together, we realized we were $50,000 short. What do we do now? They turned to me, the "fundraiser."

After about two moments of thought I knew the answer. I had to call Capt. Berger and Milton Cooper. They each gave us $25,000 over the phone and the checks arrived the next day. We had done it!

A group of us then went to Israel to help receive this planeload of Soviet Jews whom we had sponsored. We went specifically for that purpose though we stayed a few days longer. None of us who participated will ever forget those moments of seeing elderly Jews descend, young families coming together with children, an exodus reminiscent of ancient Egypt. A number of men and women of the Israeli army were present to receive them as well, distributing candy to the kids and goodies to the adults. Needless to say that many of them, when they first came off the gangplank, got down on their knees and kissed the cement tarmac of Israel. They were all crying, and so we joined them. You couldn't help but be deeply moved by the whole experience. It was the best fundraising experience in which I was ever involved.

WHO IS YOUR REBBE?

T HE FIRST TIME I heard the question, "Who is your rebbe?" was way back in 1948 as I was entering the Rabbinical School of the Jewish Theological Seminary. Having come to this somewhat late, and even though I had been a rabbinical student at Yeshiva University for five years, I still had no idea about conducting services and being a rabbi for the High Holidays. So I was told that there was a fellow, Wolfe Kelman, (who himself was a student at the Seminary at that time), who possibly had positions available for student congregations for the holidays. Timidly I approached him. As I recall it was in the Seminary cafeteria. I introduced myself as an incoming student and his first question to me was, "Who is your rebbe?" I was taken aback because I realized I had none, and at that moment it seemed like a fatal flaw.

Actually I did have a rabbi who encouraged me greatly, but he was a local rabbi in an Orthodox synagogue my father-in-law Max Walfish used to frequent. But because of the situation, I assumed it would not be politically correct to use him as a reference. Besides he was not really a mentor, though on occasion we would study a bit together and there were times when we took long walks together on Shabbat. But in my mind that did not quite fit the bill or answer the questions.

That question has been with me now for sixty years. Who, in fact, is my rebbe? So as I think back I have really had many and they have had a profound influence on my life and on my unfolding. But I am not sure I agree even today with the concept of a rebbe. In the Hassidic tradition it means somebody to whom you give unflagging devotion and loyalty, to whom you bare your innermost soul, and who you accept as an ultimate paradigm of what a spiritual leader should be. Perhaps it is in my nature, or temperament. But of all the people who have had, in some cases, a profound influence over me, after awhile, I always saw their warts and shortcomings. I am not sure the fault is in the stars; it may readily be with me. But there is no one who has remained my rebbe forever.

Among my teachers, Mordecai Kaplan, Max Kadushin, and Abraham Joshua Heschel, were probably the most influential. All had a tremendous devotion to the future of Jewish life and, at some time or another, took a strong personal interest in my own development. My admiration for each of them has continued in an unflagged way. Perhaps I was looking for an emissary tsadik, or righteous man. Even Moses, our Master Teacher, had his faults as well.

In addition, I had a diverse group of Holocaust teachers: Joachim Prinz, Rabbi Weissmandel, and David Weiss-Halivni. In addition, a number of people in my congregation who were survivors and taught me a great deal, not only about continuity and courage, but perhaps even more important, about life in the old country, its culture, its religion, and its strengths. I always absorbed such knowledge with great desire, as if I were learning about my own personal roots, which in many ways I was.

In later years I could say that I was strongly influenced by Rabbi David Hartman, by Yosef Begun, by Natan Sharansky and also by my son, Rabbi Jeremy Fenster, from all I have learned a great deal, not only from texts but from life.

Often I ask myself: is a rebbe necessary? Is it important, is it possible to have someone whom you look at as a supreme example of piety and learning, and is able to give you answers to all personal problems and philosophical questions, and all aspects of life? There is help out there and it is a matter of finding who understands and appreciates your questions and can help find an answer. But I guess I have always distrusted the idea that you embrace a single person who can do all of that faultlessly. It may, in fact, be true that I have missed an element of spiritual joy by never having found one sustaining life-long rebbe. Closer to the truth, I think I try to make myself my own rebbe, to learn from experience and to try to figure out how I might get to a higher level by trusting my own learning and judgment. Have I arrived at that point? Absolutely not. I still consider myself in process and hope that maybe some day I will, in fact, be able to say that I have found what I am looking for. 'Til then, I am still in search. No rebbe – yet.

ANNETTE

DURING MY LONG tenure at Shelter Rock, I came in contact with many people who were very prominent in my life, but at the same time they disappeared and I may not have seen them now for decades, though their memory still lingers.

One of the most memorable people was a woman who served as the Administrator of our synagogue office, Annette Shubert. She was an enigmatic, colorful, unforgettable type. She wore outlandish outfits for a synagogue office. But she had an indomitable spirit and, if she took a liking to you, nothing was too much for her to do. On the other hand, if she didn't, you were in deep trouble. I later found out that there was one woman who kept trying to make an appointment with me and she was reportedly told by Annette, "Look, the rabbi is very busy, he doesn't have time for your nonsense." Naturally that did not exactly endear her to that congregant.

There were many stories about her that could be told, as for example, when she first came to Shelter Rock and I brought in a bottle of champagne to signal her arrival. At lunch time that day we each took a sip or two and went back to work. Little known to me was that if Annette just smelled the cork, she would become giddy and go into a dither. This time she actually had perhaps half a glass of champagne and before I knew it, she was lying on the floor in my office, asleep. At that point I didn't know her so well, but I decided to test her mettle. The president of our congregation, who had interviewed her and selected her for the job, phoned the office and asked to speak with her. I didn't hesitate for a moment. I woke her up and told her the president was on the phone. She thought I was kidding and, in any case, was in no condition to talk to anybody. But being very resourceful, in a moment or so she recovered and continued on with the day's work.

She stayed at Shelter Rock for a long time until, unfortunately, she took gravely ill and was in Winthrop Hospital in Mineola toward the end of her life. Just about that time our son Dan was courting a wonderful young lady, Jan Strizler. Jan and Dan were at our house for Shavuot, when I decided to walk to the hospital to see Annette.

Jan accompanied me and Annette knew we were coming. I shall never forget that meeting. There was no way that Annette wanted to meet this young lady in the condition and looking like she actually felt at that moment. So she did something very characteristic for her. She wrapped her head ala Gloria Swanson, put on a bathrobe with a large belt around her waist, fixed her face, and greeted us like she was a Hollywood starlet. Jan couldn't believe she was as ill as I had described to her and that was the only time they ever met. Before we left I said to Annette: "Shubert, you goniv, Jan thinks you are a Hollywood star instead of a Bronx bomber."

Annette brought many interesting people to our synagogue and they served us well, like Temmy Kocivar, Solange Pullman, Dorothy Levy and others. She made a big impact, not only on me and our family, but many of our congregants.

They remember her fondly, and when she died a number of them got together and bought an ambulance in Israel dedicating it to her memory.

THE COMMISSION

B EING ASKED TO join the Commission of Jewish Law of the Conservative Movement came to me as a surprise in 2005. I was asked by the then President of the Rabbinical Assembly, Rabbi Rafi Rank to join twenty-four other colleagues of this select group which cannot legislate, but does offer authoritative guidance and direction in the many Halachic or legal matters that come to our attention.

I hesitated, having once many years before turned down such an invitation, not feeling qualified. But this time at Rabbi Rank's insistence I accepted. His point was that with my long experience as a Conservative Rabbi in the Metropolitan New York Region the questions coming up before the Committee were relevant to that experience. He felt that I would be able to help.

During the course of the first sessions of this committee, I came to the realization that many were at the heart of the Conservative Movement's enterprise and touched on hot-button issues that could not be evaded. The first of such was the issue of accepting and ordaining gay and lesbian students at the Jewish Theological Seminary. Our committee could only recommend since we are not the admissions committee or the ordaining body of the Seminary. But, nonetheless, it was understood that our recommendation would carry weight with the Seminary faculty.

The issue turned out to be thorny and contentious. Many sessions were held with a great deal of back and forth, negative and pro opinions being expressed. There were considerable numbers of rabbis active in congregations, who no doubt had met gay and lesbian students over the years, who felt that the time had come to modify the severe biblical law of Leviticus 18.

This had happened to me as early as the '70's. A young man whom I knew virtually all of his life came to me with the embarrassed revelation that he was gay. He was also deeply committed to Judaism and was often in the synagogue on Shabbat morning. "Rabbi, I am gay, does that mean that I am no longer welcome in the synagogue? And if I come and they offer me an aliyah (an honor to be called to the Torah) does that mean that I have to reject it?"

His obvious sincerity and my attachment to this young man and his family was a deep one – and I almost burst out into tears. My response was intuitive. "You have as much right to be in this synagogue as I do."

But he did stop coming to Shelter Rock and ultimately found a more comfortable spot at a gay and lesbian synagogue in Manhattan, which in later years has grown so that they rent the Javits Center in New York City for their High Holidays worship.

A number of such examples happened. These had been my Bar and Bat Mitzvah kids, part of my family. I could as much disown them as one of my own children. I hoped we could so something. I bided my time.

The stubborn question persisted as to how that could be done and still remain within Halachic, that is legal Jewish norms, and this, of course, evoked bitter and at times acrimonious controversy. Generally speaking the members of the Seminary faculty that served on the Commission were against the proposal and felt that the biblical injunction could not be in any way contravened. This led to prolonged elaboration and discussion.

In the end what appears to many as somewhat incomprehensible emerged, mainly adopting the two positions, one accepting and the other rejecting gay ordination. This is a long-standing tradition of the Law Committee which used to refer to it as majority and minority reports. For some it does not offer precise enough clarity. For the new chancellor and the Seminary faculty it was a sign for them to proceed if proper candidates could be found. And so it has been. Not everyone accepted our decision with joy. But I am convinced it was correct. Modern Judaism has to be open and accepting – to those who want to be with us.

Over these last years other controversial changes have been considered. One has been the use of instrumental music in the synagogue on Shabbat where, for example, an already present guitar may be used during the service. It is still being considered. The status of a non-Jewish spouse, married to a Jew who is a member of the synagogue, and the question of burial privilege in the Jewish cemetery upon death, was also undertaken. Currently the Committee is embroiled in the discussion of what food, if any, can be eaten by an observant Jew in the non-kosher restaurant. Though this has a long history among us and an opinion was written by Rabbi Max Artz decades ago, it has come up again for review at this time. And, of course, the issue of kosher slaughter of animals has been on the front burner since the revelations in Postville, Iowa have come to light. It may turn out that history will judge the emergent Hechkser Tzedek to have been one of the most important innovations of our time, linking what is kosher to what is ethical and proper. Many people feel that it is at this hour of our history that we must once again affirm the Talmudic principle, "The law of the land is the law of Judaism" and that "the laws were given to refine human nature."

The background question that faces the Committee on Jewish Law, the "800 pound gorilla" in the room, so to speak, is to ponder whether questions such as these and others that will come up will reinvigorate the Conservative movement. In the immediate period of post-World War II, we found ourselves in a growing and vibrant situation. That has stopped. No one can say for sure where the answer to regaining our momentum lies. But many of us, and I among them, believe that this is not a time for a failure of nerve, to go back on the way we have come and the positions that we have taken. Without traditional practice as our guide, we are lost. Without the modern key, we are obsolete. We have to learn once again how to reconnect both of these elements for vital growth. And we need people committed to both ideals.

Many have this idea that in order to grow again we must embrace the entire corpus of the past. But this is simply impossible. The Bible and rabbinic law are the foundation of Judaism, but not its highest story. The rabbis' elaborations embrace the ideas and values that have kept us as a people in every generation. If we let that go, we are without resources for the future.

Naturally, there is no easy rule of thumb as to what traditions must be kept and remain in force and what can be relaxed. To some saying a bracha while eating salmon and salad in a restaurant that is not kosher, is an absurdity; to others it is an act of consecration. To some, having the guitar leading the congregational singing on Shabbat is an aberration; to some it is an inspiration. These and many others are the questions before us, but as long as we can grapple with them and listen respectfully and openly to both ideas, the result should bode well for the future of the Conservative Movement in America.

Our constituency expects us to engage in ongoing efforts to reinvigorate the tradition while preserving it. We must not let them down.

"ARE YOU STILL A RABBI?"

O N THE FIRST Shabbat after my retirement from Temple Israel in December 2003, Ricky and I returned to Shelter Rock for the morning service. As I entered the synagogue, a young man whose consecration in Aleph I recalled two or three years ago, looked at me askance, "Rabbi Fenster, are you still a rabbi?"

In one sentence that sums it all up. How do you go from being a congregational rabbi for more than fifty years onto the next phase of your life? I found out that it is quite a challenge. And it is also liberating.

So what did we do? We drove to Florida, stopping in places that we had always heard of but never been to before. Durham, Charleston for Shabbat, Savannah – they all came alive. Then we participated in a Shabbaton in Boynton Beach. It was exhilarating.

So we are sitting for ten days in a beautiful home of our cousins Aileen and Stuart Disick, by the pool no less, and all of a sudden I get this idea, which had been rolling around in my head for years, to write a memoir of my life. And to make it a "narrative theology." That is to say, how the events of my personal life affected my theological and religious outlook. Things I had never spoken of before.

The first pages poured out of me. Then we came home, and I continued. I have written now on and off for eight years. It is even hard for me to believe, but in the writing of it I have gotten a new and fresh perspective on my life. It is not going to be nine hundred-plus pages like our former President, nor is it going to contain earthshaking and sensational revelations. But I did hear Bill Clinton say, as well, that the writing of his book was a deep experience and one that he had not anticipated. What happened is that suddenly I saw connections that I had not realized before. And I am pleased to report that my life hangs together better now than I had ever realized.

Since retirement I have also written a longish essay: "The Challenge to the Conservative Movement." That also helped me clarify some issues that had been rolling around in my head.

Long before retirement, Boris Chartan, the President of the Holocaust Resource and Learning Center at Welwyn Preserve in Glen Cove, had suggested to me that it would be a good idea for me to join him and the others once I retired. Actually, the late Bishop John McGann of the Archdiocese of Rockville Centre and I had been the original religious consultants to the Center when it was formed almost two decades ago. One of the revelations to myself that I uncovered in the memoir, was the enormous impact the Holocaust had had upon me, even though I had never left Brooklyn. My father had lost his whole family and that resonated strongly within me. Powerlessness did not coincide with my view of Judaism.

Rabbi David Hartman, has written:

> "For many of us, the State of Israel represents our collective determination not to be defined exclusively by the gas chambers of Auschwitz but by the hope of rebuilding Jerusalem. We will always mourn for Auschwitz. We will never become reconciled with our people's tragic suffering and losses. We will never forget how the homeland of Bach, Beethoven and Kant became the homeland of Himmler, Eichmann and Hitler."

> "Nevertheless, we will celebrate our people's new life and hopes in Jerusalem. In returning to Israel we reaffirmed our determination not to withdraw from history but to continue believing in the possibilities of a new future no matter how ambiguous, uncertain and precarious life is."

Hartman has here stated precisely what the memory of difficult past events have done for me.

And so I began to serve the Holocaust center as a part-time Executive Consultant. The learning process was challenging, rewarding, and a prodding to get more people involved. I am mostly interested in the events of the past serving as a stimulus to understanding and accepting pluralism in our society. The inter-faith, inter-racial dialogue has suffered many setbacks in recent years. Respect for the "other" should lead to understanding. One thing we know for sure: disrespect leads to disaster. The world must be made safe for diversity.

Is that part of our tradition? It certainly is. Our rabbis spoke of, "the righteous of all nations." It is a sacred and beautiful category. If we open our eyes we see examples of it all around us. There are righteous people in all nations. It is our hope to discover and strengthen them.

I was an ardent fan of the late Ray Charles. In his singing I always heard the pain of his life, of his people and of our people. He was a blind man who helped open all of our eyes. Not all aspects of his life were totally pure. But he was a good example to all of us, that when you are down, get up, brush yourself off, and keep going. "God's anger may be for a moment, but His grace is for a lifetime; weeping may come in the night but joy comes in the morning."

So you see, the habits of a lifetime always surface. No matter where I start, I end up quoting Scripture!

In sum, let me say this: I still have the zest to serve! Still feel the fire in my bones! Thanks to God.

VITAL ISSUES FACING CONSERVATIVE JUDAISM

F OR A BRIEF time Ricky and I
journeyed to Cherry Hill in New
Jersey to be part of the United Synagogue Convention that was taking
place there. The immediate reason for our going was to participate in
the open meeting of the Committee on Jewish Law and Standards. The
goals of our committee are to deal with the legal or Halachic questions
that come up in everyday life with the members of our congregations. It is
an ongoing enterprise, because the questions are ongoing and continuous.
Our committee is made up of twenty-five people, but for these particular
meetings many were unable to attend so we tried a telephonic conference.
As it worked out, the reception from one of our members in California
was clear, but from Massachusetts, slurred. So it took time for us to get
going. The chairman of our committee, Rabbi Elliot Dorf, the Rector of the
Rabbinical School of the University of Judaism in California, asked me to
fill in some time while the mechanics were being worked out. In substance,
this is what I said to those assembled.

"The issues we hope to deal with today are important ones. Our agenda
is full. Today we will discuss whether a non-Jew needs to wear a head
covering during a service in the synagogue, and may a non-Jewish spouse
be buried with her family in a Jewish cemetery. These are important issues

to which we applied the Talmudic dicta to act, "in a way that will lead to the paths of peace."

"But more important than these two items are those that should be on our agenda but are not. They have come up at our Law Committee in the past. One has to do with the use of musical instruments in the earlier part of the Friday night service, Kabbalat Shabbat, which recognizes the reality that our services need to be more spirited and engaging to our congregants. Some dismiss it as "happy clappy." To my mind that would be a mistake. Our challenge is to remain within the parameters of Halachic norm while expanding outreach to our congregants. We need to do more to accept all those who come within our orbit and ask to be included. I remember the time when the details of Jewish law used to be argued by congregations and not just rabbis. A return to that situation, I believe, would help stimulate what some consider to be a decreasing and moribund segment of American Jewry."

"We have the right idea. We have to continue to apply it."

Let us hope we will.

BENEATH THE CANOPY

ONE ASPECT OF my life at Shelter Rock were the many special occasions on which I had to officiate. There was, of course, the continual round of Bar and Bat Mitzvahs and in addition, as the congregation grew and became older, there were more and more funerals at which I had to officiate. And then, of course, there were the weddings. Shelter Rock had become a popular synagogue for young couples to be married because of our beautiful sanctuary with 350 seats, which was not too large, and a caterer that had become well-known. There were times when I must have done a hundred weddings a year at Shelter Rock and at other places to which I had been invited.

So the aggregate number is quite overwhelming. When I contemplate it myself, I am impressed that I was able to say that I never came late for a single wedding, or forgot one, or disappointed a bride or a groom. There was one near miss, when I was rushing from the Beth David Cemetery in Elmont on a Sunday at noontime and I managed to create a "fender bender" accident. No one was hurt, thankfully. Only the papers were exchanged and the comments that come with them, but I had lost my edge to get to the wedding. I did arrive a few minutes late and it proceeded as usual. But that was the only time out of 3,000 weddings.

One of the positive aspects of rabbis having families is that they learn to view these events from the inside within their own circle. When our children and grandchildren were married, the tension and excitement was palpable. I could easily project that onto the weddings I was called upon to officiate. I can honestly say that I never approached the bimah of our synagogue without feeling a sense of reverence and solemnity of the occasion. Usually I try to relieve the tension with some off-hand remark that might be humorous. Many a time a bridesmaid would faint in the middle of the ceremony. A few times the groom or bride started not to feel well, or one of their parents. I kept my eye on everyone as keenly as I could to detect an oncoming sign, and more than once I did see someone in a state of collapse before they got there.

None, however, was as dramatic as a wedding that took place in our synagogue some twenty-five years ago. Both the bride and groom came from families that were highly respected in the congregation and long-standing participants. It doesn't happen often and so this was a very festive occasion. The father of the bride was in the haberdashery business and told me I needed a new tuxedo for his daughter's wedding. I resisted, saying that the tuxedo I had was only a few years old and I had only worn it a couple of times. He would not hear of it and before I knew it I was in the showroom of "After Six" and he was taking out what was apparently the most expensive item on the floor. I protested, but to no avail. I said, "if I pay for half" which I'm sure ran to a few hundred dollars. He said, "All right. We'll settle up after the wedding." It is ironic and unbelievable, even as I tell it today. There was a large congregation present; it was a sacred moment. Afterward, joy reigned supreme. The first dance after the chuppah is usually a long and intense one. I was dancing with the father of the bride who was ecstatic. The next moment, he slumped in his place, fell to the floor, dead. Pandemonium ensued but, unfortunately, dead is dead. I never again put on that tuxedo, but we did send it to Israel where they did use it for Purim, a time of costume and revelry.

How I was able to keep all of these brides and grooms somewhat vividly in my mind and keep the dates from getting tangled up, has always been a source of amazement. It took increased effort but as I realized the impact on people's lives at those special moments, I tried to make each one different and individualistic.

Once when Ricky and I were in Jerusalem, in order to get away briefly from the very intensive relationship which we enjoyed with our children and grandchildren, we decided to go to the movies one night. Mostly we attend American movies in Israel and it's an interesting experience watching the Israelis relate to American plots and situations. This one night we were just about being seated for the movie when someone tapped me on the shoulder and said, "You're Rabbi Fenster, aren't you?" Truth is at that moment I didn't exactly feel that rabbinical or look at myself as an American rabbi on holiday. But when I said yes, he responded, "You married my daughter." I was outwardly overjoyed which immediately turn southward when he said the next sentence, "She got divorced." That was the end of that movie for me and I wondered why he had to say that. If he wanted his money back, he would have to speak to the caterer, not to me.

But in many places that I go nowadays I do meet up with somebody with whom I had stood under the wedding canopy. And I have officiated at their children's weddings many times. But just recently I had a sign that I may be getting too old for this because apparently I had scheduled to do two weddings on the same date, at the same hour. When I realized it, I was beside myself. How do I break it to one of them that I am not going to be able to live up to my announced expectation? Both were families I knew very well and were highly respected in our community. The weddings were going to be held at prestigious hotels in New York City. For a day or two I agitated as to how I resolve this uncomfortable situation. Early one morning just a day or two later, I got a call from the father of one of the brides. His daughter had met the other bride and by comparing notes as to who was officiating, they knew we were all in trouble. I must say that the father of the bride was most helpful in allowing me to resolve this in a comfortable way, and I am deeply appreciative of his attitude. I guess he understood that the old rabbi just 'ain't what he used to be'. But I still hear the bell go off most mornings and hope to be good for another few rounds.

CONTENTIOUS ISSUES

MANY PEOPLE SPEAK, oftimes, with a depreciatory tone, of the "politics" inevitable to synagogue life. They are mistakenly confusing personality issues with what could be considered broader implications. Most often "politics" turns out to be who is saying what and when they are saying it.

Over the years I considered myself very fortunate that Shelter Rock had few ideological issues that were besetting it. It is true that at the time of its founding, there was a debate whether it should be Orthodox or Conservative. There was already then one Reform congregation in the community so that was not the issue. They settled on a Conservative synagogue, not out of ideological commitment, but simply because they thought that as a centrist movement it would appeal to both those on the left and the right. And that largely proved to be correct.

But in the late 1980's the egalitarian issue rose to the surface and became quite contentious at Shelter Rock. As a student of Mordecai Kaplan at the Seminary, we already had a strong advocate for women's rights through his teaching and his example. I had tried giving a woman an aliyah as early as the mid-1960's when I was in Jackson Heights, but I was enveloped by a wave of protest from the old-timers. I realized at the time that its time had not yet come and waited for a better day.

But that better day never came about smoothly. Twenty years later at Shelter Rock there were a considerable number of people who opposed equality for women in the synagogue. This was the time before we had a woman president of the congregation and in fact, when I came to Shelter Rock, women did not even have the right to vote in the annual election of officers. One of the first changes I managed to initiate was that in the second year I was there, both men and women voted equally. But other changes did not come about that easily.

Elsewhere in many congregations there was a spirited debate amongst those who were for and those who were against egalitarian practice. Factions that were opposed on occasion split off from their main congregation and established a new entity. The general culture was debating the issue and the feminist mystique with all of its implications was becoming widely discussed.

At Shelter Rock I tried to move slowly with full understanding of those who resisted change. I proposed that a meeting be called of the general membership to decide whether a young lady, who reaches the age of Bat Mitzvah, could have that ceremony on Saturday morning rather than on Friday night which had been the custom. Saturday morning was reserved only for Bar Mitzvah ceremonies, and I felt this would be a good way of at least symbolically designating the coming of equality. Some were even opposed to women appearing on the bimah on Saturday morning, but I insisted that they get beyond that.

At the meeting to decide the issue of Saturday morning Bat Mitzvah, some three hundred people showed up to the membership meeting. It was conducted by the President of the congregation who had a hard time controlling the noisy and very engaged group that was present. Some twenty speakers or more were heard on both sides of the issue, many quite passionate, logical and controlled. There were others angrier and less controlled. I waited until all the speakers had finished and said simply that I believed this was the time to move in that direction. As I recall it, the vote was some two hundred in favor and some one hundred against; in other words a considerable minority expressed their negative view. I left the meeting that night asking myself whether this was a victory and what the result of such a vote would be.

I found out early the next morning. One of the members of our congregation who was not in regular attendance at the synagogue service, arrived indignantly into our office by 10:00 a.m. He had already removed the memorial plaques dedicated to his father and mother in our synagogue and proceeded to throw them down on the desk in the administrative office, saying "I would never consider keeping these plaques present when

Bat Mitzvahs will be taking place on Saturday mornings!" I happened to be present and heard this impassioned declaration. I looked at him as if he had gone mad. How he equated the respect due his parents to a young lady, making a commitment to Judaism for her future, I simply could not understand. I guess there were only boys and no girls in his family. To me it seemed obvious that when you have 50% of your population that is female, you had better educate them and give them full responsibility and rights. That is to say, if you want to have a future for the Jewish values and its cultural continuity.

That was hardly the end. Within a short time an equal group of mostly young women in their thirties and forties were petitioning for a fully egalitarian service. At the same time many of the old-timers were petitioning similarly that we resist the egalitarian impulse. They saw it as an eroding of traditional values and they ascribed to it the philosophy of the slippery slope. Today you start with that which leads ultimately to assimilation and absorption.

Never caring for controversy or confrontation, I tried to steer a middle course. But it did not quite work. Some of the egalitarians began to demonize me as out of touch with contemporary Jewish life. My point was that I would try to keep the congregation so that it would appeal to both men and women of all ages, that their parents who were very often more traditionally oriented would be able to come and be comfortable, and that we would move along with "evolution and not revolution." They did not buy that formula and, looking back I would say, who could blame them. I was determined to keep the congregation together knowing that at any given time it could easily break off into smaller divisions.

Finally I devised a method by which, for at least a short time, everybody was happy. We established an Egalitarian Minyan to be held in another space in our synagogue. I would often attend myself on Shabbat morning for at least part of the service and there were occasions when they had a goodly number of people present. The service in the main synagogue proceeded as usual.

In the meantime a smaller group of more traditionally oriented people came and asked for an Orthodox service. It originally started with a group of Shelter Rock kids who had begun to attend Yeshiva University and who were told that they should not be attending a synagogue where men and women sit together. They came to tell me that they enjoyed Shelter Rock and did not want to leave. First thing they did was to fix up two rooms of our schoolroom floor into what they themselves called, "The Underground

Shtiebel." They began with a small group that had services every Friday night and Saturday. On the holidays they moved into a larger room as they attracted more and more people. So after awhile it turns out that we had three services going simultaneously. But I insisted there is to be only one Kiddush reception at the end of the service so that we would all mingle together and so that each could claim that theirs was the best. And it worked. At least for a while.

But before we came to that solution there were some tense moments. I remember once there was a fundraising dinner on behalf of the Jewish Theological Seminary being held at the Garden City Hotel. It was a gala affair with a few hundred people present from many of the Conservative congregations on Long Island. We had a number of representatives present and one of them, Jack Rosenthal, was invited to spend some moments before the dinner with Chancellor Ismar Schorsch of the Seminary who was to be the main speaker. This was all quite proper and regular except that Jack insisted I go along with him.

So there we were in one of the posh reception rooms of the Garden City Hotel, the Chancellor, Jack and me. I was a bit wary because this was at the height of our egalitarian controversy and Jack was not in favor. He was out to make a point with the Chancellor, who was the head of the Conservative Movement in all of its departments. Jack spoke respectfully but forcefully: "You see Rabbi Fenster here, he has been our rabbi so far twenty-five years and it has gotten to the point where he does not look forward to coming to the synagogue any more on Shabbat morning because of the tensions. How is a Movement going to continue when its leaders are not happy with it?" I protested immediately at the description of my distaste coming to shul on Saturday morning. But the truth is it had gotten more difficult and there were people I had begun to avoid. That was all before we came up with the new formula which quieted things down, at least for awhile.

Looking back on that whole period I have concluded that while it seems I was too timid, it definitely was the right thing to do at that time. Today Shelter Rock is fully egalitarian and has been for the last few years, and there were no major separations or walk-outs. It is a unified congregation, under the leadership of Rabbi Martin Cohen, my successor. Other issues due to economic downturn and shifts in the population have begun to emerge as major concerns. A congregation that is unified and determined to continue will no doubt be able to overcome these concerns as well.

TO GREEPORT

ORIGINALLY IT WAS my intention to complete this memoir with the year in East Hampton. Little did I know that after a few months of most enjoyable leisure that I would be asked to assume a congregation unlike any I had recently served. It reintroduced me to an aspect of Jewish life that I have not observed for as many as six decades.

Jewish life in small towns where there are few Jews and where the synagogue is only one of many religious institutions, and the smallest one at that, was something that I had of course heard of and spoken to people about, but had not witnessed since my days in Mt. Kisco, New York in the late 1940's. This new experience was what Greenport, N. Y. offered and Ricky and I readily accepted it.

In the first instance, it is different because the congregation is quite small, comprising sixty-five families. Temple Israel in Great Neck, for example, had some 1200 families when I was there. But there is great advantage to small congregations in that the people are intimately bound to each other in a most impressive way. If one of them takes sick, they can receive a dozen calls in a day from their friends and fellow and sister members. The rabbi enjoys a special status. This year when we went to Israel for a brief time, I suddenly started receiving letters from the people of the congregation, the likes of which I had never received before. People were writing to say how much they missed us and hoped we would come back soon, even though things were going well without our being present. They were most gratifying to receive.

Another outstanding aspect of the congregation is the presence of a half-dozen people who are over one hundred years old or very close to it, and in some cases beyond it. While some are physically limited, they take an active and engaged position on what is taking place in the congregation and community. They want to be part of it. One of our members, one hundred and two years old, Ethel Brown, is in the synagogue every Friday night that she is physically able to be there, which includes almost every week. And everybody wants to know whether or not Ethel was in shul last Friday night. If not, they must call her.

One of our members, Jack Levin, who was just one hundred, still plays an active round of golf and I am told that he is quite good. His younger brother, who is only ninety-seven, often plays with him as does Dr. Bill Sausmer, a retired physician who at the age of ninety is the youngest of the threesome. I am also told that they are quite serious about their playing and entertain no witticisms about it.

The synagogue building is one hundred seven years old. It has been designated a "National Historic Landmark." Of course, there have been changes and extensions in that period, but the sanctuary more or less remains as it was, with fifty permanent seats on the main floor and twenty-five in the balcony. On the holidays we move into the Assembly Room which can accommodate one hundred and fifty. I did not realize how much difference there is to the "feel" of a smaller group, how much more intimate and informal it is than having conducted services on Rosh Hashanah for, let us say, two thousand people. The relaxation quotient goes up considerably, while the enjoyment factor increases. In a sense you are talking to people, not orating at them.

Of course it must be said that the members of the synagogue of Greenport, on the North Fork of Long Island, mostly have come from New York City and have opted to a simpler lifestyle than the one they had before. Greenport is a laid-back country town. We live one block from the harbor which in days gone by was a whaling village. On Shabbat afternoon it is a great joy to go sit at the harbor and watch the boats lazily glide by on the water. The sky, whether cloudy or not, the air, the whole ambiance is totally different than suburban life. I would say you are touching the edges of nature, but you have cut out a great deal of the artifacts of an urban civilization. The talk is plain and simple and to the point. Everybody knows everything. Our interfaith activities are real and plentiful. Recently our local parish priest publicly brought up the subject of whether Pope Pius X11 coordinated with the Nazis or not. I had never heard anything quite so candid in my life and I admired his honest openness. He called for the Vatican to open their records from that time and clarify the issue.

Our ecumenical group meets to see where we can cooperate and where we are going to be hitting dangerous spots. They self-police references to Christological theology and I did not have to tell them that some of that would be embarrassing to me in the form of prayer in which I would be asked to participate. They understand the tensions and they are anxious to make it comfortable for me. I should add that I am one rabbi to twelve Christian clergymen in Greenport. But I don't feel alone.

Originally we expected to be in Greenport for just a short time. Recently we signed-on until 2012. We love the village, the harbour, the synagogue, its garden and its people. In one week we can be in the suburb of Roslyn and seaside in Greenport, savoring both.

Dr. Micah Kaplan is our president; Adrienne Greenberg is slated for the future. Recently, when Ricky's sister Billie died in Jerusalem, we were moved by the congregations expression of condolences. Tanta Billie (as she was affectionately called) did make it out to Greenport once with her husband Leon. Our congregation showed great respect for her. We are very grateful.

THE NARROW BRIDGE

S O THE IDEA of bringing this memoir to conclusion had to be deferred again. And especially in the light of the death of our son Jonathan in October 2008.

Ironically we were sitting in the succah in the lovely garden adjoining the synagogue in Greenport. We were there with our Ecumenical Minstries, a half-dozen clergymen and women who had joined us that day for a succah experience. For many it was the first time that they had visited those frail booths that we construct in the fall of the year, reminiscent of the harvest festival in Biblical Palestine. Our enjoyment of the moment was shattered by an emergency call that we received that Jonathan had just suffered a heart attack in the Park Slope section of Brooklyn where he lived, and was taken to the Methodist Hospital there. Ricky and I rushed to the hospital, driving as sanely as we could for over two hours, hoping for the best but preparing for the worst. Seeing him hooked up to all of the machines that were keeping him going, we realized how serious the attack was. He could not speak because of the pipes in his mouth and throat, but he did wave to us and we were able to speak to him. The intern told us it was serious, but that there was hope that he could ride it out.

And so it was for ten days. They removed his pipes and while speaking was not easy, he would write out messages for us, humorous and enigmatic, typical Jonathan. They were beginning to talk about putting him into rehabilitation in the same hospital so that he could gain his strength back.

But then a strange thing happened. I took sick myself. I had been taking an aspirin a day on the advice of my physician. But it caused a bleed in my ulcer and by the time I was admitted to the hospital I needed four pints of blood to restore my strength. I stayed overnight and by the next day was ready to come home.

Resting comfortably at home in the evening, suddenly our son Danny appeared. At first I thought it was awfully nice of him to come to visit. Danny was known to be exceptionally generous when it came to taking care of his elderly parents. But as he entered the bedroom I could sense that something was wrong. He was the bearer of the news that his brother had died. He did not want to tell it on the phone so he came in person from Manhattan. He was going to Brooklyn to tell Jonathan's son Michael the same sad news. He also wanted to be with him and try to soften the blow.

Jonathan's death had a major impact upon our family. Our son Jeremy came rushing back from Jerusalem and Elissa and her family from Newton, Mass.

It is probably accurate to say that for none of us Jonathan's death came as a total surprise. Jonathan was a talented, even brilliant person – enigmatic, extremely open to all people, a good friend, and an informed and engaging conversationalist. There were times when he exhibited the traits of bipolarity. There was medication to keep him stable and when he took it, he was wonderful to be with. While he had grown heavy in his last years and had trouble walking, he would manage to come out to Roslyn to see us every other week and would stay in our kitchen and talk for hours on a variety of different topics, of which it sounded to me that he was expert: economics, psychology, astronomy, social work, philosophy, Buddhism, of course Judaism, Hassidism, the Psalms, Abraham Heschel, Martin Buber.

After twenty-five years of being a social worker in a variety of different settings, in the jail at Bellevue Hospital, in juvenile family court, in a retirement home, with cerebral palsy patients, and special needs people, he had reached the point where he found it difficult to go on. It was a sad time for him and for us. He went on disability, the economic stress was not overbearing, and he seemed to be improving. Lo and behold, two months before he died, he told me he was thinking of applying to rabbinical school in Newton. Actually, he had written away for the application which he was beginning to fill out.

I know this sounds strange, but I always considered him a child of the sixties when he was growing up. He was attracted to the hippies and for a while wore his hair down to his shoulders. He would go to Washington to protest the war in Vietnam. The amazing thing was he was always in the heart of it and, as far as I know, was never arrested. Once he called from Washington in the midst of a huge rally and protest to say that he was on the roof of this church and could see the police surrounding the sit-in that was taking place. He explained that they were taking those arrested to the Robert F. Kennedy Stadium. There were hundreds, perhaps thousands, of them. He said he might not be in touch for a few days but not to worry – they would feed him well in jail. Ricky and I did not think that was the worst thing in the world, but not hearing for the next hours, I decided to call my former congregant, Cong. Ben Rosenthal who was living in Washington and serving in the House of Representatives. Once on the phone with him I asked if he would do me a big favor. "Ben, could you go over to RFK Stadium and see what you could do to get Jonathan out of there?" A few hours later he called back to say that he could not find Jonathan. He had not been arrested. He was probably floating around somewhere but he could not put his finger on it. A half-hour later Jonathan did call from a coffee shop. The next day he returned home. He had managed the protest and the evading of the arrest at the same time. That was typical Jonathan.

Looking back I remember some of the joyous moments as well. And there were many of them. Once we came back in January from a visit to Israel and took the next plane to Florida to be with my mother who was spending the winter in one of those apartments in Hollywood that dot the shoreline and offer magnificent views of the ocean. When we arrived we found, much to our surprise, that Jonathan had decided to go down and spend a few days with my mother as well. By that time my mother was in a wheelchair, getting around with great difficulty. So for the next three or four days we all sat around reminiscing, laughing, having the best time. Three generations at the height of happiness in a warm climate in the winter. You could not ask for much better than that.

But there were black hole moments as well. There were days when he didn't answer his phone. He was not sleeping, going out of his apartment or communicating. Three or four times Ricky and I went to the apartment in Brooklyn, not knowing what we would find. We would ring the bell and in a few moments Jonathan would appear, ready to go for a cup of coffee at a local luncheonette. Sitting together for an hour, we were reassured. We knew that there were problems, he was receiving expert help, but at those moments you could believe that he was coming back.

Then we tried to convince him to take the pills. He never really accepted his need for them, but for a while he acceded. After weeks, he improved. We looked for signs of the old Jonathan. We would see them for a few months. Then again, trouble. It inevitably meant he had stopped taking his pills.

A signature moment came once in the midst of a Jonathan down period. He was staying with us on Reed Drive as he often did when the world went dark for him. It was winter and snowing, usually not a bright time. Lying downstairs on his bed in the room he reminded himself that it was his son Michael's birthday and suddenly he perked up and said, "I want to get to that birthday party that he is having." Michael was living with his mother Betty in Stony Brook. It was a good hour away on a night when slippery driving prevailed. He knew the risk, but was determined. He got up, drove out to the birthday party and returned home late at night. Those were always the signs we took as meaning that he still had the determination to go on, especially for Michael whom he adored. The next day we expressed our great admiration for what he had done.

Jonathan was an extremely loyal and devoted friend. And as such there was a group that tried desperately to help him. Over the years Bob Lewin and he really opened their souls to each other. In difficult moments Bob opened up his apartment for Jonathan – to stay in when he was down until he was feeling better. Many people tried to help him and did. Jonathan was married twice, to Betty and later to Betsy. Both were good women. It just didn't work. But Bob was always standing by ready to help.

At Jonathan's funeral I remembered that he had mentioned to me a short time before that his favorite psalm was Chapter 34 which contained the phrase, "the righteous may be afflicted with many difficulties but God saves him from them all." As soon as he had told it to me I knew the meaning to him personally. In his life he was searching for the right way, which was dark and shrouded but the search persisted. He prayed for an external force to help him through, and for a time it worked. But when they told us in the hospital that he had stopped taking his pills, we knew it had not worked continually. In a sense like all of us, his life was unfulfilled. But we received many notes from a variety of sources after his death to tell us that his sweetness of character and his high ideals resonated in the life of many people. We pray that his memory will be a blessing.

Losing a child, under any circumstance, is difficult. And terrible. Jacob in the Bible says of Joseph, "My soul was tied up with his." And so it was with us.

I could appreciate my father now more than ever. He had lost a brother and a son and now so have I. Did it help that he was forty-four when Elliot died and I was past eighty when Jonathan was taken? The raw, basic knawing emotion is the same. Part of your being is gone. An aspect of your life is over. But when you have thirty or more people in your family, as we do, you know what you have to do. At dawn, if not joy, at least continuity.

Somehow or another I managed never to feel deserted. Going back to the earliest days, I felt a strong power of perseverance within. It helped me through many difficult situations early in my life and continuing later on as well. As Mendel of Kotsk said, "The whole world is a very narrow bridge. The main thing is not to be afraid."

We are standing on that narrow bridge now.

PUTTING IT TOGETHER

LOOKING BACK AT the itinerary, starting in Brooklyn, and then to Mt. Kisco, Newark, Jackson Heights, Haifa, and then for that long period at Shelter Rock and subsequently, I am looking for the thread that ties it all together. To me it is no exaggeration to say that my ties to the tradition and my attempted service to the Jewish people and beyond, was exactly what I needed to get me going and to keep me there. But there is, in truth, another element as well.

Expatiating on it does not come easily, because in my mind it is slightly tacky in describing it to anyone beyond myself. That would be the element that our family plays in strengthening my outlook and keeping me focused.

I have tried to describe my father's work ethic and my mother's genuine warmth and compassion, all of which were a big help. My sister Eleanor and I have bonded together these last years in a way I never would have believed possible. If you are smart, tensions unite rather than divide.

A major part of the strength of family life derives from our grandchildren and their children. My kids especially make fun of me when I describe my grandchildren, each one of whom I say is "special." I am not aware that I use that term but it has been pointed out to me. And I would maintain that it is accurate. They represent a diverse not-to-be denied bunch, nine in Israel, the diversity of the Sabra, and seven here, the face of America.

We have blondies like Michael, 6'2", living now in Williamsburg, Brooklyn; subsequently, Michael had decided to be a chiropractor and is studying in Atlanta. and great-granddaughter Avigayl, now seven living in Beit Shemesh.

We have Binyamin and his wife Rachel and their five children living in Ramot, Jerusalem. Binyamin is our family scholar, who I understand has made quite a reputation for himself already, and whom I talk to whenever I can, with special affection, remembering that he is the one who took me into the mikveh in Safed, which still brings back cool memories on a hot day.

And, of course there is Bracha, the oldest of our grandchildren, her husband Moshe, and their five kids. Bracha who recently turned thirty years old, really is a special person of outstanding qualities. She has more energy than anyone I have ever known, taking care of her family, cooking for, and helping as many people as she can, always inviting people over and always on the move. On her thirtieth birthday I spoke with her, reminded her of the day she was born. Ricky and I were in the Old City in the summertime, especially because we were anticipating Ellen giving birth. When the moment came, Jeremy was taking care of his wife, and I was assigned the job of bringing a taxi from the Jaffa Gate into the Jewish Quarter so that Ellen could be spirited away to the Hadassah Hospital on Mt. Scopus.

It may not sound like a very complicated procedure but it also was not easy. At that time cabs were not permitted to come into the Jewish Quarter because of its narrow streets and alleys, and there were many of them where a cab could not fit at all. Given my instructions, I proceeded to run up to the Jaffa Gate, a good part of which is uphill, not steep mind you, but uphill nonetheless. I mentioned to Bracha that if I had to do it now, she would have waited possibly for a long time to be born. But at that moment I dashed up, spoke to one of the Arab drivers who understood the emergency nature of the situation immediately and together we proceeded back to the house. It was a delicate operation, but we made it. And I recall dashing up the stairs to get Ellen and helping her down into the cab. They were on the second floor, but at the landing coming down, she had a labor pain and we had to stop for a few moments. But Ellen is a good scout and she and Jeremy were whisked off to Mt. Scopus – and the rest is history.

The arrival of the other kids was not so dramatic, but each one was welcomed with joy and thanksgiving. Sara, Kyla, Malka, Chani, Uri, Akiva and Rachel, plus Bracha and Binyamin.

One of the reasons we want to spend time in Israel is to be close to them and their families, but, as you can imagine, it doesn't quite work so easily. Our original idea to spend six months in Israel and six months in Roslyn, was detoured by these many opportunities that I was given to which I never had the strength or desire to say no.

Our American grandchildren are not any the less spectacular. Dan and Jan's kids, Zach, Ben, and Rebekah are all highly individualized, intelligent and loving. Jonathan's son Michael is a delight, as are Elissa and Bill's children in Newton, Mass., Gabe, Kayla and Isaac.

In recent years we have been able to spend much more time with Gabe than previously because he was up there near Boston. Gabe is a very bright young man who went to Wesleyan College in Middletown, Conn. We had never heard of the school until he told us that he had been accepted there. Hard to believe, but just a few days after his excited call of acceptance, we read on the front page of the New York Times that Wesleyan is the first college in America to adopt the policy of nude dormitory. For this they get forty thousand dollars a year! I immediately got Gabe on his cell phone to make sure that I understood correctly what was happening. Gabe, who is very smart and very cool and knows how to handle his grandfather quite well, assured me he has no idea what this was all about and he personally was not involved. We were concerned, as of course were his parents and so we went up to visit Gabe on a number of occasions while he was at Wesleyan. It all seemed quite normal, except that he had a rope ladder from his room that led him down to the ground. A few dozen feet away was a large telescope for those studying astronomy, which Gabe apparently used to visit for long periods of time. What can I say, that after graduation and studying for a few years in Israel, Gabe has decided to become an Orthodox rabbi. His looking into the stars has paid off. Now we are all looking forward to Kayla's wedding in Newton to Eliav, a bright and lively addition to our family.

The reason I write all this is not because I believe they are so unusual, but to bring home the point that they keep my mind focused on a contemporary life. I love being with them and keeping up with what they are doing in the present moment. In order for me to do that, I have to be up with events so that we will have a universe of discourse and so that I will understand what they are into. I cannot say what all of this meant to them, but I can hint at what it has meant to me and Ricky. As Annette Shubert used to say, "They're the best." And special.

Ricky and I are proud as well of our nephews and nieces. Johnny Holtzman lives with his wife and children, Alex and Jesse, in San Francisco. David Raphael and Jo live in Atlanta with their kids, the oldest of whom, Alya, has earned a PhD in Microbiology after years of work at Stanford. We don't see them as much as we would like but this year after a week in Delray Beach, we hope to spend a day or two in Atlanta with the Raphaels. All in all, as the old ad for Levy's Bread used to say, "It makes for a good sandwich."

And, "The last, the last is the sweetest." Our two daughters-in-law, Ellen and Jan. It sounds exaggerated, but in my mind, it is the truth. They have been and are God's gift to the Fenster family. Ellen is from Kansas, Jan from Roslyn Heights. Both are beautiful, authentic people. Kol haKavod to our sons, Jeremy and Daniel, for finding them, with help from Above. They have made us wiser, our lives richer, our hope for the future, firmer.

"THE MEMOIR NEVER FINISHES"

IT IS CURIOUS as I look back to my retirement from Shelter Rock and I began to write this memoir, that I thought of my life as a backward recording. How foolish I was! Hopefully, as long as you live, new things are happening which may be as exciting as anything of the past. And so I have discovered.

No way would I have wanted to give up the rich and deep experiences I have had since my retirement from Shelter Rock. Even a brief tenure in the congregations I served have often brought interesting new people and circumstances. When I was at the Old Westbury Hebrew Congregation in 2007 I met a fine gentleman, with whom I bonded closely, whose name is Peter Madoff. Peter and Marion, his wife, had lost their son Roger to cancer. They would often be in the synagogue and it was Peter who recommended me to East Hampton as the interim rabbi, which was an adventure all its own. Subsequently, the Madoff family attracted international notice and at this writing the drama is still being played out. I have no knowledge or insight whatever as to who was involved and to what extent in the Ponzi scheme of Bernie Madoff. But recently I heard from Peter who had been told in the summer of 2009 I had undergone a replacement of my worn out hip and as a result I was 3 weeks in the hospital and rehabilitation unit of the North Shore Hospital. I appreciated very much Peter's concern, as that of many others who had heard of my circumstance. All of that had come upon me rather suddenly and much to my surprise I had rapidly decided to do something about it.

For five years previous I was experiencing some weakness in my hip and leg and my son Daniel, the chiropractor, had taken an x-ray and told me immediately arthritis was setting in. As time went by it got worse. By the time I got to the hospital I could barely walk in. My physician Dr. Howard Guzik recommended that I go for the surgery. He never said it was a piece of cake, but somehow or another along the line that's the impression I had gotten somewhere. Well, it was not exactly that, but a month after the operation I was already walking better than I had before and looking for more improvement so that I was very happy with my decision to go ahead. And of course Ricky was with me every step of the way.

On a beautiful summer night in August of 2009, to celebrate recovery, Ricky and I met with our son Dan and my grandson Benny for a festive meal at La Marais, which has to be the best kosher steak house in New York. Benny, who is only sixteen, is an emerging star basketball player, having already played an important role in the Abraham Heschel School's victory in their basketball league. This marked the beginning of my recuperation period and we were looking forward to the evening with great anticipation. Since I needed a pint of blood subsequent to my operation, I thought it would be a good idea to indulge in a red meat steak to replenish the blood. What an awesome idea. We sat there for a number of hours relishing the occasion and speaking of future events, the possibility of a wedding in Jerusalem in October. Pondering the future is always exciting, but often frustrating. So much mystery surrounds what is going to take place. It's easy to say, as the old song does, "Que Sera, Sera" but it is not quite so easy to be so complacent. We make plans, but we wonder if we will be able to see them to fruition. Every day there are reminders that once you are passed eighty your youthful years are over. There are many doors open before you, but you know how easily one of them can shut.

So now we are planning something called a second Bar Mitzvah which Dan and Jan wanted to take place in their apartment on 86th Street in Manhattan. That was characteristically thoughtful of them, but I thought Greenport a better venue, among congregants, family and friends. And so it was. Magnificently! A second Bar Mitzvah is seventy years after the first one, so that mine would come up at the end of October. As a reminder, "with the honey there is always the sting." Since the family would be gathered, we would hold an unveiling ceremony for Jonathan that same weekend. We have already set the stone for the unveiling, upon which we have inscribed a saying from Pirke Avot. He, "greeted everyone with joy" and was, "full of good intentions." Both are true. Being at the cemetery recently I noticed that we had put on my mother's tombstone a famous saying of a poet-laureate of the Hebrew language, Hayyim Nahman Bialik, "And in their death they commanded us to life." That seemed to describe the situation quite aptly: We hope to be summoned to life. By my parents. By Elliot. And by Jonathan.

AFTERWORDS

TIME ONCE AGAIN for the annual remembrance of my brother Elliot's death. It is now more than six decades that he left us. It is no longer an open wound in need of daily care. It festered long ago, though the scar remains. He would already be collecting Social Security, but the haunting questions have not faded. It was so unfair. He never got a chance at life. Yet as I look back, from this yawning distance, perhaps there was meaning or a message to all of us. I am still undecided.

Telling myself to focus on the present, I refer to Elliot's Hebrew name which was Elimelech. He was named after my grandfather, who in turn was named for Elimelech of Lizensk, who was born in the old Austro-Hungarian empire. The original Elimelech of the Eighteenth Century was a renowned Hasidic master with a vast following. Many in the next generation bore his name proudly. His spiritual legacy is contained in the book, Noam Elimelech, which is studied all over the world.

In any case, Elliot's full name in Hebrew would be Elimelech ben Uri u' Bracha, the names of my father and mother. My father was named Uri and when he came to America he was known as Ira. He was born in Strelisk where another famous Hasidic rabbi Uri the Seraph thrived. With all of this background, you might ask, how come I didn't wind up a Hasid. I don't feel like one, dress like one, or act like one.

Not a Hasid, I see myself as an American Jew. My background is Flatbush, baseball with the old Brooklyn Dodgers at Ebbets Field, and

Jackie Robinson stealing hime, which we actually once witnessed. Add to that football at Madison High School.

The memory of my Hasidic forbears still warms me on a cold day. I especially admire their piety and passion, their wisdom and leadership. I have tried to apply their shine to this time and place and would like to believe that some of it has rubbed off onto me. It is also increasingly obvious, as I see it, that a portion of their intellectual and emotional strength has been transferred to the next generation in our family. They too are not Hasidic, but they are beautiful exemplars of intensity in religious and spiritual matters. I fully believe that their flowering in the future will be extraordinary.

To an extent even the names are the same. We have Zachary Uri in America, Uri Shmuel and Uri Krohn in Israel and Elimelech Kornfeld, of Beit Shemesh, also in Israel. They all bear names that have become revered in our family. They are already living up to and beyond expectations. May their strength increase. And with them, their parents and siblings. They are our legacy to the future.

Also, when in Israel, our time has been enhanced by involvement with Yad L'Kashish Life Line to the Old and Shaare Zedek Hospital both in Jerusalem. They have enabled us to make at least a small effort toward Tikkun Olom, fixing our world. Their leaders, Nava Ein Mor and Dr. Yonatan Halevi are a privilege to know.

ACKNOWLEDGEMENTS

Having finished the memoir, I want to express deepest gratitude to those who have helped me to this moment. First to Ha-kadosh Baruch Hu, for having enabled me to reach this day.

I cannot sufficiently express my gratitude to the Moss's, Linda and Steve, for the support, loyalty and kindnesses they have shown our family over the years. The Tannors, Neil and Eileen, have also been with us every step of the way. Profound thanks. The same with the Zelmans, Morris and Edie; the Levines, Marty and Allison, and "tachshit" – Gary Zelman and Ruthie and to the Magids and Rosenthals. The Goldmans and Stanley Rubin.

I am regretful that Dr. Saul Lieberman is no longer with us so that I could at last claim that I did in fact learn, "ishto k'gufo" (going back to my oral exam at Martha's Vineyard).

Ricky's joy and pain have long been mine. As John Denver sings to his Lady, let us hope, "that our time has just begun."

My gratitude to Sara Bloom is abiding for all of her help. Parts of the manuscript were read by Stuart Stritzler-Levine, Martin Levine, Rabbi Martin Cohen, and Mark Strauss. Of course, to my family members, who were kind enough to hear again the stories that I have told, I am eternally grateful.

Temmy Kocivar was indispensable to this manuscript. Zachary Fenster was with me until the end as a source of joy and love.

Finished and done, may it be a praise to God.

Made in the USA
San Bernardino, CA
08 July 2017